Keep on cycling !
it's fun !

Clive Parker
July 08

Pedalling to Panama

by
Clive Parker

authorHOUSE®

AuthorHouse™ UK Ltd.
500 Avebury Boulevard
Central Milton Keynes, MK9 2BE
www.authorhouse.co.uk
Phone: 08001974150

First published by AuthorHouse 3/17/2008

ISBN: 978-1-4343-5940-7 (sc)

Printed in the United States of America
Bloomington, Indiana

This book is printed on acid-free paper.

www.cliveparker.co.uk

To the memory of

David Stanley

CONTENTS

INTRODUCTION

A CAFÉ IN COLÓN

A cafe in Colón. I am the only white person around. An elderly man in the corner raises his hand and smiles at me. The ice cream is good, although the coffee is a little bitter. Panamanian coffee tends to be bitter. I had seen no other foreigners in Colón. I look at the scene around me. The main street is wide, with gardens down the centre. There are large trees, flowering bushes, and seats for relaxation, for watching the world go by. A boy leads a blind man along the street.

Signs have been erected saying 'Tourism - the future of Colón depends on it' and 'Say no to violence, say yes to peace'. I hope the fifty cents I have paid for the coffee and ice cream will make a difference. Looking at the very visible poverty around me, I doubt it somehow. I'm drinking my coffee slowly as I feel less conspicuous in the cafe.

The guide books tell you not to go to Colón unless you have to. I didn't have to. Colón is at the northern, Atlantic, end of the Panama Canal, a fascinating man-made wonder of the world. It seemed a logical place to finish a bike ride through Mexico and Central America. My ride finished at Balboa, near Panama City, and having taken a boat through the canal, I am now waiting for the train back from Colón to Panama City.

I had been through a unique part of the world. It is neither North America nor South America, and it certainly isn't European. It is, well, Central America. I felt privileged to have been part of it for several months and to have fitted in. As a foreigner travelling through this region, I aroused much interest, especially as I had chosen to travel by bike.

Despite the poverty I found a region peopled by warm, friendly, hospitable folk. I never felt personally threatened or in danger. Even in El Salvador and Nicaragua, countries recently torn by civil wars, I felt perfectly comfortable and found that people were so pleased to meet a foreigner, and to have the opportunity to talk about their views of things. People were concerned for me and for my safety and I received numerous warnings, if not outright doubt, that to cycle such a distance was fraught with danger. It seemed fitting therefore, to spend my last day in Colón, a city the guidebooks tell you to avoid.

The feeling of welcome had started as soon as I arrived at Chihuahua Airport, seven months earlier. It's a small airport and my plane was the only arrival. A large cardboard box was sitting alone on the International luggage conveyor in the customs hall. It contained my bike. There were no luggage trolleys so the customs woman summoned a porter with a barrow. 'Where do you want to go?' he said. 'A quiet corner where I can assemble my bike' I answered. He took me to the perfect spot under the watchful eye of the airport police who seemed to have nothing else to do but watch me. One of them came over to chat to me, I told him of my plans to cycle through Mexico and Central America to the Panama Canal. I said I must be *tonto*, or crazy. He said 'no not *tonto*, an Adventurer'. It felt like a good start to Mexico.

Cycling requires no technical skill, unlike most other sports. All you need are a bike and the time. I had both, plus a desire to see the countries and meet the people of Mexico and Central America.

CHAPTER ONE

DOWN TO DURANGO

I was plunging relentlessly downwards, mile after mile. Freedom. The road took no hostages. It was steep. It started at the town of Creel, 2000 metres above sea level, and should have been downhill all the way. The hand-drawn map given to me in the tourist office gave me no inkling of what lay ahead. I reached the bottom and the road immediately headed uphill again. In my fresh state – i.e. unfit - this meant pushing the bike and all its weight up the road. Eventually, the top. Phew! I had cycled into a deep canyon, or *barranca*, and was now back at the same altitude on the other side.

One moment I had been looking up at great mountains of yellow and white rock standing guard over the *barranca* and the road. Now, I was level with them. This was some road! I was on the way from Creel to Samachique, a small village populated largely by indigenous Tarahumara people.

Then it happened again. After a few miles the road found another *barranca*. Was it the same one? It didn't matter.

What did matter was that I was freewheeling rapidly down knowing the fate awaiting me was another steep push up the other side. I made the most of the downhill surge, the fresh air breezing through my hair and clothes to take away the sweat of the uphill slog I had just completed. I could see the road snaking its way down, then up the other side. There was no traffic and I felt I had Mexico to myself. The climb up the other side was hard. The bike was heavy to push. And there was the altitude. The air was thinner. I had read about altitude problems amongst mountaineers in the Himalaya. I had not expected to have problems myself simply pushing a bike along a road. Breathing became slow, and difficult. I felt dizzy so I took my time, I had little alternative. Pressing on, I was soon amongst pine trees on a plateau. I could breathe again. I had cycled through two *barrancas*.

As I was pedalling along congratulating myself the road started to go down again. I was suspicious. Was this a third *barranca*? It was. This was the big one, the same Copper Canyon or *Barranca del Cobre* that I'd seen near Creel. I heard the tinkling sound of a river below me, cascading over the rocks. The road went alongside the river for a while. I passed a lorry in a lay-by and stopped to see if I could scrounge something to drink. The climbing I had already done had made a noticeable impact on the drinking water I was carrying. I had not seen any wayside shops to buy more drink. I was dismayed as the driver was nowhere to be seen. Not to worry, I thought, the road will simply follow the river and it will be easy going from here.

Then I noticed that although the road was still going downhill, the river was actually flowing in the opposite direction. I stopped to check that I wasn't just imagining it. Yes, the river was flowing the wrong way. Round the next corner, the road started to go up. Up again. This was getting beyond a joke. I needed to drink some more water, which by now I was rationing as I knew I barely had enough. I stopped at a small white house with a crate of empty Coca-cola bottles outside, covered in dust. A neighbour said, yes, the woman who lived in the house sold drinks, but no, she was not in at the moment. Why are people never in when you want them to be? I cursed.

The lack of shops had taken me by surprise. On my last trip to Mexico, there were shops everywhere. Here there were none. This could partly be explained by the road being fairly new. On the other hand there were people around, mainly Tarahumaras, and I started saying to myself 'why can't they start up a shop, instead of sitting by the side of the road?' Of course, it's easy to say that without knowing their circumstances. In Latin America 'indigenous' usually means poor. If they have no means of getting together the money needed to start up and stock a shop, it won't happen. It's not just a case of having the money. They would also need a place to build it, maybe with permission from a landowner that would never, in practice, be granted.

There was a fourth *barranca*. It was smaller, and by then I was getting used to them. I also knew that I wasn't too far from civilisation, the village of Samachique. That was my target for the night; I was hoping there may be accommodation there. It was the only place of any significant size on that stretch of road.

I was down to my last mouthful of water, when a petrol station came into view. I put on a spurt in case it disappeared in front of my very eyes. A young man was on his knees reading a newspaper spread out on the bare concrete floor of an otherwise empty office. There were no drinks to be seen anywhere. "You don't have drinks?" I said, more as a statement than a question. I don't know who was more surprised, me that he didn't have drinks, or him that anyone would expect there to be drinks on sale at a petrol station. I could almost hear him thinking, in a clever sort of way, "Petrol stations are for selling petrol, chum, didn't you know that?" I wasn't quite desperate enough to drink petrol.

Round the corner, a road sign announced the imminence of a junction. It was the turning for the short side-road that runs down to Samachique. In Mexico road junctions are usually places of activity, as people are waiting for busses or transport of some sort. To my relief, there was a house with a small shop at the junction.

The lady behind the counter had plenty of soft drinks, but no water. That didn't matter. I bought a litre bottle of lemonade and almost downed it in one go. Then I asked her if there was accommodation in Samachique. She was certain there wasn't, but said I could camp near her shop if I wanted. What a relief. It was five o'clock, and the forty-six miles from Creel had taken longer than I expected because of having to climb out of all the *barrancas*, pushing the bike on foot. I was, to put it politely, knackered.

I looked around for somewhere to pitch the tent, but it was easier said than done. The ground was either too hard or too rough, or on a slope. Eventually, I went down into the woods below the house and found a relatively good spot where I banged away with rocks to get the pegs into the ground, and tied the guy ropes to trees. Getting tent-pegs into the ground was to become a major pre-occupation of camping in Mexico. I had a typical British tent designed for soft wet ground in Scotland, with plenty of pegs that slide in easily. In Mexico the ground is normally so hard that getting the pegs in requires a lot of energy and effort, and swearing of course. Swearing always makes a job easier; it should be included in the technical manuals. Chapter Nine – "How to swear at your car to make it work."

I was carrying my tent because distances between towns in Mexico are so great that I would have to camp from time to time. My preference would always be to stay in hotels or guest houses. They are safer and more comfortable, and I had the money to do so. I knew that with a daily cycling range of forty to sixty miles I would have no alternative to camping from time to time.

After putting the tent up, I went back to the house to calm my nerves and see about getting something to eat. The woman offered to make some *quesadillas* - cheese filled tortillas. While she was cooking them, I sat in the kitchen chatting to her two children. The kitchen was simply furnished, with a hard earth floor and a water tap standing proudly. There was no other plumbing in the house. The whole family slept in one big room, which had several beds. While eating the *quesadillas*, I asked the woman if she had seen Hersh. She had.

ڷ

Hersh was a Canadian I had met the previous night in Creel. We were staying at the same hotel. He was cycling from Alaska to Tierra del Fuego, at the southern tip of Argentina. He had cycled through New Zealand. I told him I was a long distance cyclist too, and he asked me how far I had cycled. "Sixty miles, I have just started" I said. I had cycled from Creel to El Divisadero and back as a warm up trip. Creel seemed an unlikely place to start a cycle ride, and I am still not sure how seriously Hersh took me. He was doing greater daily mileages than I intended, and although we were going the same way, he set off much earlier than me in the morning.

He had suffered many problems with his bike. A lot of spokes had broken. He had to change his wheels, and had done various other repairs. I am not very good at bike repairs, and all his stories convinced me that I was not likely to get very far.

This feeling was made worse when I discovered that my front wheel wasn't quite true. I discovered this in the hotel room in Creel, when I was looking over the bike after my warm-up trip. I couldn't understand it, as I had bought the wheel new just before I left Europe. I started thinking, how can I possibly expect to cycle to Panama with a warped wheel? I began to think in terms of maybe just going to Guadalajara instead. I thought I could manage that, even with a slightly warped wheel.

Hersh said he was camping most of the time. There are two schools of thought as to which is the safest way to camp in Mexico. Hersh's view was that it is safer to camp in a hidden spot in the trees where nobody can see you, and no-one knows you are there. The other view is that it is safer to camp where people know you are there, preferably in view of people. This tended to be my own practice. I have read about cyclists packing up and moving on if someone sees them camping. However, if you are inside the tent or away from it, you wouldn't know if someone had seen you.

Camping behind the woman's shop, I was awakened at three o'clock by a disturbance, a loud clanging noise. At first I was so scared, I dare not move. I slowly and carefully opened the tent and realised what was happening. A dog was rummaging through a litter bin made out of an old oil drum!

In the morning I stocked up with water. I left carrying three and a half litres, a lesson learnt from the previous day. This was a cumbersome weight on the back of the bike, but in the hot dry climate of northern Mexico, coupled with the uncertainty of supplies during the day, I judged that I had to set off with that amount each morning. I never ran out again.

The road to Guachochi was less brutal than I had experienced the day before. Before long I had left the *barrancas* and hills behind me, and was in Cowboy Country.

Much of northern Mexico is cowboy country. The majority of men you see wear cowboy hats, cowboy shirts, jeans and boots. They are not going to fancy dress parties; it is their normal day to day wear. Even a man running a small *abarrote* or general store where I stopped was in cowboy gear. He assured me that Guachochi was only twenty kilometres away, and that the road was mainly flat. His little daughter peered at me bashfully from behind the rack of biscuits.

Stopping at *abarrotes* soon became an essential part of my cycling routine. They provided an opportunity to buy drink, which I was determined not to run out of again. The drinks were kept in a fridge, and I preferred to buy a cold drink, rather than drink whatever had been baking in the sun on the back of my bike. Another thing I liked about stopping at *abarrotes* was that I could chat to the owner, and whoever else was around. And of course, travelling on a bicycle, they frequently wanted to talk about me and my journey. It quickly became apparent that I wasn't seen as 'just a tourist'. There was evidently something different about me.

The following morning on my way from Guachochi to Balleza I stopped at an *abarrote*, standing in pine woods in the middle of no-where. It was well-stocked and run by a mother and daughter. As I stood there sipping my coke, a truck pulled up and an elderly couple got out, the man wearing a straw hat. The couple were talkative and mentioned the forthcoming Presidential elections. They couldn't say who was going to win; it was going to be a close call. They asked about my journey and referred to me as an adventurer. I was beginning to like this. After ten minutes of conversation, the man suddenly said 'toothpaste please' as if he had just remembered the purpose of their journey. They had come out with no money, but the shop owners produced a well thumbed exercise book under the counter where credit was recorded.

In Balleza, someone had seen Hersh. 'When?' I asked. 'Yesterday'. It had taken him two days to do what had taken me three. He was distinctive because he was carrying his luggage in a trailer, and had both the Canadian and Mexican flags flying from it. Shop owners noticed him even if he didn't stop.

The ride from the mountains down into Balleza was through broad open country divided into a patchwork by dry stone walls. They made me think of Northern Britain. I wondered if they had been introduced by the Spanish, as there are dry stone walls in parts of Spain. It was about ten miles downhill, so I arrived in Balleza on a 'high'. The town had an amiable atmosphere but no monuments or attractions of merit. Inevitably I seemed to be the only foreigner staying there. The family running the somewhat run-down, but clean, hotel where I stayed did their best to make me welcome. When I enquired about restaurants, the wife offered to cook me a meal in her kitchen. I wanted a beer first and she sent me to the *cantina*, or public bar, on the edge of town. When I walked in I was immediately approached by two men a little worse for wear. They told me they were drunk – well, could have fooled me! They had seen me earlier in the day, cycling down from the mountains, and wanted to know where I was going. They wished me well as I left with my two bottles of Corona.

Back at the hotel, I sat at the wooden table in the centre of the cramped kitchen and chatted to the lady while she cooked my dinner. Her husband was outside trying to fix the car. He was making a lot of noise. Meanwhile her ten year old son sat watching me. His mother regretted that he drank so much coke. She said she thought he would end up working in the United States as there was little work in that part of Mexico. Her brother was already there, earning good money. I asked her if they would use a *coyote* to get her son into the United States. She hoped not, as they could be dangerous.

The word *coyote*, as well as being a prairie wolf, is used to describe men who illegally smuggle people over the frontier between Mexico and the United States. The United States has increased frontier patrols in recent years and it is a thriving business. I have heard of people paying $6,000 for the services of a *coyote*. There is serious talk of building a fence the length of the frontier, to keep the Hispanics out. Not only Mexicans, but people from all over Central America make their way north by land.

Fences and walls are not new. Many medieval towns had walls built around them to keep invaders out. In those days invaders weren't looking for jobs, just more material things like horses, food, and women. In 1961 the Berlin Wall was built. A twist in history, it was designed to keep people in, rather than out. It lasted until 1989, when the collapse of communism led to the collapse of the wall, so to speak. I predicted at the time that the west would have to build another one, to keep economic migrants out. My prediction turned out to be a right, but in the wrong continent.

Many Mexicans want to enjoy the American Dream, and are prepared to go about it illegally. As a transit route for Central Americans with the same objective, Mexico is a buffer state for the United States. There is an agreement between the two whereby people from Central America who are caught in Mexico, believed to be travelling to enter the United States illegally, are repatriated by Mexico. This keeps the problem one step away from the United States, and helps keep them happy. President Vicente Fox of Mexico considered it important to have good relations with his northern neighbour.

It strengthens Mexico's hand when dealing with the issue of Mexicans working illegally there, currently a big issue in both countries.

President Bush sees merit in giving legal status to people who are working in the United States and contributing to the economy of the country. This is one of the few things I find myself in agreement with GWB about. If an economy gets the benefit of people's labour, both in generating wealth, and in doing jobs that other people don't want, then those people have a right to be recognised and have the same benefits as other workers. This means they get 'plugged in' to whatever health and social security systems there are. It also means that by ceasing to be illegal, they are less likely to be exploited. I heard a number of stories from Mexicans who had been paid low wages and treated badly, because their employers knew that they would be too afraid to complain, due to their illegal status. Put simply, giving people legal status means treating them like human beings.

Not everyone agrees on this though. Bush has had difficulty getting this over, because of protectionist attitudes. People see even jobs that they don't want as 'their' jobs. It's like the attitude of a spoilt child 'It's mine and you're not having it.' People only want immigrant workers on their own terms. The jobs that are unpleasant, hard to fill. Jobs no-one wants unless they really need the money. Mexicans fit that bill perfectly. The signs of poverty don't need prising out of the desert.

While I travelled through northern Mexico the subject of working in the United States frequently came up. I met many people with family there, as well as people who had worked there and returned home. It saddened me that a country as vast and potentially successful as Mexico should lose so many of its people to a richer neighbour. I began to see Mexico as a missed opportunity.

I left Balleza early in the morning as it was about sixty miles to Hidalgo del Parral, known locally just as 'Parral'. Impatient to be on the road again, I skimped on breakfast to save time.

It was a hot morning. The road was hilly. There were no *abarrotes*. I began to get hungry. I wasn't carrying much food as I don't usually eat much whilst cycling. However, at mid-day the lack of breakfast began to take its toll. Feeling weak, I sat under a tree by the side of the road. An open gate led into a barren field. My stomach groaned with emptiness. For the first time since leaving Creel, I didn't want to carry on.

I remembered the woman in the hotel had said there was a junction further ahead, with a military checkpoint. I told myself that where there are soldiers there has to be food. That encouraged me to carry on. After struggling for a few uphill miles, I saw the checkpoint in the distance. Then a row of buildings. Arriving at the checkpoint, I realised that the row of buildings was a row of cafes. Now I know what it is like to see an oasis in the desert. I asked the soldiers which café was the best. They directed me to a small one almost at the end, and I was very quickly devouring a plate of steak, rice, beans, chips, and salad. It was washed down with .....coke!!

I don't normally drink multi-national drinks as I don't agree with the practices and policies of these companies, which are aimed at stifling competition from small local firms. However, their products are almost the only drinks in Mexico that come in returnable glass bottles. I had considered the environmental impact of doing such a long cycle ride in hot climates. Many drinks come in throw away plastic bottles, an apt description, as people simply throw them away. The roadsides of Mexico and Central America were festooned liberally with discarded drinks containers thrown out of car windows. The explosion in the volume of food packaging has taken these countries by surprise. The rubbish disposal infrastructure can barely cope. I was going to drink five or six bottles a day for six months and I didn't want to add to this burden. Whenever I could, I ordered drinks in returnable glass bottles.

I felt much better with a full stomach and said goodbye to the family running the café. I passed the checkpoint again, and asked the soldiers what its purpose was. They were searching for drugs and guns. Since the checkpoint looked permanent, and people knew about it, I couldn't imagine many drug traffickers and gun runners being taken by surprise.

I was closing in on Parral, my first large town since starting out. The road became a dual carriageway and was busier. The centre of Parral was hard to find, for some reason. When I did find it, I had my first, and only, refusal from a hotel to my request to keep my bike in my bedroom.

My bike was precious to me. It was an essential part of my luggage. I depended and relied on it, like a cowboy would his horse. It was therefore natural that I would want to sleep with it in my room. The lady running the first hotel I tried in Parral flatly refused to let me take the bike into my room. She added insult to injury by saying I would have to leave it just inside the glass front door to the hotel. There was nothing to lock it to. It was obvious to everyone except her that it wouldn't be safe there. She wouldn't budge, so I looked for another hotel.

The young man on reception at the one round the corner was wearing a France replica football shirt. A good start, I thought. 'Of course' he said 'You can take the bike into your room'. Nothing is perfect though. I had to change rooms during the night because of the uncontrollable noise of the air conditioning system.

I had cycled 280 miles. Parral was a large town, with facilities I hadn't seen in the mountains, so I decided to rest there for two days. I needed to do some laundry as well. It was a well timed choice as there was a music festival in the town, with free concerts in the *zocalo*, or main square.

One evening I went to a good open-air concert by a series of local rock performers. One band had an excellent drummer. Drummers are to bands what goalkeepers are to football teams. They lurk quietly at the back, in a world of their own. Occasionally they demonstrate a moment of skill, of brilliance, and make everyone go 'wow'. This drummer did just that. He played solo for a minute, and earned a fabulous applause.

Some long distance cyclists carry music tapes or CD's, and a device to play them on. I regarded this as unnecessary weight; there is plenty of free music to listen to. Music in bars, music on TV, music in the streets. It's all around, why carry your own?

Parral's place in history was as the latter-day home of Pancho Villa. It was also the place where he was ambushed and killed.

Pancho Villa was, like Robin Hood, a hero to some people, a villain to others. Robin Hood was certainly unusual; he robbed the rich to help the poor. Normally, it is the other way around, so the rich get richer and the poor poorer. Pancho Villa's history was a bit more chequered. At the age of sixteen he killed a man who was attempting to abduct his sister. This brush with the law led him into banditry and cattle rustling. In 1909 he settled in Chihuahua to run a horse trading business. It was here that he became connected with revolutionaries plotting to overthrow the dictator Porfirio Díaz. His qualities of fighting and leadership were identified as essential for the planned revolution, and he became a leading figure in the struggles that followed.

After the revolution he settled in Parral, where he met his untimely end at the age of forty-five. I was there on the anniversary of his death. I went to see a re-enactment of the deadly ambush outside the Pancho Villa Museum. A 1920's Ford came round the corner, with seven people in it. When it approached the museum (formerly a hotel), shots rang out, and the people in the car fell out, injured or dead. Five were dead. Amongst them was Pancho Villa. Moments later, men rode past on horseback, to finish the task, riding away triumphantly. They were never identified, or at least, nobody said they knew them. The sort of life Pancho Villa led; he will have made plenty of enemies.

I left Parral along the main road to Durango. It wasn't particularly busy. A sign gave the distance to Durango as over 400 kilometres. It was daunting. It seemed a long way. Five days, I reckoned. The map showed very few dots to indicate towns. One, called Las Nieves, was forty-seven miles from Parral. The curator at the Pancho Villa Museum thought there was a hotel there. That was my target for the night. After that, I was less sure of targets.

I crossed the state boundary between Chihuahua and Durango. Like the United States, Mexico is a federation of states. The title of the country, according to my visa, is *Estados Unidos Mexicanos* – the United States of Mexico. The State of Durango is in a different time zone, one hour ahead of the State of Chihuahua. For the first time in my life I cycled across a time zone. One moment it was one o'clock, the next it was two o'clock. I had lost an hour of my life. Stopping in a café for lunch, I checked the time, just to make sure.

On the café wall was a notice issued by the State of Durango, announcing an amnesty for cars and vehicles not properly licensed. I had seen many cars and trucks with United States license plates, mainly from Texas. At first, I assumed they were American tourists. Then I thought they were Mexicans who lived in Texas and were back for a holiday. Finally someone suggested to me they were mainly stolen and smuggled across the frontier. Either that, or it was simply cheaper to buy new cars in the United States. The story changed so much I never quite got to the bottom of it. If they were illegal, then they were probably uninsured too – a worry for me if I got hit by one. At least an amnesty was on offer, probably the right thing given the number I saw.

Las Nieves spreads itself along the wide main road. There are two hotels there, a filling station with a mini-supermarket, and two bus company offices. All were set back different distances from the road to give an unplanned feel to the place. I found a room at the hotel opposite the mini-supermarket, handy for buying cold beer. In the evening my mind worked on the problem of accommodation for the following night. I had the idea of going to a bus company office and waiting for a bus to come in. The drivers, I reasoned, would know the road well through driving back and forth along it, and I could ask them for advice. A bus arrived, going from Durango to Ciudad Juarez. The driver was very smart in his black trousers, white shirt, and tie. He looked busy, but he found time to talk to me.

He said the next town was Rodeo, over a hundred miles away. I knew I couldn't go that far in one day, so resigned myself to camping. However, that wasn't my only concern, as I needed to buy water on the journey. If I was going to camp, I would need to be sure of water supplies for two days. A lot of water, in the hot Mexican desert.

"There's nothing between here and Rodeo", he said. "Nothing?" I bleated. "Not even a little *abarrote?*". "Nothing" he repeated. The woman in the office nodded. "No shops" she said. The driver reckoned I should set off with at least four litres of water.

I thought about what he had said, and it seemed unlikely that there would be a hundred miles of road without a single shop, even in the Mexican desert. There were people living there, after all. I made it plain to him that when I said 'shop' I simply meant somewhere to buy water, not somewhere to buy a new shirt, some saucepans, and a car battery. The driver saw my point. "Yes" he said, "there are simple shops which might have drinks and biscuits, nothing more." "That," I said, "is all I need".

In the morning, I wanted a good breakfast before leaving Las Nieves. My hotel didn't do food, so I went to the other and ordered scrambled eggs and coffee. After twenty minutes, nothing had appeared. How long does it take to scramble eggs, I was thinking. Then I noticed the elderly cook sneaking through the front door carrying a bag of eggs! Sure, they did breakfasts, but nobody had planned to get some eggs in.

The road was a pleasure to cycle. It wasn't too hilly and traffic was light. The scenery was broad and open, with mountain ranges in the far distance. Cattle ranches with high fences lined the road, making camping problematic. Scaling a fence with a baggage-laden bike and camping amongst cattle were both unattractive ideas. I pedalled on optimistically, telling myself that something always turns up when you want it to.

There were plenty of long distance busses, which I found comforting because if anything awful mechanically happened to the bike, such as total collapse, I could flag one down and be rescued. I noticed the bus drivers waving at me. This was my second day on this road and some of them will have seen me the previous day. This added to my feeling of comfort over the next few days, as I felt that the bus drivers were looking out for me and monitoring my progress.

Late in the afternoon I got to the junction for Torreón. There was a filling station, but it was closed. A shop was closed also. The sun had gone in. The whole place seemed desolate and deserted. I expected tumble weed to blow down the street any moment. A woman piling plastic bottles onto a rather battered pick-up truck told me I may be able to camp at the road maintenance depot. I looked at it, but it wasn't inviting. As an afterthought the woman added that there was a village five kilometres up the road.

When I got there it was located to one side of the road, behind a fence. A track to it went through a gap in the fence. Pedalling around the village, I found a large well stocked shop, with young men milling about outside. People inside were scrutinising the contents of the shelves.

I bought a few things and tentatively asked the woman if there was anywhere to camp. 'You can camp anywhere, the village is perfectly safe.' she said. I pedalled off, hoping the young men hanging around outside the shop didn't watch where I went. A track at the edge of the village led to a place that looked ideal for camping. Flat grass, next to a river bed, with a row of houses in the background. The ground looked a little hard.

Testing the ground with a tent peg, I attracted an audience of four boys. One of them kept spitting compulsively onto the ground. I made a mental note not to put the tent where he had been spitting. The audience was too much for me, so I wandered off for half an hour, along an unfenced road, watching some cowboys rounding up cattle on horseback, in the yellow evening sun. They looked handsome in their cowboy hats and they knew it. Their work looked impressive. Maybe they were showing off. They asked me where I was going. I said 'to the next village', not wanting to own up that I was contemplating camping on their land. I didn't contemplate for long, as I realised that the cattle could return. I went back to my original camping spot. The boys had gone, so I unpacked the tent. One of them, Roberto, saw me from his house and came over.

He helped me put the tent up, which I appreciated as the ground was hard. He was seven and liked school. He had a catapult which he periodically aimed at imaginary eagles in the trees. He told me that wolves would come and eat me in the night. He also had odds and ends in his pockets, like an interesting rock that he gave me. A good old fashioned boy, I thought, not infected by Playstation

Two! The other boys never came back, and I went to sleep not long after eating supper. I felt confident camping within sight of the houses, as there would be watchful eyes on me.

In the night I was awoken by the noise of horses grazing intensively, right next to the tent. Oh no! I lay there for five minutes wondering what to do, I didn't want a horse treading on me in a tent, in the dark. I made as loud a noise as I could and they galloped off, never to be heard again. In the morning when I awoke, the tent was surrounded by chickens. Roberto had told me it was common grazing land for the village.

The next day, sitting on the ground outside an *abarrote* having a drink, I was joined by Francisco, a sixty-five year old Mexican who had been living and working in Dallas the day President Kennedy was killed, in November 1963. He described the day to me, and I enjoyed listening to him. For many years after, they said that everyone could remember what they were doing when President Kennedy was killed, which was true in his case.

Francisco spoke hardly any English. Encounters like that made me appreciate the value of learning Spanish before I did this trip. Being able to chat to virtually anyone made a big difference to travelling through a country of a hundred million people.

Later in the afternoon, I stopped at another *abarrote*. I sat on the grass and was joined by a man who had lived in Texas and came back to Mexico as soon as he had made some money. It was home after all. He now worked locally in construction, having learnt his trade north of the border. He reckoned there was plenty of work locally.

His story is not unique to this part of the world. He could have been a Turk talking about Germany. People have always migrated. What is relatively new is the existence of countries, borders, frontiers and nationalities. For much of the time the human race has been on the planet, these concepts did not exist.

In primitive times there were tribes. Now we are more tribal. We label ourselves not only by nationality, but by regions, localities, neighbourhoods, which football team we support, our religion, even which side of the motorway we live on. One minute we are 'motorists', the next minute 'consumers'. Why can't we just be 'people' any more?

The following day the road seemed to go over a giant sheet of corrugated iron. For miles it was dead straight, and went first gently up, then gently down, repeatedly mile after mile. It was neither flat nor hilly. It was strange. The ups and the downs were of equal length. I was aiming for the town of Rodeo, where the bus drivers had told me there was a hotel. It was right beside the main road, and had a variety of rooms. I was given one at the back, away from the traffic noise, which I was glad of. Later, returning from the shop with a bottle of beer, I noticed that the rooms at the front were occupied by groups of young men, travelling north for the riches of the United States.

Getting an evening meal in Rodeo was a challenge. Mexicans eat a full meal at lunchtime. In the evenings, they tend to eat *tacos*, which are cooked and sold at *taquerias* - stalls by the side of the road. *Tacos* are light tortillas, which are filled with spicy meat and freshly chopped lettuce and onion. Quite often the women cooking them are working for themselves, carrying all the food and cooking equipment from their homes to their sites every evening. *Tacos* are cheap and tasty, but don't satisfy a hungry long distance cyclist.

A discouragingly empty restaurant on the main street was closed. The owner pointed at a pizzeria over the road, up some stairs attached to the side of the building. I climbed the stairs, went in and took a seat. I shared the place with a couple who were having a romantic date. Maybe they hoped to have the place to themselves. They were laughing and giggling a lot, so the date must have been fun.

The following night, I again had to camp. I found a spot near a village, in a field of maize. There was a pond nearby, its surface covered in insects; and a tree where I could sit and watch the sun go down over a nearby lake.

I was getting closer to Durango, the state capital. The farmland changed from cattle to acres and acres of apple orchards. They were planted in neat rows that went on for ever. A man with a large beer belly was standing in the middle of the road, both feet on the white line, selling bags of apples. He had a captive audience as there were *topes* on the road, so traffic moved slowly.

Topes are speed humps, a feature of Mexico. They are everywhere. Seemingly the law allows anyone to build *topes* provided they pay for it themselves. As a result, villagers club together to pay contractors to install them; it helps protect them and their children from the menace of speeding. There are normally warning signs. What they lack, sadly, are gaps for cyclists, so I had to continually watch out for them. Some are simply ridges of concrete, which can be somewhat painful for a speeding cyclist. Sometimes I had to stop and walk over the *topes*, rather than risk damaging my wheels. In spite of that I didn't begrudge them too much – seeing the way Mexicans drive I regarded them as a necessary evil to save lives. Looking on the bright side, the sign warning you of *topes* means there will probably be somewhere to stop and buy a drink.

As I wobbled over the *topes*, the apple seller tried to persuade me I could carry five kilos of apples on the bike. I saw his point. They were cheap enough. He was carrying a five kilo beer belly, after all. However, I resisted the temptation, and continued down to Durango. It was time for a well-earned rest in a city.

CHAPTER TWO

THROUGH ZACATECAS
TO GUADALAJARA

Durango was busy. There was traffic everywhere, and I wasn't used to it. Trying to turn left across the opposite traffic, I lost my nerve and crossed the road using a pedestrian crossing.

The city has many grand old Spanish colonial style buildings. There is an imposing cathedral facing onto the *zocalo*. The *zocalo* is the living heart of the city, a park with trees and benches where people sit, talk or just watch. Children play. Men wander around selling helium-filled balloons. Around the *zocalo* and surrounding streets are a number of hotels. I pushed my bike around looking at them, trying to work out which one might be quiet, and not too expensive. The first one I went into was beyond my budget. The doorman understood my game and discreetly pointed to the one next door.

It was an old hotel, with many internal rooms around a courtyard. They were quiet. I was given one with a large rotating fan hanging from the ceiling. I was glad not to have the noise of an air-conditioning unit. There was cable TV, ideal as I was planning a couple of rest days here and I would be able to watch Champions League football. I went down to reception to ask where I could buy a bottle of beer.

"You can't take alcohol into your room."

After two weeks on the road, I had developed a routine when arriving at a hotel, which generally involved having a shower, then lying on the bed drinking a bottle of beer. The night before, I had been camping in a field with no shower, no bed, and no beer. Her announcement was therefore a complete shock. Keeping my cool, I reasoned that if I went out with a small rucksack, she was unlikely to offend my dignity by searching me when I returned. I was right, and the beer I brought back tasted somehow better for being against the rules.

I liked Durango. It was pleasant to sit in the *zocalo*, watching the world go by. I was in no hurry to be a tourist, as I had cycled 538 miles to get here. My first priority was to relax.

Writing my diary, it wasn't long before a man came to sit on the same bench as me. He started a conversation, and predictably he had lived in the United States, in Los Angeles and Chicago. I asked him directly if he had gone there illegally, paying a *coyote*. He had.

"Isn't that a bit dangerous?"

"You do foolish things when young. The lure of money is all that matters. I wouldn't do it now. I am a lawyer and OK financially. In the United

States I worked as a barman, was exploited, and had no access to welfare or health services. Good reasons to come home to Mexico."

I asked him about Mexican politics, and why I had the impression that most leading politicians are white, or creole, whereas most of the population is either *mestizo* (mixed) or indigenous. He didn't think it was racism. One factor was that lots of Spanish people came to Mexico in the 1940's, fleeing Franco. They were politically minded and joined the political classes in Mexico in a big way. Their descendants continue in that role. It was easier for recent immigrants to Mexico to maintain their whiteness by bringing wives and families with them, unlike the original colonisers who were mainly men.

I told him that many people in Spain had warned me that Mexico is very dangerous, with lots of bad people. He was surprised, as he thought Mexico was a very safe country, except the capital Mexico City. He thought the Spanish attitude was a superiority complex - "well, they're only Indians" or words to that effect.

I needed to find out about hotels between Durango and Zacatecas. The tourist information office only covered the state of Durango, and as much of the road is in the state of Zacatecas, the woman who worked there had to go by her own knowledge rather than use official information. Determined to be helpful, she phoned her colleague in Zacatecas to confirm that her information was correct. Such helpfulness in Mexico was common. It was so different from the warnings I had been given whilst living in Spain, that Mexicans were all 'bad'.

Maybe the endless Hollywood westerns I watched as a child had something to do with it. Cowboys and Indians. And Mexicans. Mexicans were always bandits, desperados, cattle thieves and murderers. Suspicious looking dark men with moustaches. A Hollywood plot to plug the idea of white Anglo-Saxon superiority. In those days, it was easy to get away with using negative racial stereotypes.

Durango town hall is an imposing building, built around a courtyard. The wide staircase leading to the offices of the higher officials on the first floor has colourful murals depicting the history of the region. Strife between Europeans and indigenous people, between workers and owners, feature significantly in the murals. Walking up the staircase, studying the murals, evoked a powerful feel for the harshness of the arrival of the Spanish and its effects. The grandeur of the building reflects the wealth that the town had managed to create for itself amongst all that brutality.

The city had few middle class trappings. There was a coffee shop, but for a town of its size it wasn't very busy. Bookshops were hard to find. A lavish department store called Sanborn's had a book section. It usually had more security guards than customers. On the other hand, there were many shops selling cheap clothing and cut price cosmetics. Wealth created by the cattle ranches in the area didn't trickle down much.

Durango became prosperous because of its position on the road from Mexico City to Santa Fé, and for silver mining. The silver mine overlooking the town is now closed, but I went to the museum there. It has superb views over the city. Returning to my hotel, I stopped at a roadside kiosk for some freshly squeezed fruit juice. I don't know what the fruit was, but it was bright red. I remember the colour because it gave me a stomach upset. I spent much of the night in the bathroom, staring down at the red fluid beneath me. Waking up at nine o'clock I didn't feel like moving. I dragged myself down to reception to ask when check-out time was as I had been planning to leave Durango that morning. "Two o'clock" she said. Great, I went back up to bed and slept till twelve. I then faced the reality that I wasn't going anywhere, and went back to reception to pay for another night.

The room was 250 pesos and I offered her a 500 peso note. She said she had no change. Change was a game in Mexico; people always said they didn't have any. I don't know where all the notes and coins went; shop-keepers and business never had any. The hotel only accepted cash. It was almost full. It was inconceivable that they didn't have any change – how had all the other people paid? She was adamant that I would have to go to a bank to get change, so off I went, hoping that my fragile stomach would last out. There was a long queue in the bank, but the security guard took pity on me and ushered me directly to a cashier. I just made it back to the hotel in time.

The delay of a day was a blessing in disguise, as I pedalled out of Durango on a Sunday, when traffic was lighter. My destination was Vicente Guerrero, along the main road to Zacatecas. The countryside was very hilly, and to my right were ominous grey clouds. I saw some other recreational cyclists, rare in Mexico. They waved to me. Then the clouds got closer. The days had been dry so far and my waterproof jacket had worked its way to the bottom of the pannier. I had to do a major re-organisation of my careful packing to find it. I plodded along in the rain, looking around at the hills enveloped in cloud. The scene reminded me of Rannoch Moor, an unexpected comparison.

When the rain stopped, I arrived at a filling station that did hot chocolate. It was so welcome. People were staring at me in my waterproof jacket, designed for the British mountains. 'Well, it's raining, what do you expect', I was thinking, hoping they could hear my thoughts.

The rain passed, and on I went. On the outskirts of Vicente Guerrero there was a rodeo. A man was organising the parking. He tried to organise me, but I realised I could get a reasonable view over the fence. Cowboys waited eagerly on horseback in a pen, for their turn to be released into a long paddock. At the same time, a bull was released into the paddock from an adjoining pen. The cowboy galloped along. The bull galloped along. The cowboy had to lean over, and bring the bull down to the ground. This had to be done before either had reached the end of the paddock.

It was not as easy as it looked. Many times, the cowboy failed to ground the bull. There was a scoring system, which I never managed to understand, and periodically the audience would applaud. After I had seen enough I went into Vicente Guerrero.

The family run hotel was simple and cheap. I wasn't fooled by the VISA sign on the door, which looked out of place. The woman couldn't explain it and wanted cash; maybe a child had put it there for fun. I was given a room at the back, with curtains that didn't quite close and a small television that didn't quite work.

There was a lot of traffic in town that evening. Furthermore there were two traffic wardens. The traffic was going round and round, and as there was a small roundabout in the centre of town, with a fountain in it, the traffic wardens were needed to keep the traffic moving. The drivers of the vehicles were mostly local young men who had been to the rodeo, and they were driving round looking for friends and for girls. They went slowly causing a traffic jam. One of the traffic wardens said every Sunday the farmers come into town from miles around for the rodeo and to meet friends.

In the morning I decided to clean the bike chain and gears, so I went to a petrol station to buy some diesel. First, I needed a bottle to buy it in. I bought a drink, drank it, and presented the bottle to the attendant. In Mexico petrol stations are normally attended, so I didn't have to fiddle around filling the little bottle myself. I already had an old toothbrush with me, ideal for cleaning the chain with. Whilst doing this, I noticed the pedals wobbling a bit on the axle. They weren't supposed to. I ignored it for a while, and then persuaded myself that mechanical problems seldom go away, they invariably get worse. I instinctively knew the bottom bracket was wearing out.

The bottom bracket is the axle around which the pedals rotate. Was I carrying a spare? Come on – I'm an amateur at this game, what do you expect!

I tried not to panic. My dream of cycling to Panama started to look silly. However, I knew the bike was still ride-able for a reasonable distance, and there would surely be a bike shop somewhere that could help. I continued cleaning, to give myself a bit of thinking time. This is a ruse I learned years ago from a boss who smoked a pipe, in the days when it was OK to smoke in the office. At meetings, if he was asked a tricky question, he would start to light up his pipe. This gave him enough time think his way through the problem. It was not the done thing to interrupt pipe smokers. Lighting up was seen as a physical necessity, like going to the toilet.

I decided to see if there was a bike shop in Vicente Guerrero, and if not I would continue cycling to Zacatecas, where there surely would be one. If there wasn't, Guadalajara was a bus ride away. I was certain there would be a repair shop there.

Having mentioned the possibility of catching a bus, I will now declare my hand regarding 'rules'. I have read books by long distance cyclists who set a rule that they had to cycle every inch of the way. They argue that not doing so would somehow invalidate their journey. I had no such rule. My primary aims were to see the country, meet the people, and enjoy myself. Using transport if I needed to would not conflict with these aims.

I had a subsidiary aim too. Having worked as an accountant for years – where timescales, deadlines, targets, and objectives were part of my daily chore, I was going to be free from all that on this journey. No rules, no timescale, and no objectives apart from the general ones I have just mentioned. The idea of catching a bus if the bike needed repair did not concern me at all. Did I use transport on this journey? Well, you'll have to keep reading to find out!

A traffic warden directed me to a bike repair shop. Walking in, I knew I wasn't going to get very far. The shop contained two shelves with a random assortment of spare parts, a glass cabinet with rows of brake blocks lined up on display, and tyres and wheels hanging everywhere. A teenage boy, the only person working there, was trying to inflate a boy's tyre. He took one look at my bottom bracket. "You'll need to go to Zacatecas." he said. "Will I make it?" I asked nervously. "Yes, you'll even get to Guadalajara if you need to." he added confidently.

His confidence gave me confidence, so I checked out of the hotel and set off.

I must admit, I was annoyed with myself. Some years ago, one of my accountancy jobs was with the train maintenance department of British Rail. I learned about the practice of Planned Preventative Maintenance. Under this theory, if an important vehicle component is expected to fail after, say, 25,000 miles, it is routinely replaced after 20,000 miles to avoid a breakdown whilst in traffic. This might appear at first sight to be wasteful, but it avoids greater waste and inconvenience through having to deal with broken down trains full of passengers. Complaining passengers.

I had clearly not learnt from this. I kept telling myself it was obvious the bottom bracket would take a lot of wear on my journey, and that I should have replaced it before setting off. I was wallowing in hindsight and being hard on myself.

The green country-side on the way to Suchil was calming, and helped sooth my self-critical impulses. I had chosen a minor road, as the day before I had been on the main road which had too many big lorries for my liking. According to my map, the minor road continued through the mountains all the way to Zacatecas. It was quiet and cycling was pure pleasure.

I stopped in Suchil for a coca-cola, and to my surprise saw a giant mural painting of Pope John Paul II on the church. It was the biggest picture of him I have ever seen. Catholicism is still strong in Mexico almost 500 years after its arrival.

After Suchil, the road climbed steadily. I could see it ahead, snaking its way up into the hills. The green-ness was a change from the arid country I had experienced north of Durango. A shop owner confirmed it was the road to Jiménez, the last town before a mountainous stretch to Zacatecas, according to my map.

I nicknamed two o'clock the crazy hour. This is when the secondary schools close, and if I was cycling near one at that time, the roadsides would be thronged with teenagers on their way home, or waiting for lifts. A foreigner cycling past was sometimes too much of a temptation, things were shouted, jokes were cracked, and sometimes they tried to race alongside me. It was always in fun, never threatening or malicious. Mexicans are far too polite for that!

Today I made the mistake of stopping at an *abarrote* during crazy hour. Within minutes I was surrounded by inquisitive teenagers wanting to know all about me and my bike. It wasn't fair; I was supposed to be finding out about Mexico. Instead, they found out all about me. I eventually escaped from them, after giving them enough material for their next geography lesson. The road continued to climb upwards, punctuated by small villages and roadside turnings. A bus going in the opposite direction had 'Zacatecas' on the front. Odd, I thought. Then a deep valley opened up before me. The road took a dive down into it. Gathering momentum, I passed a teenager on a bike. He decided it was going to be a race. Down I went, and down he came too. He was determined to pass me. He was riding recklessly and a collision would not have been good news for me or my bike. At his age, he probably didn't care, but I still had to think about the practicalities of getting to Panama in one piece. I slowed down to let him pass.

This was an aspect of the macho culture prevalent in Mexico. Many men thought I was racing and tried to egg me on. I frequently received shouts and cheers from men in passing vehicles, and it never occurred to them that I was unlikely to be racing as I was alone. Maybe they thought I was such a good racer that I was miles ahead of all my competitors. Blasting their horns at me was a constant annoyance, as it generally made me jump rather than encouraged me. Eventually I got used to it as a consequence of being amongst people who were naturally friendly.

Boy racers were a different kettle of fish. They tried to out-macho me. I am past my prime, cycling hundreds of miles with over ten kilos of luggage. Is it a fair race for a 16 year old with no luggage and fresh legs to enter into a race with me? I think not, but that is the essence of machismo – it is really cowardice. A one sided race you are sure to win.

I continued to Jiménez, past the large detached houses on the outskirts, and then rows of old adobe houses, a few of which were shops. There was a billiards hall too. At the end of the road was a church. I could not see which side of the church the road went. It seemed to end at a wall.

"Where does the road go?" I asked a group of workmen, who had just finished filling in a hole in the road. A lot of workmen for such a small hole. One of them said "The road ends here, it doesn't go anywhere." I said my map showed it went to Zacatecas. They all agreed it didn't go anywhere.

It was five o'clock, and I had cycled a long way downhill into this valley. The wooded hillsides were bright in the late afternoon sun. I asked if there was a hotel. "No, you'll have to go back to Chalchihuites." I was impressed they could pronounce it, because I couldn't. I was too tired to go back and felt deflated that I had cycled into a dead-end.

The workmen formed themselves into an ad-hoc tourist assistance committee. Someone thought there was a track through the mountains to Zacatecas, but it was very hard to negotiate. Gradually, the discussion became more focussed on how they were going to find me accommodation for the night. They were discussing possibilities of finding me a 'super-basic' place I could stay in the village.

I took little part in this decision-making. I decided to go with the flow, to see what happened. When you travel alone for a period, you are making constant decisions. Little decisions, true, but it is constant. Where to go, where to stop, where to stay. It gets a bit of a bind, so I simply decided to switch off my 'decisions' button, and let the villagers decide for me. I felt I was in good hands.

Readers may be wondering why on earth I should trust my fate for the night in a gang of Mexican workmen. By now I had been in the country long enough to feel completely at ease with its people, especially in rural areas. I did not feel in danger at all. I had experienced so much kindness already on the road that I was happy to be in their hands. I knew that Mexicans are, by and large, good people.

As I listened, they were discussing who might be prepared to let me have a bed for the night. We went to a house at the top of the village. I was shown into the living room with my bike. It had two beds, some religious pictures, a few chairs, and a book-case containing mainly ornaments. A computer on the bottom shelf of the book-case looked a little out of place. The house belonged to one of the workmen, and his wife went out the back to clean the shower so I could have a wash. While I was waiting the three sons came in to see me, one by one.

After my shower I joined the men of the family who were gathered round the bonnet of a truck, peering in. There was no engine. Another truck arrived, carrying an engine which was unloaded with much pushing and grunting. One of the sons, Miguel, showed me their roosters, each in a different pen. I had never seen a cockfight so he took two roosters out of their separate pens and put them on the ground facing one another. They got into combat mode, extending their feathers like a colourful ruff. Once I had seen the roosters aroused, he put them away before they started fighting.

Miguel took me to his grandparents' house, in the middle of the village. He had a bike, so we rode along together. The house was behind the billiards hall in the main street. His grandfather showed me a room at the back of the house where I would be sleeping. It had three beds, a mirror, and not much else. The toilet was in a separate building. They had set up a line of string to switch the toilet light on whilst lying in bed. Simple, but effective!

Miguel suggested we went to the village sports field, to see what was happening there. It was outside the village, on a piece of flat ground next to the river. Some teenagers were playing football, and two men were practising basketball. They asked us to join in. I didn't tell them I had never played!

After ball-bouncing for a while I remembered my hunger from the day's cycling. Miguel said his grandmother was cooking some *tamale*, so we went back. *Tamales* are made from corn dough mixed with meat and tomato or chilli, and steamed in corn husks. They are served together in a large pot. Each one was different, and I wasn't sure what was in each corn husk until I had taken one. That was part of the fun.

The kitchen was full of implements, meat and onions were hanging up to dry. There was no running water, and Miguel scooped a cup of drinking water out of a large plastic container. I bought a tin of beer from the billiards room bar. I went to bed soon after - I had to get up early because the bus to Zacatecas left at five the next morning!

I was already up at four thirty when Miguel's grandfather came to check that I was awake. I gave him some money and staggered through the village in the dark to find the bus. The driver was standing next to it in the street. I hoped it would be a long distance coach, with luggage compartments underneath big enough to take bikes. It was a local bus. The only compartment contained the driver's bucket and mop, with little room for anything else. The driver said he couldn't take bikes.

I showed willing by removing the front wheel, hoping it would make a difference. The driver showed willing by opening the rear emergency door, and said I could push the bike in there. I was saved. The bus growled its way through dark villages, picking up passengers. The colonial buildings of Sombrerete looked forbidding in the dark. By Fresnillo it was getting light, and the driver stopped for a coffee. He didn't announce it as an official coffee stop, but I could see what he was up to. I wandered into the café and joined him for a coffee while the other passengers dozed on the bus.

We arrived in Zacatecas. The bus station is perched on a hillside, high above the town which sits in a bowl in the hills, a bit like Leeds or Sheffield. Shoving the front wheel back into place, I was mobile again and freewheeled down into the town. Next to the cathedral I asked a traffic warden for advice on accommodation. He had a list of hotels in his top pocket, with the prices in a column on the right. I went to the cheapest, which happened to be nearby, behind the cathedral.

A man mopping the courtyard saw me peering in through the front door, trying to work out why it was so cheap. He was Eduardo, the owner, and he offered me a room for a price even lower than that on the list. It was a special offer for me. "What's the catch" I asked. "You have to share the bathroom". I looked at the bedrooms and selected the best one, on a corner with a view of the cable-car going up the mountain. The other window looked up the street. I liked the room, I liked the guest house, and I liked Eduardo. Sharing the bathroom was a bit academic.

Walking round Zacatecas I couldn't understand why it wasn't very touristy. It had cobbled alleyways winding round narrow streets. It had baroque churches, stout stone houses of the wealthy, and was surrounded by picturesque mountains. The town had made its wealth from mines – silver, copper and zinc. It had a feeling of self-confident importance, and had all the facilities you could ask for. There were even cafés selling real coffee. I decided to stay for a few days.

I had chosen a good guest house, and grew to like Eduardo and his wife. They were both artists and spent evenings in the kitchen drawing. Eduardo told me about the art galleries in Zacatecas. His wife enthused about the light, which was good for artists, and about the cold weather in winter. It is the second-highest city in Mexico, 8,000 feet above sea level. One evening Eduardo sold some pictures to some people from Jerez, and was happy for me to mingle with them whilst they looked at his work. His wife enjoyed watching football on TV, and one evening we both watched Jaguares came from behind to beat America 4-3 in a league match, with only ten men. The Mexican League is exciting as they play attractive attacking football. Another evening we watched England play Poland. An important game for the English, it seemed.

Visiting one of the art galleries Eduardo had mentioned, I saw a life-size plaster cow wrapped in bubble-wrap. It could have been on display. I wasn't sure whether it was 'art' or not, so I spoke to the curator about it. "It has just arrived from Switzerland" she said, "We haven't got round to unwrapping it yet." I was relieved. I thought for a moment that the bubble-wrap was modern art which hadn't quite made an impression on me. You can never tell with modern art.

Eduardo and his wife were so wrapped up in their art, they didn't seem concerned about marketing their guest house. That suited me, because all the time I was there, I was the only guest. The 'shared bathroom' was shared in name only. Eduardo let me use the kitchen, and took me to the local market where I could buy fresh fruit, vegetables, and chicken components. I use the word components, because the stall-holder only had whole chickens on display. You told her which parts you wanted, and she sawed them off with an electric saw, a bit like buying shelving from a sawmill.

I enjoyed resting in my corner bedroom, watching the world go by from my two windows. The sleepy morning air was always brought to life by the bottled gas delivery trucks driving around touting for custom with a recorded voice blasting from a tannoy. "El Gas" it repeated, over and over again, the word 'gas' slightly elongated as if to emphasise. One morning it was raining and I lay on my bed watching the cars skidding on the wet cobbles, wondering if they'd make it up the hill.

The local arts festival began with a performance by a German group based on the life and work of Pablo Neruda, the Chilean poet. It was performed in the *plaza* outside the cathedral, and involved actors, fountains, music, fireworks and fire. It teased all the senses. It was incredible. I had never seen anything like it. The Spanish word '*espectacular*' was inadequate to describe the display. Afterwards, gob-smacked, I was interviewed by the local radio station, who wanted a foreigner's view of the show. I gave them some jumbled Spanish about Neruda's ideals being popular in Scotland.

Another spectacular worth visiting was the fountain which is accompanied by classical music and coloured floodlights. The display is perfectly synchronised to leave the spectator agog. Local people went there to watch it while they ate ice creams. It only operates at certain times of the week while it gets dark. The shadows of the ancient aqueduct above add to the atmosphere.

I couldn't resist a ride on the cable-car. It was constructed in the 1970's and connects the El Eden mine above the town with Cerro de la Bufa opposite. A guide gives you information on the length and height of the cable-car run, punctuated with witticisms about how many seconds it would take to crash to the ground. It is a scary ride, wobbling along 800 metres above the streets. The Cerro de la Bufa has good views and is decorated with statues of local worthies such as Pancho Villa!

Readers may recall that I needed to repair the bike. A good tactic when looking for a bike shop is to stop someone with a bike and ask them where one is. I stopped a *muchacho* and he led me through the streets for about fifteen minutes until we got to a shop. He helped me explain the problem to the man. Another example of Mexican helpfulness. When I said I lived in Scotland, he said, "Is that near Chicago?" There may be a Scotland Illinois for all I know, but I was by now used to explaining that Scotland is attached to England.

The shop didn't stock components in European sizes. They only did light (i.e. easy) repairs. They suggested I go to a bigger shop in the neighbouring town of Guadeloupe. I went there but couldn't find it. I considered other options - wait till I get to Guadalajara or get one sent out from Glasgow by courier. That wasn't as daft as it sounds, as Zacatecas would be a lovely town to be holed up in while I waited. I phoned the shop in Glasgow where I had bought the bike and asked about having a part flown out by courier. They said it was possible, but then asked me a lot of complicated questions about serial numbers. It was all beyond me.

I went back to my room at Eduardo's to brood. From the window I spotted a cyclist pushing a bike out of a house on the other side of the road. I ran down and asked him if he could recommend a cycle repair shop. "Yes" he said "Bici Taller Burro". Which broadly translated means the 'donkey man repair shop'.

The man gave me directions and I found it easily. The donkey man replaced my bottom bracket inside an hour. I went for a test run up Cerro de la Bufa. At the top, I got into conversation with two Californians, one of whom asked me what psychological preparation I had made for my trip.

The question took me by surprise, exposing a trans-Atlantic cultural divide. I have never considered seeing a psychologist about anything, whereas it is common in the United States. I have no idea how a visit to a psychologist would have improved my trip.

The new bottom bracket didn't feel right. It wasn't tight. I took it back to the donkey man and he agreed to replace it again. Some of his friends arrived, and took the Mickey out of him for not doing it Right First Time, as they say. The new bottom bracket he fitted is still in use today. He changed the handlebar tapes, and adjusted all the cables, all without charge. There was much humour. His friends were keen cyclists, and gave me route advice for leaving Zacatecas. They said their friend called his business the donkey shop as an attention grabbing joke. He wasn't a donkey really.

They noticed that my tyres were on the wheels the wrong way round. This was a new one on me. They showed me the direction of travel arrows marked on them, so the tread is used to maximum effect. I had never noticed that before. They changed them round in ten minutes. The bike now having had a complete overhaul, I went for another test run up the mountain. It was perfect. I was ready for the road once again.

So far, I haven't mentioned punctures in this book. I have used a bike since I was about four years old, and have probably mended several thousand punctures since then. For ten years I cycled to and from work in Glasgow. The combination of wet roads and broken glass is deadly and I suffered many punctures as a commuter in the Scottish rain.

This is why after a bit of research I invested in German Schwalbe tyres, designed for cycle touring. They are widely recommended. I had cycled 637 miles to Zacatecas without getting a single puncture. I was impressed. The trouble was I didn't dare tell anyone in case it precipitated one! In engineering terms that is absurd. Simply talking about something doesn't make it happen. However, there is a degree of superstition in everyone, so I kept my secret to myself.

Zacatecas is at a crossroads in the centre of the country, giving me a choice of routes. My aim of getting to Panama made it logical to go to Guadalajara. In the meantime, however, Hurricane Stan had hit Chiapas, Guatemala, and El Salvador with such force that many homes and roads had been washed away. There had been deaths, and thousands were homeless. Every night there were pictures on the news, so I could monitor things further south. I was glad I wasn't there as I would be in the way of the rescue operations. People had no water. It was an emergency of vast proportions.

Normally, the rainy season in Mexico is from May to September, and September is the peak month for bad weather. I deliberately timed my trip to coincide with the dry season, October to April. Starting at Chihuahua in the north west of the country I was furthest from the hurricane zone around the Gulf of Mexico. However, the further south I cycled, the closer I got.

What I couldn't plan for was how they recover and rebuild by the time I reached the affected areas, about December. I knew the frontier with Guatemala was closed because the bridges had been washed away. When this happens, they usually rebuild in a matter of days. However, if I needed to change plans Zacatecas would be an ideal place to do this. I could turn back northwards, go through Monterrey, and into Texas. A bit different, but in my heart I knew that I really wanted to go to Central America.

I decided to keep going, monitoring the news. The option of turning northwards and heading for Texas would continue to be viable until I reached, perhaps, Oaxaca. I had plenty of time.

There are two roads from Zacatecas to Guadalajara. The main road is direct. A minor route wanders through Jerez and Tlaltenango, crossing a few sierras. It looked more interesting, so I left Zacatecas bright and early on a Sunday morning, after saying an emotional farewell to Eduardo. He was sad to see me go, and I felt touched. However, all travellers know when it is time to move on.

The altitude of Zacatecas meant that the road descended easily from mountains to cattle ranches. I revelled being on the move again, with a new bottom bracket. I looked forward to being in Jerez, which Eduardo had told me was lively on Sundays.

He was right. The place was packed. The streets were busy with local ranchers, dressed in cowboy outfit. These weren't city people posing as cowboys, they were cowboys. They wore Wrangler jeans, button-up shirts with twin pockets, and leather boots. They looked handsome and serious. Many drove round in their pick-up trucks, eyeing up the crowded pavements. Others came into town on horseback. They could sit on their horses, drinking beer. More macho, and less risky with the police. The girls had to be similarly dressed, or they wouldn't be taken seriously.

I took a room at the Hotel Plaza. It was small but cheap, and had the bonus of a roof with a view of the *plaza*. The owner showed me the way to the roof, and said I could take a chair and some beer up there if I wanted. He even found a light chair that would be easy to carry up the stairs. That's what I call service.

Staying in so many hotels, I gradually formed an opinion of what makes a hotel good or bad. I don't think there is an absolute answer, to be honest. A consistent factor was that family run hotels tend to give better service. You get problems at hotels where the owner is absent and has left poorly paid employees in charge, indifferently watching television at reception.

After a shower and a beer I set out to explore Jerez, and find something to eat. The *plaza* was the focal point of the town with mature trees giving shade from the relentless sun. Children were playing, and toy sellers tempted them with things to play with.

As it got dark, I took a couple of bottles of beer up to the hotel roof to watch the sunset. A full moon rose slowly over the surrounding woods. In a corner of the *plaza*, a band was playing for about twenty people in a group, all wearing cowboy hats and clothes, dancing to traditional music. I went down for a closer look. It was a birthday party. It is common is this part of Mexico to hire a band for a birthday, and hold the party in the street. People stood in the *plaza* watching. The boot shiners were doing a good trade.

The hotel owner warned me there would be a disco next door until midnight. At ten o'clock many of the people in the square started to go into the disco. Most wore cowboy hats. It looked strange. I couldn't imagine many discos in northern Europe allowing in so many people wearing cowboy hats. Maybe they slept in them too.

At midnight the disco closed and quietness fell. The young people filed out, still wearing their hats. I slept well.

In the morning, I left for Tlaltenango, seventy-two miles away. It was a long day typified by hills, mountains, and stops for drinks and ice creams. I arrived in Tlaltenango feeling good at having cycled such a distance. I pedalled around looking at the hotels. The Hotel Plaza – another one – looked promising. At another a fierce looking woman sat in reception. I could read the price list hanging on the wall without having to bother her. I preferred the look of the Hotel Plaza so went back. They had two types of room. Some overlooked the *plaza*, and some were internal. They were a bit expensive, so I decided to look for somewhere else. In my haste, I accidentally let the bike fall to the ground.

The manager came running out to say that he was authorised to offer me discount. Losing a potential customer was more than he could take. We agreed terms, and I took a first floor room with a view of the *plaza*. It had a wide double bed, a large bathroom with hot water, and bed-side tables with lamps. It's surprising how many hotels lack bedside lights. In cheap places you can expect minimal furniture. When you pay more you deserve not to have to find your bed in the dark, having turned off the overhead light with the switch conveniently located by the door on the other side of the room.

I think some hotel owners have never actually slept in their hotels.

Tlaltenango was a busy market town, with a lot of clothes shops. People were well-dressed. It lacked a decent restaurant though. I could choose between more *tacos* from the street chefs, or a burger and chips. I was tired and hungry, having sauntered over seventy-two mountainous miles, so I went for the latter. I washed away the taste with an ice cream. I haven't mentioned Mexican ice creams before, which is remiss of me. They are exquisite. The range of flavours is unbelievable, and many are made with fresh fruit. I became addicted to them, especially a brand called La Michoacána.

In the morning I had to ask for directions out of town, due to the usual absence of signposts. Conflicting directions made me go round in circles a few times before finding the escape route. The road climbed high. A view opened up over a long valley which seemed to stretch for ever. I stood looking at the view for a while, not realising that the road went down into the valley. The descent was exhilarating. Then the road climbed up again, onto another sierra. It was steep and I was pushing the bike a lot. At the top was a police check-point, near a small cafe. "They are looking for drugs" said the cafe owner, as his little son popped open my bottle of Coke.

I was heading for a big city, Guadalajara, and made the most of the mountain scenery. My plans after Guadalajara were a little unclear. I spent the night at a roadside hotel on the outskirts of Gárcia de la Cadena. I lay in bed thinking about the ride into Guadalajara. It is Mexico's second largest city, with a population of four million. It would be like cycling into Birmingham, something I would never contemplate doing. It was going to be scary, to say the least, and I was worried.

Gárcia de la Cadena lies at the foot of a hill. Climbing up it the next morning took my mind off Guadalajara. Ten miles before the city I cycled past its landfill rubbish dump. The entire morning harvest of urban rubbish pounded past me in big smelly lorries. The road had no shoulder. The rubbish lorries were large and noisy, as well as smelly. And of course, they all came back empty after dumping their load. The sun was hot. To say it was unpleasant is a monumental understatement.

I stopped at a shop and sat under a canvas canopy tied up with baling twine. I was out of the sun, but the lorries weren't far away. A lot of little girls were playing, and I became their centre of attention for a while. A woman came out to serve me. She described the route into the city centre and told me not to worry as the traffic goes so slowly it is safe.

Feeling more assured, I followed her directions, which were good. Soon I saw the towers of the cathedral ahead of me. She was right about the traffic, too. It was slow and there was a service road next to the dual carriageway for much of the way, so I could avoid most of the traffic. Near the cathedral I asked a traffic warden if he knew a central, economical hotel. He pondered for a moment, and then came up with a suggestion close by. It was opposite a shop that sold chilled beer. So far so good. The receptionist showed me a comfortable double room which I could have for the single rate. When he showed me how to work the TV, on came Real Betis –v- Chelsea. I had reached Guadalajara, my first significant target. I had a bed, beer, and football. What more could I want!

CHAPTER THREE

ACAPULCO HERE I COME

I had cycled almost nine hundred miles since leaving Creel, and Guadalajara was my first major city. Cycling such a distance without encountering any significant cities emphasises the sheer scale of Mexico. I spread out my map on the hotel room floor and looked at where I had come. Suddenly, the prospect of reaching countries to the south of Mexico looked achievable.

Pondering the various options, I decided I would head for the Pacific coast. First, I needed to get out of the city. No matter how I looked at the map, it was difficult to go in that direction without using motorways. That didn't appeal. I was told they were dangerous, and illegal anyway.

I went to the bus station to find out about a bus to Manzanillo. I liked the sound of the name, and the bus ride would be perpendicular to my main direction of travel. Taking the bus would not significantly reduce the distance cycled.

In Mexico, most bus stations are on the edge of town. This is good for taxi drivers as it keeps them busy. Maybe I should have taken a taxi like everyone else. I cycled. It is nine kilometres from the city centre, along an unbelievably busy dual carriageway which ends at a motorway intersection. I stood there for a while, staring at the motorways, trying to work out where to go. I asked passers-by how to get to the bus station. They pointed up a motorway. I cycled a little way up it, took fright, and turned back.

I asked some more people, hoping they would give me more acceptable advice. No, it was the same. I braced myself and cycled about half a mile along the hard shoulder, traffic whizzing past my left shoulder. I got to a footbridge. Two workmen in shabby clothes were pushing shabbier bikes over it. I stopped to ask them the way, and they pointed over the bridge to a small road next to the motorway. The ordeal was over; I crossed the bridge and took the road, past a line of waiting busses and cheap cafés. I went into a new terminal still under construction. Some workmen wearing hard hats shouted at me, and told me the real bus station was next door. I had to dodge taxis nipping about like demented bluebottles before making it onto a broad concourse lined with bus company offices. I walked round looking at the times and fares displayed on boards behind each company's desk, glad that shopping around wasn't too great a test of my linguistic ability.

Before committing myself, I took in a breath and thought. I knew that there was no way I was going to cycle along motorways to get to the Pacific coast, so I took the plunge and bought a first class ticket to Manzanillo for the following day, with the most expensive company. No charge for the bike. Sometimes you need to push the boat out, and my reaction to the stressful ride to the bus station was to want a relaxing bus ride, laying back on a reclining seat and looking at the scenery.

Cycling back into the city centre, I was more aware of my chaotic surroundings. Shops and factories had been thrown up with little regard for planning or aesthetics. Advert hoardings were stuck up everywhere, competing with each other for attention and money. Vivid colours were the order of the day in the advertising industry. There were frequent sets of traffic lights, and traffic moved slowly. A teenager cycled behind me. When we stopped at traffic lights we chatted. He liked cycling, football, and most sports. He found it hard to keep up with me. Without realising it, I was getting fitter after all these miles.

I went to see Guadalajara town hall. Sitting in the council chamber looking at the murals, I got into conversation with an American man. He was twenty-five and had short hair. He had been to Germany for his job. I asked him what his job was. "I'm a soldier" he said. He was going to Iraq in January. We had a long talk about the Iraq War....for him it's his job; he has to do what he's told. He said we're supposed to learn from wars, but we never seem to. He thought we will never know the true motives of the politicians about the Iraq War. I confessed to my disappointment that Tony Blair seemed to have lied about the 'weapons of mass destruction': as far as I was concerned, the war was really a dishonest manoeuvre to control oil supplies.

He was an engineer and was going to Iraq to help them build new schools. He was well motivated, and I felt pleased that I had found common ground with an American soldier in having concerns over war. He was a Texan, from El Paso. It was his first time in Mexico, which seemed remarkable as he lived in a border town.

The following day the young man who worked on reception gave me a hug when I said goodbye, as if I was setting off on a pilgrimage somewhere. We had got on well, my comings and goings had brought a bit of excitement to a job he found boring. I pedalled back to the bus station a lot more bravely this time, knowing the way and less fearful of the brief sprint I had to do along the motorway hard-shoulder.

The bus to Manzanillo had wide, comfortable seats, and we were given a drink and a sandwich. The pleasures of first class travel! After a brief stop in Colima, we were soon in Manzanillo. The bus station was a few miles out of town, up a dusty track in what was little more than a clearing in the woods. Women were carrying shopping along the track. I asked them the way, and they described a route alongside a railway line taking massive freight wagons to and from the port. I could see docks and wharves on the other side of the railway line, and dock workers whistled in encouragement as I breezed past. The ride into town took twenty minutes enabling me to say that I cycled to the Pacific Coast, after all!

It was good to see the sea again after weeks in the desert and mountains. Before starting my journey, I had lived in Valencia in Spain for a year. I was missing being near the sea. As soon as I checked in to a hotel, I went to the waterfront. I found a bare-walled bar with little character and two ladies serving. Or I should say, waiting to serve, as I was the only customer. At least I could choose the seat with the best view of the sea! I sat there with my beer, smelling the sea. It was fantastic. I bought some *tacos* from a *taqueria* over the road. They smelt and tasted equally good.

I was staying in the old town, some distance from the beaches and hotels that now comprise the resort of Manzanillo. In the heart of the old town you could imagine the resort didn't exist. There was a market, streets full of shops, and on the seafront a pier. A naval ship was tied up at the pier, and sailors were practising their diving skills from dinghies. I walked to a rocky headland, where a platform gave good views of the sunset over the Pacific. I never saw sunsets over the sea on the east coast of Spain.

One of the shops in town sold bottles of wine. This is unusual in Mexico as Mexicans don't normally drink the stuff. The weather is too hot. Shops only sold wine at places where there were foreigners. Mexicans call all spirits *vinos*, and once when I asked in a shop for some wine, I was given a bottle of brandy, which wasn't quite what I had in mind. In some Mexican states anything stronger than beer has to be sold under supervision. Looking at the wine on display, I noticed that bars were padlocked across the front of the shelf so you couldn't move the bottles. An assistant came over to help me. I explained to her that in Europe it is normal to drink wine with our evening meal. As I left, I heard her telling a colleague "You know, in Europe, they drink wine with their dinner." "Really? How strange" was the reply.

The tourist information lady in Manzanillo had a wealth of information at her disposal. She and her leaflets were crammed into a minuscule blue and white kiosk on the waterfront. If she had needed to bend to scratch her foot, she may not have managed; such was the smallness of her kiosk. She told me about a turtle sanctuary thirty miles down the coast at Cuyutlan. I decided to go there. Leaving Manzanillo knowing I had an easy day ahead of me, I dallied a little bit on the road.

Cuyutlan is at the end of a dead end road that leaves the coastal road before Armería. It goes through swamps with palm trees leaning over the roadside. Apart from the sounds of birds it was almost deserted. From time to time I heard mysterious plopping noises in the swamps as I pedalled past, but I never worked out what they were. Suffice to say, I lived to tell the tale! The tarmac ended just before Cuyutlan, so I pedalled into the village along a dirt road. It was a curious place. A resort out of season. There were food shops and a row of shops selling swimming gear, towels, and tee-shirts. There was a noticeable lack of customers. The girls working in them looked up hopefully as I passed, but I didn't see anything I needed.

There were plenty of hotels to choose from. I was drawn to one right on the seafront that looked as if it was falling down. The owner said a room was ninety pesos and invited me to view two of them. I took the better of the two, as it seemed a bargain. It had a view of the sea, and plenty of ventilation as one of the windows was broken. In front of the hotel, on the sand, was a row of *palapas*, offering freshly caught fish. They had roofs made from palm branches, to shelter customers from the hot sun, making them look ramshackle. Some had been busy at lunchtime, but others clearly had not. On the beach there was no electricity supply, cooking was done over open fires. The food was kept refrigerated with chunks of ice and stored in cooler boxes. I was wary of this, as the day was very hot, and ate in a restaurant in the village.

I asked the owners of the hotel why it was in a bad state of repair. It had been damaged in an earthquake four years ago and the previous owners had run the place down. The present owners bought it three days before my arrival to restore. This story was later corroborated by two other people I met, and there were certainly plenty of workmen around. The new owners had lived in the United States for years and retired back home to Mexico to live. I got the impression that buying a collapsing hotel was more of a hobby than a business. The woman confided in me that they had plenty of money and didn't need business ventures at their stage in life!

The Director of Tourism for the area visited for lunch. I was introduced to her, as I was the first non-Mexican visitor since the new owners took over. Fame!

I went to the turtle sanctuary, full of anticipation at the thought of seeing some real live turtles. It was at the end of a road along the shore, and consisted of two sections. One was a building which housed the café, information centre, offices and general amenities. Opposite was a large area with a low roof covering a number of circular and oval tanks, each surrounded by a wall about two feet high. These contained the turtles.

I spent two hours there, learning about their work, and watching the turtles. They crawl ashore during the night and lay their eggs in the sand. The sanctuary staff gather eggs off the beach, incubate them so they hatch, then keep them in tanks for three days before releasing them back into the sea. Some Mexicans regard turtle eggs as a delicacy, and go along the beach looking for them, which is illegal. It is also illegal for restaurants to offer them for sale. People ignore the law if they can get away with it, as there is money to be made. The day I was there they had 500 baby turtles in a huge tank. They also have a few adults of various ages for study. Mexico is host to seven out of eight varieties of turtle in the world, all of which are threatened with extinction because of the precarious way in which they lay their eggs. I was heartened that Mexico takes species preservation seriously and has several sanctuaries.

Cycling back into Cuyutlan I saw a bit more wildlife than I had bargained for. A snake shot across the road in front of me. It was about a metre long and was moving fast. I was glad we hadn't collided. It was only the second live snake I had seen since starting. I saw plenty of dead ones, killed by early morning lorries and left as carrion.

From Cuyutlan my next destination was San Juan. Pedalling slowly through Armería looking for somewhere to stop for a drink, I heard a voice behind me say "Hablas Español?" I turned round and saw another cyclist with identical gear to mine - panniers, tyres, even cheap cycling shorts from Decathlon (nine euros fifty, and good value!).

The Basque flag was flying proudly on the rear carrier, and the irony of asking if I spoke Spanish wasn't lost on me. His name was Endika. He was cycling from Alaska to Chile, and had done eight thousand kilometres so far, making me feel a bit small. He was worried that his tyres were more worn than mine! He had left Alaska five months before.

We chatted about our journeys and plans. I mentioned my concern about the hurricane damage further south. He said the Guatemalan frontier was open again as the bridges had been replaced. We cycled along together for a while, but he was planning to stay with a friend in Colima, so we separated at the next junction. We exchanged email addresses and still keep in touch.

The power to maintain contact by email is a new luxury for long distance travellers. Twenty years ago, if you travelled it was hard to keep in touch. You could phone home and write letters. Fine. If you met people whilst travelling, you normally lost contact as soon as you parted, unless you were particularly determined. Several times on this trip, I arranged to meet people whom I had already met elsewhere on the journey, simply because we had kept track of each other by email. It sounds like Big Brother, but it was tremendous to be able to do that. When travelling you can feel isolated at times, but reading and sending emails makes up for this in a big way.

The excitement of meeting Endika kept me going into San Joan. Most of the buildings were hotels and the place was deserted, so I pedalled up and down the single street looking for the best value hotel. It was out of season and I was the only guest for the night. I finished off the day's cycling with a swim in the sea, having the yellow swathe of sand to myself. The town's only shop resembled something out of an old Western film. As there was no restaurant open I had a 'picnic' in my hotel room.

The morning sun streaming into the room woke me early. Leaving San Juan the road became hilly and remote. Up and down I went, peering nervously into the jungle on each side of the road. People said there were no hotels and I knew I would have to camp. There were signs on the road asking us not to hunt the jungle fauna and to take care of it. You certainly knew there was fauna in there, you could hear it grunting, squawking, and rustling in the undergrowth. There was no way I was camping in that lot. A large spider as big as my hand crossed the road in front of me. I didn't know if it was poisonous and had no idea if it could jump. I didn't wait to find out.

The road suddenly climbed high, as if skirting a mighty glen. The hard work in the jungle heat was unwelcome. Damn it, everyone knows coastal roads are supposed to follow the line of the sea and be completely flat, so you can amble along listening to the waves swishing against the rocks. I hoped my effort would be rewarded by sweeping majestically down to the sea, like the Mountains of Mourne in the well-known song.

At five thirty I had only two hours daylight left. The road passed around a cliff top and I spotted two deserted golden beaches, about 1000 feet below - encircled by jagged rocks, poking out of the sea like wolves' teeth. Mercifully, the road rolled downhill for a couple of miles to a bridge over a dried out river, the lowest point in the road. I looked for a way to the beaches. I was also thinking about how

I was going to eke out my limited supplies of food and water. I asked a couple of teenage boys to show me the way to the beach. We passed a field where some people were harvesting melons. I offered to buy one. The foreman wanted ten pesos, a good price for a five kilo melon! I had no change, but one of the villagers reached into his pocket and paid the ten pesos for me. The generosity touched my heart. He was proud of the fact that he had once lived in Washington, where he had seen snow!

The two boys took me to the beach and helped me put up the tent. They were curious to see how it went up as they had never been camping; in fact they had never left the immediate vicinity of their village. We watched a medley of crimson, orange and yellow as the sun went down. The boys went home and I had the beach to myself. Although the two boys knew I was there, they assured me the village was safe. It had a population of 120. I ate as much of the huge melon as I could, and the waves lulled me into peaceful sleep.

The following morning I passed another long distance cyclist; an American living in Peru and returning home to Colorado. He had flown from Peru to Mexico City. Seeing two long distance cyclists in as many days improved my confidence as I realised that I was not alone. Even, dare I say it, normal.

Furthermore, a shop owner where I stopped for a drink had seen Hersh, the Canadian cyclist I met in Creel five weeks before. We are a small and noticeable breed!

I continued through beautiful coastal scenery, with hardly any traffic. The next night I rented a wooden cabaña on the beach at Nexpla. Cabaña may be too grand a word for what was no more than a large garden shed on stilts, with a bed in it, and a hammock on the veranda. It was lovely lying in the hammock, listening to the sea. An Australian, living in Canada, had been in the cabaña next door for a month. He was happily lost in his thoughts most of the time I saw him. He said he was a surfer, although I never saw him surfing. Nexpla was a surfing resort plonked in the middle of nowhere, a collection of motley beach cabañas waiting to disappear under the next tidal wave.

In the morning, the beach was lined with local fishermen using hand lines to catch fish. It needed a lot of patience, and they had been there since before it got light. Their families were waiting for the fish they would catch. It was a paradox that the beach was shared by rich surfers from affluent countries, and poor fishermen wearing the surfers cast off clothes, scraping a living from the same blue waters.

It was tempting to stay with the surfers and fishermen at Nexpla another night, but I pressed on to Lázaro Cárdenas knowing I still had plenty more coast to come.

Lázaro Cárdenas was a hive of activity. Streets lined with stalls selling everything you could imagine. Plastic goods, electrical goods, clothes, kitchen utensils. It was all there. People shouted, music played. This wasn't a quiet back-water. Buying and selling made people hungry and there were stalls selling *tacos* and pizzas. It was manic. Sometimes I got the impression that the whole of Mexico was in the middle of a retail bonanza. Lázaro Cárdenas was determined not to miss out.

The town was originally called Melchor Ocampo. A man called Lázaro Cárdenas was the state governor of Michoacán from 1928 to 1932, and President of Mexico from 1934 to 1940. During his presidency, he put into effect land distribution that created more peasant communal holdings or *ejidos*. He nationalised the railways and, even more controversially, the petroleum industry. The latter was done in 1938 to deal with a pay crisis which the petrol companies would not resolve, culminating in a strike in the industry. Britain and the United States didn't like losing control of their investments and boycotted Mexican oil. Mexico sold it to Nazi Germany, so Britain broke off diplomatic relations. Oil nationalisation has proven to be for the long term good of Mexico, enabling oil reserves to be redirected into the Mexican economy. There are parallels with what Hugo Chávez is doing in Venezuela today.

Lázaro Cárdenas was a popular President, and is credited with doing much for the poor. He died in 1970 and the town was re-named after him in his honour. There are other towns in Mexico named after politicians. Two are named after Vicente Guerrero, a rebel leader in the independence struggle against Spain, who became President in 1829 and was assassinated in 1831. In the United Kingdom we have airports named after Robin Hood, John Lennon and George Best – but politicians? Hmmm, please spare us that one.

Two spokes in the rear wheel had been loose for a while, but I had been ignoring them, pedalling on regardless as if on a suicide mission. There was a cycle repair shop opposite my hotel, so I wheeled it in for advice. The two men looked at it and told me to do nothing. Let sleeping dogs lie. Advice confirming my opinion is always welcome, I am human after all. I had done a hundred miles since I first noticed the problem, so I was inclined to leave it until I got to Acapulco. They then fiddled about with the gears, and charged me twenty pesos for doing so. That annoyed me intensely as I had no problems with them. I had been taken for a ride, which annoyed me after their agreeable advice about the spokes.

To restore my equilibrium, I went for a coffee at a café called El Sabor de Gloria – The Taste of Gloria. I sat alone on a trendy wrought iron bar stool, looking at the paintings and modern art on display. The café seemed a little out of place in a working town like Lázaro Cárdenas. Gloria, the owner, told me about her life. She was from Mexico City, but preferred the tranquillity of Lázaro Cárdenas. She felt a good quality café would bring a bit of civilisation to the place. She had created her own niche market. Gloria enjoyed talking to me so much that she refused to allow me to pay for my coffee. I will have to be pleasant and interesting more often.

After coffee, my next task was to change hotels. I had inadvertently chosen a hotel next to a set of traffic lights. It was a Friday night, and I had been kept awake by the sound of music booming from the cars waiting at the lights. All night long, as the song goes. I would never make the same mistake again. Finding a different hotel for Saturday night, I made a different mistake, as I failed to ask whether there would be a wedding party in the hotel. There was, next to my room. After two sleepless nights in Lázaro Cárdenas, I am surprisingly benign in writing about it!

My mileage was now 1,030. I had passed 1,000 miles, a psychological achievement. The downside was that my milometer was only set for three digits, so in one fell swoop I went from 999 miles down to nought. Not three noughts, just nought. All my achievement wiped off the clock. I wasn't having that again so I re-set the milometer to four digits.

I left Lázaro Cárdenas confident of making it to 2,000 miles, but stopped after only ten in a village with very colourful flower beds down the middle of the street. I sat outside a café and ordered a coffee, and as an afterthought some biscuits, which were brought to me in a cereal bowl. A pick-up truck arrived and three men got out. One of them joined me so he could practice his English. He lived in California, and was back home for a holiday. His name was Jessie, a bit unusual for a Mexican. "I'm really Jesus," he said "but Americans don't like it. They think it's blasphemous to be called Jesus, so I now call myself Jessie."

Jesus is a common first name in Spanish speaking countries, and Jessie's experience of Christian intolerance appalled me. What would Jesus himself had thought if he knew that one day people would find his name unacceptable? He may not have been surprised as he was himself a tragic victim of religious intolerance.

I had a long day ahead of me so I didn't sit long with Jessie. The next dots on the map were close together, Ixtapa and Zihuatanejo about seventy miles from Lázaro Cárdenas.

Ixtapa didn't impress me. It was almost indistinguishable from Benidorm except that the accents were American rather than British. True, there were plenty of hotels, but they all reached for the sky, with prices that did the same. There were large houses with high fences and alarm systems. There was money here. The road through it had a cycle lane, the only one I saw in Mexico. I was the only cyclist on it, so I felt it had been built especially for me!

The road to Zihuatanejo went uncompromisingly uphill. It was getting late and I was close to exhaustion. I was determined not to stay in Ixtapa so I carried on. It was a good decision. Zihuatanejo was a real town, with people, shops, and ice cream parlours. Finding a hotel was difficult. It was not a lack of hotels – to the contrary, there were plenty. The difficulty was that after my experiences with noise in Lázaro Cárdenas, I became excessively fussy. I walked around each hotel like a pompous official from the Noise Executive, determined to locate a source of noise to justify not staying there. There was either traffic or air conditioning units. I was told they don't make any noise, but I didn't believe it.

I found a small family run posada in a quiet backstreet. No air conditioning, no traffic. And, I was assured, no wedding parties! I liked the family instantly. They took to me too, so I decided to stay a few days. I needed a decent break from cycling. I wanted to lie on the beach and go swimming. True, I wasn't far from Acapulco, but

I thought Acapulco might be expensive, so I decided to have a holiday in Zihuatanejo.

⚲

Zihuatanejo is by a wide deep-water bay which is a natural harbour. The bay has cliffs, rocks, and sandy beaches. There was plenty to do. Some days I walked along the rocky coastal footpath to Playa La Ropa for a swim and a fish lunch at one of the beach restaurants. There was a motor boat taxi, but the walk was more fun. Other days I went down to the harbour to watch passengers come ashore from American cruise liners. The bars always put on traditional cowboy dancing, even though we were miles from cowboy country. The tourists loved watching the dancers twirling around each other romantically, an image of authentic Mexico.

On my last day I explored a minor road along the river bank. It led to the grand entrance to a large residential complex. I sat on a wall for a rest, and the security guard called me over to sit near his checkpoint, as the wall was in the shade.

He was studying an English grammar book, called English for Hotel Receptionists, and he asked for my advice on pronunciation. The word 'leisure' was giving him some grief. Our chat turned into an impromptu English lesson. He worked there twelve hours a day, six days a week, and found it boring because hardly anything happened. He said the pay was not good, but he wouldn't be specific on what he actually earned. His book was published in 1978 and included quaint phrases like 'Would you care for some more?' which now seem a bit dated.

After five days in Zihuatanejo I continued down the coast, aiming for a hotel at Papanoa. It was right on the cliff-top and was extraordinary, not least because of Victor, the eccentric owner. When I arrived he was sitting at a corner table in an otherwise empty restaurant, playing dominoes with a local. He said I was lucky to get a room as the place was normally full and he was expecting a hundred people on Friday. As it was Friday that day, I had no idea what he meant. He asked me to pay 600 pesos, which I told him was outrageous. I hadn't paid that much anywhere in Mexico. He then asked me how much I wanted to pay. I suggested 400 pesos and he said he would compromise on 500. It was expensive but the hotel was in a good location, and there was something appealing about Victor's eccentricity, so I decided to stay.

After a shower, I went back to the restaurant. There was little sign of activity, apart from Victor and his domino friend. When I asked about food, Victor said "I have some lovely coffee if you want", a number of times, as though trying to seduce me with it.

Meanwhile, the armed security guards were scrutinising girls on the beach through their binoculars.

Victor kept his loose change in a plastic carrier bag. In the morning, when I paid for my breakfast, the woman in the kitchen had to find Victor, to get him to find the plastic bag, so she could give me change.

I heard more about Victor later.

After a good night's rest, I left the hotel and continued along the road. There was more traffic than the day before. After a couple of hours I spotted two bikes with panniers coming towards me, from Acapulco. I stopped as we drew level. They stopped too. They came over to my side of the road, as there was a place where we could stand away from the traffic roaring past. They were Gavin and Leo, two young men from London, cycling from Panama to San Diego.

They had started in July, in the rainy season. They were having a last fling of freedom before starting serious careers in law. They had a deadline - flights booked back to London and new jobs to begin. This put them under more pressure than I was, travelling with no particular deadline. There was another contrast between us; they were using the opportunity to raise money for charity. I had decided to avoid the pressure of charity sponsorship as I wanted to protect my independence. If I packed in and caught the bus the rest of the way, no-body would lose out except me.

Their charity was Casa Alianza, an organisation dedicated to helping street children in Mexico and Central America. Casa Alianza[1] started work in Mexico in 1988, providing shelter and support to orphaned and homeless children living on the streets. Street children are vulnerable, easy to exploit, easy to ignore. Casa Alianza helps rebuild their lives by providing support, somewhere to go. It believes in helping a child in all ways – physical and mental health, nutrition, a roof, and clothing. The basics that many of us take for granted. I admired Gavin and Leo for their enthusiasm and commitment towards these children, the likes of whom we had each seen on our travels through this neglected part of the world. Casa

---

[1] www.casa-alianza.org

Alianza operates in Guatemala, Honduras and Nicaragua, as well as Mexico.

Meeting Leo and Gavin was tremendous for my morale. It was a defining moment in my journey, because I had been heading southwards with a vague idea of getting to Panama, but doubting whether I could actually do it. Meeting two guys who had come from the very place I was aiming for suddenly made my ambition achievable. It was too good to be true. We swapped emails and kept in regular contact, exchanging advice and encouragement.

In their first email I learned that they too had stayed at Victor's. Like me, they had been presented with a totally unrealistic room price, and had been more successful than me in knocking Victor down. He told them the hotel had been full the previous night (i.e. when I was there almost alone), so he seems to have delusions of grandeur. It hadn't occurred to Victor that cyclists travelling in opposite directions might stop and chat!

At the entrance to San Jeronimo was a turret with armed look-out men surveying all who passed. A sign above the door declared "Tourist Information and Security", so I went in to ask the vigilantes about hotels. They said there were cabañas to rent on a beach seven kilometres away, at the end of a side road. The road was well decorated with pot-holes. I wobbled along carefully to a village called Hacienda Las Cabañas. Small white houses needing some maintenance were strung out along both sides of the road, their doors open to let in some air. People sat watching the world – i.e. me – go by. Some waved as I passed. Small shops were trying to make ends meet by competing with each other to sell the same meagre range of food and drinks. The scruffiness of the houses and their occupants gave away there wasn't much money here.

The little road ended on the bank of a river at a place called Paraiso, or 'Paradise'. I didn't expect the road to end abruptly on a river bank beside a stone pier. The Tourist men in San Jeronimo hadn't mentioned that. I stood there gaping in disbelief at a sandy isthmus covered in palm trees on the other side of the river, living up to its name of Paradise. There was a row of *palapas* on the isthmus like those I had seen at Cuyutlan.

Boatmen were looking for customers, and one of them took me across in his green wooden motorboat. It crossed my mind that a bike might be a problem on a sandy isthmus with no roads, but I preferred not to think about it. I was in the mood to go with the flow and let things happen. It's more fun sometimes.

The boatman took me to a *palapa* called Sandra's as he was friendly with the people running it. A man came over from Sandra's and helped me push the bike across the sand to a shaded place on the beach where he said I could camp. He helped me put my tent up. At first I was nervous about loosing tent pegs in the sand. I needn't have worried; he showed me a better way of pegging a tent into the sand by digging down to the wet sand to put the pegs in! In spite of years of camping, I didn't know that. We live and learn.

Nearby a young Mexican was lying in a hammock next to his tent, drinking Sol beer. His name was Sergio from

Monterrey and he worked for Sol. He was combining a business trip with a weekend on the beach, so he had plenty of Sol with him. He plied me with a bottle as soon as we started talking.

I had a fish supper at Sandra's. As darkness fell I was brought a lamp made from an old mayonnaise jar, a bit of string, and some paraffin. Simple but effective. I took it back to my tent so I could write my diary by its light. A man camping nearby with his family came over and invited me and Sergio to their bonfire to join them for drinks and a chat. *Un rato* they called it. They were from 'DF', Distrito Federal, as Mexico City is called. They were regular visitors here, and explained that the beach camping area is informally divided up amongst the *palapas*. If you eat at one of them, they don't charge you for camping.

Our bonfire *rato* went on until late. The look on Sergio's face was a picture when he finally reached the bottom of the ice box and found there were no more bottles of Sol to dispense. The best part of the evening was lying back on the velvety dry sand watching for shooting stars in the clear sky.

I didn't sleep in my tent as I wanted to experience sleeping in a hammock. I am unlikely to do it again as tossing and turning was so awkward that I kept waking up. My rough night was rewarded by seeing the sun come up over the sea. The lagoon behind the isthmus was beautiful, with leaning palm trees and so many wild birds. The shoreline was lined by local men fishing with hand lines, making it look so easy.

I asked the *palapa* man for a boat back across the river. While I was waiting, he showed me some baby turtles he had hatched out from eggs he found on the beach. He would release them into the sea in two or three days. I was touched by his caring nature, and crossed the river feeling content with my night on the beach.

Cycling back towards the main road, I realised I had left my crash helmet festooned to a post on the beach! I wasn't going to carry on without it, so I had to pedal back to the pier, ask if I could leave my bike in the shop, and find a boatman willing to do the return trip for me. One took me in a boat with no engine which he had to punt across the river. On the way back ten minutes later, with my helmet, the boatman asked me how much it had cost. Telling him made me realise how unaffordable something like that is to so many rural Mexicans. The money he asked for punting me over, in relation to the time it took, was a fraction of the British Minimum Wage! I could hardly resent it.

The main road was quiet as it was Sunday. I enjoyed the relative tranquillity and put my foot down a bit, as I knew I had a good chance of reaching Acapulco. I was expecting it to be expensive and touristy, and didn't anticipate staying there long. I had been proven wrong before on this trip, and it was about to happen again.

CHAPTER FOUR

ALONG MEXICO'S PACIFIC COAST

Acapulco is exotic. Dramatic. It sweeps around a wide bay, with stunning views of coastline and the Sierra Madre. It originated as a port for the trade with China. Now there are many large modern resort hotels, used by jetsetters from around the world.

I nearly didn't make it to Acapulco. Before I got there, I came across a long stretch of road works, controlled by traffic lights. Pedalling hard to get through on green behind a stream of cars, I didn't quite make it, and the lights changed. A convoy headed by a large bus was bearing down on me. Surely the bus driver would slow down to let me get out of the way. But the look on his face said he wasn't going to. I jumped, complete with bike, landing headfirst in a bank of soil at the side of the road. In the stunned moment that followed, a couple of things clattered off the bike. While the pick-up driver behind shouted to see if I was OK, the offending bus passed on as if nothing had happened.

A close shave. Why was I travelling by bike, for heaven's sake? But the answer was simple: you see more. You are more equal to the people you meet, so interactions are easier and more relaxed. One bad driver doesn't change this, I told myself as I limped gingerly into Acapulco's Old Town.

The Old Town, centred on the zocalo or square, has many narrow and busy streets lined with shops, cafes and restaurants. Most of the voices around me were Mexican, a sure sign that this was the right place to look for an economical hotel. While I was wandering around checking out the options, I was stopped in a street by a Canadian wanting to borrow my pump. He and his friend had brought bikes from Canada on the roof rack of their van, but one of them had a flat tyre. Remarkably, they had no means of pumping it up.

I found a hotel I liked, and checked in for a few nights. I went to La Quebrada cliffs where divers dive into the sea twice a day, to raise money. It is spectacular and very well organised. One by one they climb up the cliffs where, after saying a prayer at the shrine, they carefully scrutinise the waves waiting for the right moment to dive. One display is during the day, the other at night. I went to see both. The night-time display is dramatic as they dive in to the sea carrying burning torches, which extinguish as soon as they hit the water. What started as a few local boys having a bit of fun has now been somewhat commercialised. You pay to get in, and then as you leave the divers thrust a large sack for donations into your face. Many people didn't seem to mind paying twice. If professional footballers did the same after a football game, they would probably get booed off the pitch.

There are several beaches in Acapulco. Whichever one you lie on, you are aware of a constant stream of people walking along the sand trying to sell you things. This is another side of Mexico's apparent retail bonanza. For many people without jobs, wandering around selling things is the only way they can hope to scratch together some money. I bought some very tasty home baking from one lady. Another offered me a massage. When I asked her how much she wanted, I think she was being a bit optimistic. Maybe she was trying to flatter me by over-estimating my wealth. I fancied the novelty of having a massage on the beach, so we negotiated a price that was both affordable to me, and fair to her. That's how 'market forces' should work. She said it was a hard way to earn a living, she usually found around ten customers a day.

The absence of welfare benefits in Mexico means that people who don't have a job either have to depend on their families, or resort to whatever means they can to earn a living. There are people selling things everywhere. Some of them see foreigners as prime targets, as we generally have more money than Mexicans. We can afford to travel to their country, so we must be rich. Some days, wandering around Acapulco or along the beach, I felt relentlessly targeted. Taxi drivers will walk up to you and ask if you want to go somewhere. Sometimes they wouldn't believe you wanted to walk.

It can be a bit oppressive. I had to come to terms with it as an inevitable consequence of being amongst poorer people. Sometimes it annoyed me. I had to tell myself that the exasperation I was feeling was nothing compared with the exasperation of poverty.

Another aspect of poverty that was evident in Acapulco was the street children. Many were orphans. Two I spoke to simply said they had no parents. At night they needed to be off the streets and out of harms way, but that didn't always happen. They hung around the restaurants hoping for money or food. The cashier at an Italian restaurant I used told me that there was a refuge where they could go for food and somewhere basic to sleep. You could see how easy it would be for them to slip into child prostitution, drug abuse, the slippery slope to no-where. Sadly the work that organisations such as Casa Alianza do can only scratch the surface. They should be able to do more, childhood is the most precious and vital part of a person's life. I saw children with lost childhoods, and wondered what hope they had for a decent adulthood.

After four enjoyable days in Acapulco I finally said goodbye to its beaches. The climb out was dusty and steep, with busses and lorries pounding up the hill after me, like lions stalking their prey. I saw a sailing ship at the Navy base and wondered if it was the one that was in Greenock for the Tall Ships Race a few years ago. The climb was hard but the views at the top worthwhile - beaches, coasts, and bays that all looked idyllic. Then the road sped me down to the sea again. All my work lost, but not wasted because the views had been worth it. I stopped for a drink at Rubi's neat little shop. A dog with three legs limped past, making the most out of life. A lesson to pessimists.

The road became quieter and more beautiful. I stopped at a fruit stall to buy bananas. The man wouldn't charge me. "*Un regalo*" he said, a present. "You need fibre". Spontaneous kindness, not uncommon in Mexico, is always a pleasure. He asked me what language is spoken in Scotland, which prompted a discussion about English and Gaelic, and the status of indigenous languages in Mexico.

San Marcos was very likeable. There was a hotel on the main street where I was offered a room for a hundred pesos. It was full of ants. I showed them to the receptionist, who said it was the only room for a hundred pesos; the others were 150 because they have TV. I borrowed a broom to sweep them out, but the ants had other ideas. They had checked in first, it was their room, so they marched straight back in again. I decided to upgrade to the room next door, one with TV. When I switched it on, a football match was about to start - Jaguars -v- Chivas. I just had enough time to nip over the road for some beer and pistachios, have a shower, and lay back to enjoy the football. Sadly, Jaguars lost 2-1. I have acquired a soft spot for them since watching them with Eduardo's wife in Zacatecas. Thank you, ants.

The following morning I managed an early rise and was on the road for eight twenty. Saw a tortoise crossing the road, and did an emergency stop to help it. I wanted to make sure it got off the road. Stamping my feet didn't make it move any faster, so I lay the bike down, picked up the tortoise, and carried it over the road. Then a line of traffic came round the corner, headed by a lorry. Phew! After twelve miles I stopped for a hearty breakfast. The waiter minced about with attitude and tight jeans, and was clearly not impressed with me. I asked him what Cafe de Olla was, he said he didn't understand, and I said, "It's a question - what is it." I ended up going into the kitchen, and the two girls there told me it was a type of ground coffee. It was very good too.

I camped on a beach again. It was another one where you could camp underneath palm shelters in front of a *palapa*. Playa La Bocana, on the estuary of the Rio Marquelia, was signposted from the town of Marquelia. I had a very pleasant evening socialising with some Germans camping there too, who were students in DF Mexico. We discussed whether the hand-fishermen on the beach do it for fun, or out of necessity. I suspect the latter. They have to survive. The *palapa* even had open air showers, so I could have a shower at bedtime and enjoy looking up at the stars as I lathered up.

The Germans, like me, were drinking Victoria Beer. That didn't surprise me as Germans like beer with flavour! There are many different brews in Mexico, suiting a variety of tastes. I quickly discovered that the popular brands exported to Europe are not necessarily the best. Victoria and Pacífico had become regular favourites of mine. I also had a passion for one called Bohemia, which has a very distinctive bouquet almost resembling an expensive white wine. Bohemia is always dearer, and not available everywhere. It has to be savoured. It is a good aperitif before dinner. In Mexico beer is normally served with a bowl of sliced limes, which the drinker squeezes directly into the beer. If it is very hot, some salt is brought too. I never saw lemon shoved down the neck of beer bottles by barmen, like you see in Europe.

The night was still, apart from a barking dog. I woke up to see the sun rise over the sea from the tent. I packed up and returned to Marquelia, to regain the main road. Later, I was sitting at a table outside a shop drinking some water, when a man came and sat with me. He asked me about the United Kingdom, what countries made it up, and whether they were all equal. A good question. He then pointed to all the litter in the street near where we sat, and asked me if it was the same in Europe. A difficult question to answer. I had noticed a lot of litter in Mexico, maybe I was becoming starting to forget that it's a growing problem in Europe too.

It was two o'clock and another thirty miles to Pinotepa Nacional. I judged that I could make it before dark. The first fifteen miles were fairly flat so I got a good pace on. Then there was an almighty hill I wasn't expecting. A bit late in the day for that sort of caper. At the top I stopped at a roadside kiosk for water. Maria turned off her radio to serve me, and said "Don't worry its downhill all the way now." She gave me a remarkably accurate description of all the landmarks I would pass, and said "its fifteen minutes by car, so it will take you twenty-five on a bike". Mmm, such confidence in my fitness. It wasn't entirely downhill, but I will forgive her that one!

In Pinotepa Nacional the teenager on hotel reception said it was against the rules to take bikes into bedrooms.

> "That's the first time in Mexico I have heard that", I said. Recalling the woman in Parral, I knew it wasn't quite true. A bluff is always worth trying.
>
> "How many cyclists have you had here?" I went on.
>
> "You are the first".
>
> "Show me where it is written in the rules then."

He took me into the office, where the boss was. The boss agreed that in my special circumstances, I could take the bike into my room. My special circumstances seemed to be that I wanted to stay in his hotel, and I had a bike with me. I gave him my thanks.

I walked around the town looking for an evening meal. On one side of the main road was a plaza. On the other side was an imposing white church with a giant tower. A lot of people were going in and out of the church. The town was busy. My comings and goings were barely noticed. The plaza was lined with *taquerias* doing good trade. People sat in rows under canvas awnings, chatting and eating. A jovial, round-faced woman shouted to me to join in. It was tempting, but I was becoming a little bored with Mexican food. I spotted a Pizza place down a side street. Brilliant. International food at last!

From Pinotepa Nacional I went to Puerto Escondido, crossing into the State of Oaxaca, then Zipolite. I had been to both places before, they hadn't changed much. I even stayed at the same hotels. That may have been a mistake in Puerto Escondido as the hotel was for sale, and rather run down. In spite of that, it felt good to be somewhere I had already been, for the first time in two months. It is nice to explore new places, but equally nice to be somewhere familiar. My previous visit had been four years before, when I had done a 300 mile circular cycle trip from Oaxaca down to the coast and back again. That trip had made me realise I wanted to see more of Mexico.

From Puerto Angel the road turned inland to Pochutla, so I knew it was going to be mountainous. I stopped in Pochutla to go to the bank. I heard a man behind me said *"Hola amigo"* – hello friend. "We are not friends" I said, somewhat defensively. Then I realised he was the man who had served me at the restaurant the previous day in Zipolite. He remembered that I liked good coffee, and sent me to a new coffee shop along the road, where I made a pig of myself with two cups of real coffee, and two portions of apple pie. I needed them for the stretch of road ahead.

I pedalled through the hills contemplating my general state of health and mind. After two months, I still felt very well, and was probably fitter than normal. I couldn't register any psychological toll apart from realising that I had been a bit irritable for a few days. There was no particular reason for it; for some reason I was being over critical of Mexico and Mexican people. Perhaps I was just missing Spain or Scotland or somewhere. Maybe I had reached the point where familiarity with my surroundings was making me critical, as if I belonged there somehow.

I came to the conclusion that what had made me irritable was seeing a lot of dirt and poor maintenance in Mexico. I also saw a lot of people sitting around doing nothing. I thought to myself "why can't they clean or mend something?

The visible effect of poverty was troubling me, particularly rural poverty. I was travelling mainly in rural areas where people simply don't have money to spend on anything other than bare essentials. Making things 'look nice' or repairing something that wasn't totally essential was beyond them financially. So it got left. Things became dirty and went without repair.

I recalled speaking in a village to a man who had lived and worked in Denver (Den Bear as he called it). He said in the United States people expect high standards of workmanship, whereas in Mexico people accept poor workmanship and low standards. He spoke about racism in the United States. Maybe Americans go to Mexico and see dirt and poor maintenance, and think "Mexicans are dirty and lazy". It was easy for me to think that too, but deep down I knew it wasn't true. They are victims of a country with rich and poor, nothing in between. In Europe we have millions of middle classes to keep the place spic and span. They barely exist in Mexico.

That night I sat in an internet café blasting off my thoughts to a friend. I realised some teenagers were reading the email over my shoulder to practice their English. I suppose I asked for it, as I had been sniggering at their discussions about finding boyfriends or girlfriends on the internet. I love internet cafes in small towns as they are the modern meeting places of local teenagers, and have a fun atmosphere. The teenagers were really lovely people; I was embarrassed they may have seen I was being critical of their country. They didn't deserve that, and I felt ashamed of myself.

About a hundred miles separate Crucecito from Salina Cruz. My map showed only one village, a place called Santiago Astata. It was going to be a remote stretch of cycling, so I made sure I set off with plenty of water and some food. After twelve miles I stopped at a small roadside shed, where a cheerful man sold drinks. He gave me some fermented pineapple juice, which was surprisingly pleasant. Chickens scurried about, on the eternal hunt for scraps of food. We sat on a rough wooden bench at the front of the shack. The shopkeeper started talking about bird flu, an epidemic spreading across the world, and on the point of breaching Europe. His son then arrived, on a small motorcycle. He was a bird expert and had been on a roadside hill since six o'clock, watching birds. He had watched me cycle past through his binoculars. He showed me his book "Birds of Mexico" and described enthusiastically the number and variety of birds that could be seen in the State of Oaxaca. Over three hundred different birds. As we sat, he pointed out a hummingbird, which was hovering motionless over some flowers. It was so small; I probably wouldn't have noticed it on my own.

The road continued its manic helter-skelter ride over the valleys that were taking the mountain rainwater down to the sea. Deep ravines, steep hills. I pressed on, unsure of finding accommodation in Santiago Astata. The road passed to one side of the village, with one road in. The junction was lined with shops and cafés, which all looked a bit rough. I was prepared to camp, but had a feeling that something might turn up. I asked the pharmacist if she knew of anywhere I could stay. "The Metro" she said," everyone knows where it is". I went into the village and asked people for directions, finally arriving at a building that looked a bit like a hotel. It had no signs. There was a small shop at the entrance. The stout woman on guard said there was a room available for 130 pesos. She went to prepare it. When she took me to the room, I wondered what she had meant by preparation. It was dirty and I had to flush the toilet away. I asked for a towel and she looked at me with complete amazement.

As if asking for a towel weren't bad enough, I asked for a key. Startled, she said she had none. I would have to stay in my room as she locks up and goes home at seven. I was amazed. I told her a hotel is not a prison, but she wasn't moved. I told her I wanted to walk round the village and buy food. She said she would wait till I got back. Sure enough, when I got back she was there, arms folded, waiting to go home. I resigned myself to a night in prison. I wandered around the internal courtyard, like a zoo animal looking for a way out, a breach in the defences. Luckily I discovered that although she had closed the doors, she hadn't locked them, as some of the other rooms were used as computer classrooms. A young man was still working in one of them. He appreciated my predicament about not wanting to be locked in, and showed me how he would put the padlock in the lock without actually closing it. An old, well known trick.

Re-claiming my freedom, I was able to have another walk around the village. This time I was joined by a group of teenage boys who wanted to talk about football. By now I was a village celebrity - as soon as they approached me one said "you are cycling through Mexico aren't you?" I sneaked back into The Metro like a naughty public schoolboy. The Metro was a bit of a rip off, but at least it was secure.

My plan was to continue to Salina Cruz, from where I would turn inland through the mountains of Chiapas.

Approaching Salina Cruz a wind got up. It was of course a headwind, and the road ahead went uphill before rounding a headland and entering the town. I huddled against a roadside shop to build up my energy. The cheerful lady said it was often windy there. I was approaching the Isthmus of Tehuantepec, the narrowest part of Mexico. Winds swept across from the Caribbean to the Pacific, drawn by the air currents caused by differences in temperature.

The headland gave an impressive view of Salina Cruz. The town is grey, with numerous houses speckled on the dry hillsides around. It is a port, with an oil terminal and light industry. A railway snakes its way through the town, connecting the port with the state capital of Oaxaca, 250 kilometres away. Freewheeling down into the town, dodging in and out of heavy traffic, I heard the horn of a railway engine, blasting every few seconds. The railway, used only for freight, goes through the centre of town along the side of a street. The street was busy with people, and the train driver had to be vigilant and assertive. People scurried everywhere, getting out of its way. The groaning freight train made its way down to the port and in its wake normality resumed.

After my night in the Metro, I needed somewhere a bit more comfortable. Salina Cruz is a commercial town with a range of hotels so I found what I wanted behind the main square. The following morning was a Sunday. It was 20th November, although the significance of the date didn't immediately register with me. There were parades in town. Groups of children dressed in traditional clothing marched into the square, and stopped in front of the mayor and his officials to pay their respects. They performed dances, or made human towers by delicately balancing on top of each other. Some of the boys did colourful acrobatic displays. Mexico was enjoying itself.

Curiosity got the better of me, and I asked a girl in a shop what the parades were all about. "It's 20th November, the day of the revolution." she cheerfully assured me. I felt daft that it hadn't dawned on me that every town has a 20th November Street.

Mexican history is pock-marked with revolutions. The one celebrated on 20th November is the anniversary of start of the war in 1910 to overthrow the dictator Porfirio Díaz.

Like many dictators, General Porfirio Díaz started out as a revolutionary hero. He had been an important military figure during the latter part of the 19th century, winning power by leading a rebellion against President Lerdo de Tejada in 1876.

Under his rule, there was political stability and the development of new industries and railways. This brought much needed investment to Mexico. As is often the case, power went to his head. The spoils of his endeavour did not reach the bulk of the people. Soon there was unrest. In 1906 there was a miners strike at Cananea in the State of Sonora. Díaz moved swiftly to end the uprising, leading to a massacre at the mine. This sowed the seeds of the inevitable revolution.

Presidential elections were scheduled to be held in 1910. It was clear that Díaz was planning to be re-elected. In early 1909 Francisco Madero founded the Anti Re-electionist Party. Madero came from a wealthy family and had studied business in France as well as in the United States. He published newspaper articles arguing against the re-election of Díaz, in the name of democracy and freedom for the people of Mexico. Support for Madero gathered momentum. The Anti Re-electionist party nominated him to run for President in the 1910 elections.

Díaz reacted by imprisoning Madero, who heard the results of the elections whilst in gaol in San Luis Potosí. He learned that Díaz had declared himself President of Mexico again through an electoral fraud. After the election, Madero was released from prison, but in the meantime he had drafted the Plan of San Luis Potosí, calling for the nation to rise in rebellion on 20th November. Uprisings took place throughout the country, including one led by Pancho Villa, whose story I told at Parral. Villa captured the northern town of Ciudad Juárez, the loss of which prompted Díaz to resign and flee. Fresh elections were held, and Madero became President.

Revolutionaries always agree on one thing – the need for revolution. Beyond that, disagreements set in as the post-revolutionary agenda becomes dominated by questions of what to change, how to change it, and at what pace. The 20th November revolution was no exception. Madero believed in gradual, evolutionary change; more radical reformers wanted Fast Bucks from the revolution. The next ten years saw violence, counter-revolution, and civil war. Madero was assassinated. His death was one of many, it is estimated that almost two million Mexicans perished. When fighting finished in 1920 the economy was in a parlous state. The poverty which had had spawned the 1910 revolution had got worse.

Reading about this depressing period was a foretaste of what I was to experience in Central America. A never ending struggle to get out of the circle of injustice, poverty, failed revolution. A fight so desperate that the desperate no longer fight. In Mexico, you could be excused for thinking you were merely studying history. In Nicaragua, what you see can break your heart.

CHAPTER FIVE

THROUGH THE MOUNTAINS
OF CHIAPAS

Santo Domingo Tehuantepec is a small town with a large name. It is known locally as Tehuantepec, the original name used by indigenous people. When the Spanish arrived in this part of Mexico, they wanted to assert a Christian influence and many towns and villages were given saints' names as prefixes. Today the prefixes serve as a reminder of the colonial past, and as a device to confuse tourists. Asking people if they know the way to Santo Domingo will get you nowhere.

I pedalled into Tehuantepec on a Sunday afternoon not quite sure what to expect. It was market day, a noisy, chaotic hubbub. I checked in at the Hotel Oasis, which had character in a quirky sort of way. Paintings by the owner were hanging on walls, sculptures rested on shelves. A giant tree grew in the central courtyard. I asked for a room on the top floor, which gave me a very pleasant outlook over the tree to the surrounding countryside. I then set about exploring the rest of the town. The market was busy and I strolled around buying fresh strawberries and apples and chatting to the stall-holders. I seemed to be the only tourist in town, and they were interested to hear about me, my journey, and my country. They were curious to know what fruits and vegetables we eat in Britain.

I bought some sewing machine oil, which I could use when I ran out of cycle oil. The chain and gears had needed more oiling than I expected because of the dry, hot weather. From now on, the bike would have to make do with sewing machine oil.

The market straddled the railway line linking Salina Cruz with Oaxaca. Stall-holders spread their wares out on the railway line. This struck me as being a tad reckless, as I had seen a train only the day before. I asked the strawberry seller about it, he said the trains were so infrequent that they took a chance, knowing they moved slowly through the town blowing their horns. They would have time to clear the tracks if a train came.

The reason the railway went down the main street is that when the railway company sought power to build the line, the President of Mexico insisted it pass a certain house in Tehuantepec, seemingly because he was having a liaison with the lady living there. His train would be able to stop discreetly, allowing him to visit her without people noticing.

So discreet of course, that everyone seems to know about it!

The most quirky thing about Tehuantepec was the taxis. I use the word taxi loosely. Buzzing around the town, adding to the goings-on of market day, were numerous three-wheeled motorcycles with wooden platforms built on the back, behind the driver's seat. The wooden platforms carried people, shopping, and goods. There was a flat fare anywhere in the town, and they were getting a lot of trade. They were narrower than a car, and much nippier, so they could get through the narrow lanes with no trouble.

I went into an Internet café to send some emails. It was full, but one of the local teenagers offered to finish what he was doing so I could have a session. I was becoming well accustomed to this spontaneous Mexican kindness by now. I was also beginning to take it for granted that small towns always had several internet cafes. In Europe an Internet café can be hard to find, particularly in small places, as most families have computers now. In Mexico, not many people can afford to buy a computer. President Fox encouraged the banks to make it easy for people to get finance to set up internet cafes as part of his strategy to modernise Mexico. Most of the customers are young people; surfing, chatting, emailing. Being part of the twenty-first century.

When I left Tehuantepec the following morning it was windy. I was about to cross the Isthmus of Tehuantepec, which has no mountains to buffer the wind. My map showed a place called La Ventosa - The Windy Place. I battled into a head-wind, cursing that cyclists always seem to have head-winds and nothing else. The road changed direction slightly and the wind did too. It became a side-wind. This was worse, believe it or not. Initially I was thankful that the wind was coming from the other side of the road, rather than blowing me into it. However, the wind was so strong that I was leaning heavily into it to avoid being blown off the road. This meant that every time a lorry or a bus passed it created a void in the wind, sucking me into its side. The lorries had big intimidating wheels. I was frightened.

I pulled into a farm turning for a rest, and to think about what to do. There was no doubt that the wind was dangerous for cycling. I could go slowly and carefully to the next town, Juchitán, spend the night there, and hope it would be less windy the following day. I thought it was unlikely that the wind would drop overnight. It had been windy for a couple of days, and it was getting worse. I considered taking the bus. I had no rules to break by doing so, and I had to think of my own safety. If I were flattened by a lorry, simply because I was avoiding using a bus, that would serve no purpose.

I carried on slowly to Juchitán. On the edge of the town I saw the Second Class Bus Station. Without hesitation, I went in and bought a ticket for the next eastbound bus, leaving in forty minutes. It didn't bother me that it was 'only' a second class bus. I would have to mix with the plebs! Waiting for the bus, I became conscious of a man shouting 'Oaxaca Oaxaca' (pronounced "Wah-hucca Wah-hucca") every twenty seconds or so. He was standing guard at the entrance to the bus bays, and his job was to alert passengers to the imminent departure of busses. Each time he shouted it, he never noticed that nobody had arrived in the bus station since the last time he shouted, so his calls fell on deaf ears. Which was just as well, as his call was somewhat ear piercing. When he called the bus to Tuxtla I made my way on board. My seat was next to the cracked window pane.

After leaving the bus station, the bus stopped outside the market. The pavement was choked with people waiting to get on. They had all their shopping with them; bowls boxes and baskets crammed full with fruit, vegetables, and bags of meat. The bus quickly filled up. A woman sat next to me, her young son perched precariously on her lap. She apologised to me for his feet dangling on my knees. I said I didn't mind. She dropped her bottle of drinking water, so I lay it between us on the seat. Meanwhile a musician struggled through the crowded aisle, playing his guitar and singing a medley of Mexican songs. People appreciated him and tipped generously before he jumped off at the edge of town.

The bus passed through La Ventosa, which looked distinctly unwelcoming. The landscape gradually became more mountainous, and I thought the wind was dropping. I was getting fed up with being cooped up in a bus when I wanted to be cycling. I took a chance and got off when the bus stopped at Tapanatepec, surprising the driver as I had bought a ticket to Tuxtla. Finding a hotel was easy; there was one right in the centre of the town. Finding staff was not so easy. I waited alone in reception. The phone was ringing. The mobile phone next to it on the table started ringing too. There was nobody to be seen. It was like being on the Marie Celeste.

I wandered along the corridor into the courtyard, and a woman came out of one of the bedrooms. She was the owner, and she told me her foot had been hurting. I suggested a massage, which she thought very funny. She showed me a room, but it was a bit dark. I asked her if I could have a different room. In the meantime, she had showed another man a room upstairs. He wanted a different room, I wanted a different room. She thought this was very funny. She gave us both a handful of room keys so we could choose for ourselves. As I wanted a lighter room, she recommended one with a view of the patio, as she called it. I peeped inside. It was at the end of the top floor, and had a large picture window looking down the valley to the sea. It was incredible. I went back to the lady and told her it was perfect. I nipped out to buy some food to eat in my room. I went from shop to shop, assembling a meal from tinned tuna, tinned peas, fresh tomato and onion, which could all be mixed together into a salad. I bought some bread too, and some beer to wash it all down with. It was delicious.

Although I wasn't carrying a cooking stove, I sometimes chose to eat cold food in my hotel room rather than go out looking for a restaurant. I couldn't always face up to the tyranny of restaurants. The tyranny that says you can only eat what's on the menu. The tyranny of staff serving you at the pace they want. And of course, the risk that you might not actually like the meal once it is brought to you. Eating cold food in my room avoided all of this. Besides, it was private and more fun.

The menu oppression was sometimes frustratingly inexplicable. I recall in one restaurant, I fancied fried eggs on toast for breakfast. I could see from the menu that they obviously had eggs, and they obviously had bread. However, the waitress told me quite sternly that I couldn't have fried eggs on toast *because it wasn't on the menu*. Such an unhelpful attitude towards customers was, to say the least, maddening. Some people enjoy being as inflexible as they can.

After my meal, I discovered a spiral staircase that led onto the hotel roof. I took a chair up to sit watching the sunset. To the north, I could see the mountains of the Sierra Madre de Chiapas.

At Tapanatepec the road divides. The main road follows the coast to the Guatemalan frontier at Tapachula; a quieter road goes up into the Sierra Madre de Chiapas, making its way through Cintalapa to Tuxtla Gutierrez and San Cristóbal de Las Casas. I wanted to see these towns and the mountains at close quarters. The main road to Tapachula looked as if it would be straight forward cycling, but the mountain road caught my imagination. In the morning I stocked up with water and set off.

The climb was steady. I paced myself for a long haul. After a while I could see the Pacific Ocean. I kept stopping for a 'last look at the Pacific' without actually knowing whether a turn in the road would give me another glimpse of it. There was little traffic, and I was treated very courteously by those drivers who did pass me. No doubt they realised the punishment I was letting myself in for. As I got higher, the wind returned. I was no longer in the lee of the mountains. The wind was fiercer the higher I got. The road snaked its way uphill and the wind direction changed as the road turned this way and that. I had to push the bike up steep bits where the road went into the wind. The frequent bends and wind gusts made it hard to predict what was coming next. I pushed my bike round one bend, and a gust smashed into my face so violently that I could barely stand, let alone walk with a bike. I stood there for a minute, leaning as strongly as I could into the wind. I wasn't enjoying myself at all. Whoever said cycling was fun obviously hadn't done this. The gust died down and I was able to move again. In the middle of all this, I crossed the boundary into the State of Chiapas. My emotions were confused. On one hand I was fed up with the conditions, but on the other hand I was excited about finally getting to Chiapas. It is the most easterly of the Mexican states and it would be my last part of Mexico before crossing into Guatemala. Another country!

The road suddenly reached a plateau and to my amazement the wind stopped. I pedalled into a village called El Jardín and went straight to the first shop I saw to buy something to eat. The shop had tables outside where you could sit. There were people milling about waiting for a bus. They looked at me suspiciously, giving the village a Wild West feel. I sat at one of the tables nibbling something from the shop, but I needed something a bit more substantial after my ordeal of the climb into the wind. Some workmen were polishing off their lunch at a little roadside dining room. The lady running the place offered to do me a plate of ham and eggs. A large fluffy tortoiseshell cat wafted about looking for something to eat. She was out of luck, when I finished my plate was empty.

From El Jardín the road undulated to Cintalapa. The sky was grey, it looked like rain. There were green wooded hillsides, and pine trees everywhere. It felt like I was in Scotland. I knew I was going to like being in Chiapas.

Cintalapa isn't mentioned in the guide books. A pity, as it's a charming little place with lively streets full of shops, all leading to an attractive plaza with a large church along one side. I headed straight for the hotel on another side of the plaza, and settled into a room with a balcony and a television. The television was an imperative, as I needed a rest day and there were two Champions League football matches the following day.

The owners of the hotel were pleased to have a foreign tourist staying. They were surprised when I said I wanted to stay two nights, and even more surprised when I spent most of the following day in my room. I don't normally lay on bed all day watching football. However, when you have cycled for several days, including the gruelling uphill slog into the wind, you are entitled to pamper yourself.

I slipped out to buy an ice cream between the two matches. The hotel owners no doubt wondered why I wasn't going out much. Whilst the second game was on, there was a knock at my bedroom door. It was the man who ran the hotel. "We have noticed you are alone" he said, "would you like *una amiga* for the evening?" "No thank you" I said, "I'm watching football – it's Liverpool." I think he was as startled with my response as I was with his offer.

When I left in the morning I thanked him for his kindness, to show that there were no hard feelings at having my football interrupted.

From Cintalapa it was fifty miles to Tuxtla Gutierrez, the capital of Chiapas. I kept my head down and pedalled through green hills pausing briefly in Juichipilas to have an ice cream. I loved the cycle-taxis, three-wheeled bicycles with a covered seat for passengers at the front. The town was on a hillside so these were hard work for the drivers, especially if they had slightly obese passengers. Some of them were resting opposite the ice cream parlour. They cheered me on as I left for Tuxtla.

I cycled nervously into Tuxtla. The road was busy and was narrow. I found myself in a huge plaza. It must have been the biggest I saw in Mexico. The top end was dominated by a large white cathedral. At the opposite end was the town hall, equally grand. In between were acres of space. Amongst the multitudes of people I noticed the boys selling sweets.

Poor people have to tune in their children to the drudgery of earning money early on in life. In Tuxtla there are many kids walking around with hand made wooden racks strapped to their chests. They sell sweets, chewing gum, and individual cigarettes out of packets. I sometimes think that a reliable indicator of a place's relative poverty is the ease with which you can buy a single cigarette. In Tuxtla, it was easy.

The sweet sellers were mostly young boys, missing out on an education so that they could make a bit of money for themselves and their family. Or for the owners of the wooden racks. One boy told me he worked for himself, buying the sweets every morning from a wholesaler. Others said that the wooden racks were owned by businessmen who also walked around the city centre making sure that the boys weren't resting or chatting idly. They had to be maximising their sales at all times. I don't suppose the boys had a trade union.

Other boys earned a crust cleaning people's shoes. They had well made little wooden boxes to carry their brushes in, and another to sit on whilst brushing. The two boxes fitted together so they could be carried. Francisco, who was ten, charged me two pesos (about eleven pence) to clean my boots. He said he would get twenty customers on a good day.

Francisco's story illustrated the general lack of disposable income in Mexico. The day before, in Cintalapa, I had tried to buy a newspaper to check the television times. Finding a newspaper shop was difficult. People I asked in the street had no idea where one was. I realised I had seldom seen Mexicans reading books or newspapers. Newspapers were a luxury they could manage without. When I eventually did track down a newspaper, I went to a brilliant rooftop café to read it. I was the only customer. In Europe people enjoy sitting in a cafe to take in the atmosphere. I looked down into the plaza below me, and saw many Mexicans sitting on the benches, gazing into space. Each time I went to that café I sat alone. Reading a newspaper over coffee was beyond the pocket of most Mexicans.

The concept of doing things for fun hardly exists in Mexico. On beaches I had only seen foreigners swimming for fun; the Mexicans go there to fish for food or to sell things. Poverty takes the fun out of life. I am not talking about western suburban 'poverty' where people get a big mortgage and then don't think they can afford to go out for a beer with their friends. I mean grinding poverty where people have to focus on survival.

Tuxtla Gutiérrez is definitely a town worth hanging out in. I hung out there for three days. I quickly became a regular customer in a café on the main street, where I had been drawn in by the rich aroma of Chiapas coffee. On my second visit Juán, the owner, started to make my coffee exactly as I liked it the moment I walked in. That's what I call service. It was in this café that I read in a newspaper of the death of George Best, the football hero of millions of people, myself included. I was brought to tears, and Juán came over to console me. Football is almost the only thing that elevates grown men to an emotional level.

Juán said there was a league match that day in Tuxtla. Jaguares, the local team, were paying Santos in a meaningless end of season fixture. "They haven't qualified" he added. I needed this bit of information interpreting, because I always thought a league season simply ended with someone being champions and a small number of teams getting relegated. Not so in the Mexican League. Teams play each other twice, and then the league splits in half. The top half plays a series of knock-out matches to determine who will be the champions. This is controversial, because the league leaders at the time of the split don't always get to be champions.

Meaningless fixture or not, I had to go. I had seen so many league games on TV that I wanted to experience one live. Besides, I could make the fixture my own George Best Memorial Match. Juán reckoned the best place to get a ticket was a shop called Farmacía de Ahorros – the discount chemists.

I went to the nearest branch for a ticket.

It was a hoot, because the young staff told me that there was a special promotion on and if I bought a First Aid Kit, the tickets were only seventy-five pesos each. I said I didn't want a First Aid Kit as I was cycling, so how much was a ticket on its own. A hundred and twenty pesos! The staff all gathered round and started showing me the contents of a first aid kit, to prove what a bargain it was. First, out came a bottle of alcohol and a syringe. Then some throat pastilles - "For shouting Jaguares, Jaguares", I said. Then a bandage. "For throwing on the pitch" they said....all very amusing, and as usual I had become the centre of attention in a Mexican shop.

I left the shop basking in the warmth of the people, carrying a ticket and a first aid kit. I gave most of the kit to the hotel receptionist, keeping the alcohol as it could be useful in an emergency. The label said, rather regretfully, "Not to be drunk".

I got to the ground by catching a *colectivo*, a small mini-bus or a van with seats. It is interesting travelling in *colectivos* as the passengers natter to each other. As more people get in the coins for their fares are passed forward from person to person to the driver.

Outside the ground there were stands selling football souvenirs. Women were preparing *tacos* as if an army were expected to drop in. I found the entrance shown on my ticket, and to my dismay saw that I was on the sunny side of the stadium, in the heat. This was the catch to the special offer – I needed the free first aid kit to counter the effects of heatstroke.

The atmosphere was vibrant as people had drums, pipes, and other musical instruments, playing what could have been traditional Chiapas war music. The stadium was a cauldron of heat and I wished I had paid more for a seat in the shade. People walked around selling soft drinks and beer, which they carried around in plastic buckets full of ice. The drinks were in glass bottles, the seller had to pour the drink into a plastic cup and keep the glass bottles. A tremendous weight to carry in the scorching Mexican sun.

After a minute, Jaguares scored. The lineswoman flagged for offside - *Fuera de juego*. Yes, that wasn't a printing error, lineswoman. You didn't need to know Spanish to realise that the shouts of "Puta, Puta" was a swear word. I thought at first I was seeing things, but studying her movements for a minute or two, it was obvious she had the curves of a woman that no transvestite can successfully emulate. Especially on a football pitch.

The result was 5-1 to Jaguares, which helped cultivate my soft spot for them. Santos' solo goal was impressive, a well aimed overhead kick.

I went back to my regular café where Juán explained that FIFA had sanctioned female officials in Mexico as an experiment. There are three lineswomen (linespersons?) and one referee (referess?). I thought it was odd to have such an experiment in a macho conservative country like Mexico, and he thought that was funny.

Here we are, talking about football. The international language. When I decided to learn Spanish my logic was that if I could speak two world languages, I should be able to communicate with most people I met. In my calculations I had forgotten the importance of football to so many people in the world, irrespective of their maternal language. I remember a few years ago, I was driving around Poland in a van which had the St Andrew's flag painted on the side, and the Polish word for Scotland on the back. As I was parking in the middle of a town square one day, the parking attendant very proudly said "Kenny Dalglish" in a strong Polish accent. Apart from that, he knew no English. We shook hands. Our meeting was sealed as a friendship through the third language of football, which knows few frontiers. It creates common ground from which a conversation can begin, and lead perhaps to more. That is one of the good things about the Wonderful Game.

There is of course more to life than football, and the next day I set off on my bike to see the Sumidero Canyon. I had seen pictures of it on the internet, and it was worth a look. There are two ways to see the canyon. There is a boat trip on the river that goes through it. I planned to do that later, but first I wanted to see it from above. A minor road climbs up into the mountains from Tuxtla, and skirts along the edge of the canyon to a restaurant. This is the perfect way to get birds eye views, savouring the boat trip for later. The canyon is three miles long, and at its deepest part the rock faces tower 1,200 meters above the level of the river.

The road zigzags its way up above the level of the river. The climb was steady, but travelling without my panniers and other paraphernalia enabled me to make light work of it. There were four viewing stations on the way. From each of them I peered down into the canyon, like an eagle searching for prey. I could see boats full of tourists. From the viewing bases they looked more like little insects. I couldn't wait to see it from water level, so the following day I checked out of my friendly Tuxtla hotel and pedalled the twelve miles to Chiapa de Corzo, from where the boat trips operate. There was a lot of competition for my custom. I compared prices and played it cool by wandering off to find a hotel room before committing myself to any particular boat operator. I booked into the cheapest hotel I could find, in a back street overlooking the river. I might later regret it, but sometimes you have to live dangerously.

Returning to the boat wharf, I purchased a ticket from my chosen company, and waited to be called onto the boat. The boats were open, with a dozen or so seats facing the direction of travel. Each boat had an operator and a tour guide, and of course a motor. The sun was reflecting mercilessly off the water surface and I was glad I had thought to bring my sunhat. When the boat was ready we all took seats at random. We left with the boat listing to one side. I felt uncomfortable. Meanwhile, the tour guide was doing his utmost to make the trip sound exciting.

> "If we are lucky, we will see some crocodiles" he said, in unmistakeably clear Spanish.

> "And if we are unlucky" I was thinking, "the boat will capsize and we will all be eaten alive!"

At this point the guide must have been reading my thoughts, because he suddenly noticed that the man on the opposite side of the boat from me was very large, maybe twenty stone. I weigh at most ten stone, on a good day. The guide got us to swap places and the boat stopped listing. I breathed a sigh of relief. We were saved from the crocodiles.

The trip was awesome. The cliffs are sheer, steep, and gob-smacking. It was even better than I imagined. We stopped to look at some crocodiles. I was more than a little suspicious as they didn't move at all; someone suggested they were wooden fakes, put there to impress the tourists. No-one was tempted to test this theory with an outstretched hand, mind you, so we have to give the boat operators the benefit of the doubt. Innocent till proven guilty. The Cañon de Sumidero is a little known wonder of Mexico. That figures, because Mexico is a little known wonder of the world.

We returned to Chiapa del Corzo and I walked around the town to see what it had to offer. It has a large plaza which was fenced off with corrugated iron for renovations, making the town seem claustrophobic. Around the edge of the plaza were numerous artisan craft shops, competing for trade from tourists passing through the town to visit the canyon. It was depressing that there were so many craft shops for so few tourists. Not one of them stood out as being different in any way. I had seen this before in Mexico, the band-wagon effect. If there was demand for a craft shop, there was never one craft shop doing well, but twenty identical ones doing badly. It was economic desperation rather than common sense. Prices were competitive as they undercut each other, giving away trinkets for much less than the tourists could afford.

I returned to my cheap and basic hotel for a rest. I sat out on a terrace at the back overlooking the river, with a beer chatting to the owner. He described the floods caused by Hurricane Stan. The river level had risen ten metres and encroached his grounds. It explained why part of the hotel had collapsed. He had been a worried man, watching the river rise and wondering if his livelihood was about to be rinsed away. Then, as suddenly as it had risen, the water level receded. He was luckier than some. As we talked the sun went down. He identified birds passing above the river in the evening air. Small fishing boats were returning to base. It was idyllic. An impressionist painter would have been busy with his brushes and oils.

Meanwhile, an indigenous family arrived. There were five of them and they crowded into a single room the same size as mine. They were as quiet as mice.

Remembering my stomach, I went out to find a meal. The restaurants were closing and I ended up in a showy eating place with a plate of dull, overpriced lasagne. The young waiter wanted to practice his English on me and wouldn't leave me alone. It was a relief to pay my bill and leave. At the town hall a map of Chiapas was hanging on a wall. It had all the towns listed, together with their height above sea level. The following day I was planning to cycle to San Cristóbal de Las Casas. Its altitude was given as 2,200 metres. Chiapa del Corzo was shown as 400 metres. Even allowing for a margin of error, that was going to be some climb. 1,800 metres or nearly 6,000 feet.

I had never cycled up a 6,000 foot hill before, and I went to bed feeling a little edgy!

I was in the shops when they opened at eight the following morning, making sure I had enough food and drink for a climb. I managed to leave the hotel before nine – early for me. The hotel owner wished me luck, and said that if he was younger he would like to be doing what I was doing. He was seventy. It was a nice farewell.

The climb started immediately I left Chiapa De Corzo and continued for thirty miles. The views were outstanding, and there was hardly any traffic. I stopped where some indigenous women were selling things that looked a bit like potatoes. Most of them spoke no Spanish and when I asked what they were selling they had to find an interpreter. As I got higher, I saw many people travelling on foot. Mostly barefoot. There were women in brightly coloured woven clothes, carrying huge bales of firewood uphill on their backs. Some of them wore bands around their foreheads to spread the weight. No matter how much they were carrying, they always returned a cheery *buenos tardes* as I pedalled past. Their life was hard, but it didn't stop them being pleasant to me.

At a bend in the road I stopped for a *refresco*. The woman running the shop said there was hardly any climbing left. She was right; the road went down for a short distance, up again, then finally down into the town of San Cristóbal de Las Casas nestling in the green mountains of Chiapas.

I had finally arrived, after my long uphill marathon. To my surprise, it was only five o'clock. I had cycled forty-four miles and was 6,000 feet higher than when I woke up. To my surprise I didn't feel tired, even having the energy to pedal around, pedantically judging the numerous hotels on offer. It was November, so it wasn't peak season and the hotels were keen to do a deal with me. Discounts were offered. I knew I could be fussy. The town had a good feel to it, and I sensed I wanted to hang out there for a while. I settled into the Hotel San Martin.

It was to be my home for the next seventeen days.

CHAPTER SIX

SAN CRISTÓBAL DE LAS CASAS

For several days my eyes had been giving me trouble. They kept watering up, and felt a bit sensitive. I knew I wasn't in mourning, so I went to see a doctor.

It isn't difficult to find a doctor in Mexico. In the centre of towns, many of them have surgeries next to a pharmacy, with a waiting room open to the street. You can see from the pavement how many people are waiting. I nipped into one with no queue. The doctor listened to my story then inspected my eyes. He said they were irritated through cycling into the strong winds. His diagnosis did not surprise me. I hadn't been wearing my sunglasses much, as I felt they would spoil the view. Looking back, that was a bit silly of me. The doctor noted my personal details, gave me a prescription, and told me not to cycle for a week. The bill was twenty pesos, about one pound twenty.

So my prolonged stay in San Cristóbal de Las Casas started under doctor's orders!

San Cristóbal de las Casas is a name that catches the imagination. The name translates as St. Christopher of the

Houses, so I immediately wondered why St. Christopher was of the houses. The town's name contains a riddle in that it was not, in fact St, Christopher who was of the houses, but Bartholomew.

Bartolomé de Las Casas was born in Seville in 1474. In 1502 he went to what was then Hispaniola (now Haiti) where he established an *encomienda*. The system of *encomiendas* was created by the Spanish Crown, to give favoured individuals land in the new world with the rights to the labour of Indians, who were then put to work on the land. It was slavery in another name. In return for receiving the king's generosity, they were expected to civilise the indigenous people by converting them to Christianity and protecting them. This was a sixteenth century version of the current vogue for converting people to western ideas of free trade, and 'protecting' them from the evils of alternative economic systems.

Unlike some modern free trade advocates, Bartolomé had a social conscience. He became a priest in 1510 and later converted to the Dominican faith. Seeing the ills of the *encomienda* system, he returned to Spain and wrote a pamphlet called "A Very Brief Account of the Destruction of the Indies"[2]. It petitioned King Philip II to change the system.

It is a compelling read. It catalogues many brutal acts carried out by the Spanish conquistadors. Massacres, murders, and destructions of communities are described in a plain, no-nonsense style that leaves the reader in no doubt that this was a very cruel period in the history of

---

[2] First published in English by Penguin in 1992, and reprinted in 2004.

the Americas. The writings are based on what Bartolomé saw himself, and accounts he heard first hand from other people. History may have glamorised the conquest, but Bartolomé describes it as "...really and truly nothing other than a series of violent incursions into territory by cruel tyrants."

He could have been tried for treason or heresy, but the King listened to his arguments and eventually passed new laws reforming the system. Perhaps the King had little option, as Pope Paul III had heard Bartolomé's point of view and issued a decree in the meantime declaring that Indians were fully capable of receiving the message of Christ. Much of Mexico tried to ignore the new laws. In 1545, Bartolomé was appointed Bishop of Chiapas. He used this opportunity to campaign for the rights of Indians. He acted as advocate in many disputes, and earned himself a reputation as a champion of the rights of indigenous people.

His ultimate role was as Protector of the Indians at the Spanish court in Madrid. He died there in 1566, at the ripe old age of ninety-two.

The town of San Cristóbal was founded in 1524. Father Bartolomé was an early influence in the history of the town, and in recognition of this the town was later re-named San Cristóbal de Las Casas in his honour.

My objective having been to the doctor and told to rest was quite simply to do that. Rest. I felt I deserved it, having cycled nineteen hundred miles to get there, including one or two hills. My hotel was just round the corner from the main square, the Plaza de 31 de Mayo. After returning from the doctor I drifted around the Plaza to see what was going on. Like many in Mexico, it has a bandstand in the centre. This one is a little different, in that the bandstand is elevated and underneath it is a café. The café had no seats free, so I went instead to another café on one side of the square. The young men working there as waiters were eager to serve me, and I enjoyed the atmosphere. By carefully selecting my seat, I could sip my coffee whilst enjoying a good view across the plaza to the stalls where men sold newspapers, laid on the ground for people to see.

The coffee, by the way, was excellent. Chiapas has the perfect climate and landscape for growing coffee, and this café certainly knew how to serve it. There was a roasting machine just inside the door, and the aroma hung around like an invitation you couldn't refuse. While I was there I saw somebody reading a guide book, and I asked if I could borrow it so I could read what there was to see in San Cristóbal. If I was going to be here for at least a week, I needed some sort of cultural programme to keep me amused.

Mentioning the guide book leads me to own up to the fact that I had been travelling in Mexico for almost three months now, without carrying a guide book. Some people will recoil in horror. "How can you go anywhere without a guide book?" I hear them saying, in disbelief. "You won't know where to stay, where to eat, or how to get money!"

I have always travelled. My earliest childhood memory is of a family holiday when I was four, at the Ingledene Hotel in Ardrossan, Ayrshire. At the end of the road was

South Beach station, and I could stand at the level-crossing gates and watch the steam trains roar by. I was curious about the places the trains were going to. I knew then that I wanted to travel. As I grew up I became fascinated by maps and train timetables. I would spend hours looking at them for interesting sounding places, and seeing if you could get there by train. As soon as I could, I would take myself off somewhere on an excursion, to see what other places were like. I was learning to be an explorer.

Although guide books existed, they were in those days beyond my budget. I had to take pot luck. That for me is part of the fun of travel – not knowing what to expect, looking around for somewhere to stay, and going by your nose when hunting for food. Uncertainty is part of the adventure. In recent years I have seen many people using modern guide books simply as Instruction Manuals. You see them earnestly striding through towns, their guide book in front of their nose, determined to get to the recommended place first, before all the other readers find it. I have heard people say "We can't stay there; it's not in the guide book!" I have even heard people arguing over the price of a room, on the grounds that their guide book quotes a lower price. These people are neither explorers nor adventurers. Guide books can create a situation where businesses are condemned to a place in obscurity simply because a guide book chooses not to list them. Or they may have opened after the guide book was written. Selective listing by guide books creates a funnelling of visitors, who virtually ignore everywhere else, as if it doesn't exist. During my ride through Mexico I went to and stayed at many delightful places not listed in guide books. It's a shame others missed them.

Some guide books in particular seem to be aimed at young back-packers who need to be warned about and protected from all the "dangers and annoyances" you could imagine. They are becoming surrogate mothers for people who finally break free from the parental control of their natural mother and go travelling. The wording of highlights listed in certain guides suggests to me "Written by eighteen year-olds, for eighteen year-olds" would be a suitable marketing slogan. One guide book to Central America lists dancing all night in a nightclub as one of the highlights of Panama. Not at my age, I'm afraid! Guide books can be patronising to women too, stating that women travellers should not go to certain places in Central America. Women I met who were travelling alone thought this advice was utter nonsense. However, my view of guide books did not prevent me from looking at them when I had the chance!

The following day I went back to the same café and the same man was sitting at the same seat, reading the same guide book. I asked if I could sit with him for a chat. His name was Rinaldo and he was from Gent in Belgium. He had quit a job as a bar manager to see a bit of the world. We got on very well and agreed to meet there again the following day for a coffee. I suddenly realised that for the first time in three months I had a social life. An appointment to meet someone for a coffee!

One thing you miss when travelling, is having a social life. You can't phone friends and arrange to meet for a coffee or a beer, like you can when at home. Pedalling alone through Mexico, although I was never lonely at any time,

I had become acutely aware that I was never spending any time with anyone I knew. Now, in San Cristóbal, I had a social circle of one!

After I met Rinaldo, later that evening, my social circle doubled in size. An American staying at my hotel saw me fiddling with my bike and came over to talk to me. He was a doctor from New York, working in Mexico on a relief programme following Hurricane Stan a few weeks before. He was a keen cyclist too, and he rather mysteriously had a bottle of Laphroig malt whisky with him, which he wanted to share with me. I did not hesitate in accepting his invitation, and he brought it into my room where we had a lovely evening talking about travel, cycling, and his work in Mexico.

He was working in a remote village in south western Chiapas, near the Guatemalan border. He described some of the conditions he found there, in an area that had been ravaged by the hurricane. The villagers valued the work of a doctor. His surgery officially started at ten o'clock. Most people in the country don't have watches; they get up when it gets light without knowing the exact time. He is always woken up at seven thirty by people standing outside his room talking to each other "Is the doctor in there?" he can hear them saying. He goes for a shower with his towel round his waist, and they say "Are you the doctor?" The range of things he saw was immense, sometimes the whole family turned up for a consultation, with a variety of different complaints. The lower standards of hygiene than what we take for granted in Europe didn't help – many people had intestinal worms for example.

The villagers may have appreciated Ryan's help; on the other hand, I sensed from what he said that modern medicine has to compete for respect with a culture where the medicine man always gave some kind of herbal potion to cure whatever was wrong with you. In today's terms, this means an expectation that the doctor will at least prescribe vitamins, even for an ailment where no medicine is required. This struck me as a bit ludicrous in a country where the diet, based on rice, beans, maize, and an abundance of fresh fruit, is awash with natural vitamins. If vitamins were prescribed for the sake of it, their fate was simply to pass through the body as being surplus to need.

That wasn't my only concern. Local people expected medication in the form of injections. This was the normal practice, in spite of the risk carried by repeated injections to the body. This concern was brought home to us a few days later. We went for a hike together to see if we could get to the summit of Mount Huitepec, one of the hills that surround San Cristóbal. We got to the base of the mountain by catching a *colectivo* from the edge of town. Unsure of the route, we followed a path that seemed to go up. We paused at a clearing where a house had just been built and a local man came by. We asked him for directions. He was limping badly so Ryan asked about his leg.

He said it was an injury caused by an injection. A doctor had once given him an injection in his back-side, and it had caused semi-paralysis of the leg. It seemed a harsh price to pay for whatever the doctor thought was the problem.

I sensed from meeting Ryan that however well-intentioned medical aid programmes are, there was always going to be a problem of overcoming the ingrained culture, however flawed it might be, before any real success could be measured. Sometimes people use this kind of experience as an argument against making any aid donations. My view is that this is too simplistic. You have to accept that, like the seeds in the bible, some aid will fall on stony ground. That's the price we pay for the aid that does actually achieve something. As long as some good is done, you have to accept the bad as well.

Another little excursion I arranged with Ryan – as part of my rapidly expanding social life in San Cristóbal – was to cycle into the hills to a nearby village called Chamula. First, Ryan had to hire a bike. Finding the cycle hire shop was quite a challenge for our Spanish skills, and when we did find it we discovered the owner spoke English and German, as well as Spanish.

It is uphill all the way to Chamula. At a junction we stopped for a rest and looked back at the view of San Cristóbal. We passed some Tzotzil Indian women carrying huge piles of firewood on their backs, and as usual received a very cheerful *buenos dias*. They wore brightly coloured clothing woven and dyed in the area. Arriving in Chamula by bicycle we were the centre of attraction. We were surrounded by a group of teenage boys who wanted to know everything about the bikes and my ride from Chihuahua. I realised when describing my bike and tyres that my Spanish had acquired a Mexican accent. That was fine for Mexico, but I needed to lose it again before returning to Spain, as Spanish people tend to laugh at the Mexican accent like English people laugh at the Welsh accent.

Chamula is famous for its open air market and the church, which are groomed for the arrival of tourists. We were told that we could not photograph local people as they believed that having their photo taken took away some of their spirit. Then we saw a stand selling postcards, some of which were of local people. Clearly, they could lose some of their spirit for commercial post-card fees.

We bought tickets to enter the church, locked our bikes together in the small square in front of it, and went in. The atmosphere was lovely. There were hundreds if not thousands of candles burning, giving a shimmering light. It was animated without being noisy. There were no pews. Groups of people sat on the floor in front of their own candles, worshipping. Cut grass and pine needles were spread out on the floor. People sat with candles holding onto chickens patiently awaiting their sacrifice. The church was said to be run this way to make Christianity more acceptable to ordinary people. I can see nothing wrong with making religion acceptable to people. Too often the focus is on making people acceptable to religion.

Outside again, boys asked us for pesos. Their voices whined, as if to add to the appeal. I was annoyed they were spending their childhood begging rather than playing football or whatever. With a childhood spent doing that, it becomes ingrained not to enjoy life.

Returning to San Cristóbal, I met Rinaldo for a coffee in The Usual Place. It wasn't actually called that, but neither of us could ever remember the name of the café where we always met, so we christened it The Usual Place by accident.

My hotel was on the Real de Guadalupe, the road that leads up from the Plaza de 31 de Mayo to the Church of the virgin of Guadalupe. I arrived in San Cristóbal at the start of the Festival of the Virgin of Guadalupe which ran until 12th December. The street was lively, with brass bands, fireworks, and other jollities. There was always something happening, that made you stop and look when on your way somewhere. One night when I came out of the hotel, a band came past - not marching, but all huddled in the back of a *camioneta*, with the big base drum hanging out of the back, strapped to the chest of the drummer. They played perfectly, in spite of that. It looked, cosy, surreal, and so Mexican. Being winter, it was quite cold in the evenings, I am sure they would have benefited more from marching!

A bizarre feature of the Real de Guadalupe was that it was a one way street, with the direction of traffic flow being downhill, away from the church. During the festival, numerous parades and processions go up the hill to the church. This meant the police have to do a complicated piece of work to halt and divert the traffic coming down the hill, in the face of the pilgrims and their accompanying musicians going up the way. Sometimes groups of barefoot runners came past, wearing special headscarves and carrying banners from their village.

One evening I walked up the Real de Guadalupe to the church. I sat on the steps looking over the view of the town. Some boys kick a football around. The sun goes down, turning the sky crimson, grey and deep, deep blue.

A woman is preparing hot food to sell. She has invested in a trestle table and folding chairs. She means business. She even has china crockery and real glasses. Everywhere there is a buzz. Foreign tourists mill about with locals, forming a cosmopolitan scene. There is constant activity – music, street vendors, boot blacks. The buzz conveys a mood of enjoyment.

Rinaldo had enrolled for Spanish classes at a cultural centre and language school. We were both aware of the 1994 Zapatista rebellion, which rocked the rest of Mexico, and watched a film about it there. The film was a bit long, but made the point well that successive Mexican governments had failed to grasp the question of the exploitation of the mainly indigenous population, and their ensuing poverty. A man in the audience hissed every time the film showed President Salinas, who was in power from 1988 to 1994 and left power with his reputation tarnished, to say the least, because of his failures over the rebellion.

One outcome of the rebellion was the creation of autonomous villages, where the inhabitants have a greater say in local affairs. I saw some of these villages when I caught the bus to Palenque.

I went there to see the Mayan ruins. Cycling to them would have been a big hilly detour from my planned route to Guatemala. Resting in San Cristóbal under orders from the doctor gave me the opportunity of making a detour from my route by bus, and a change of scenery for a night. Besides, cycling to Palenque would have involved a significant loss of altitude which I would have had to work hard to regain on the way back. The decision to go on a bus-ride was not difficult.

The bus journey took five hours, passing through autonomous villages proudly displaying signs announcing their status. Coffee beans were laid out on plastic sheets to dry in the sun by the side of the road. Men were raking them over, a slow laborious task that makes you wonder how the price of coffee in the supermarkets of richer countries can reflect a fair wage to the growers. The short answer is that it doesn't. Middle men and supermarkets use their buying power to ensure that most of the money we pay for coffee goes into their pockets. The growers get next to nothing for their hard work, for the risk of failed crops, or a poor market price. Capitalism says that profit is the reward for risk. That is fair, I cannot argue with that. However, in coffee production the biggest risk is carried by the growers, who make the smallest profits. There are three answers to this; foment a revolution, buy Fair Trade coffee, or ignore it. Some dream about being a revolutionary like Che Guevara but in practice few of us make it past the Fair Trade stage. Individually we have too much to lose; that is how capitalists get away with it.

I took the bike with me on the bus, so I could cycle from Palenque bus station to the ruins. The men checking tickets at the entrance to the ruins told me to lock it to the fence next to them, so they could keep an eye on it. The ruins are set in the midst of luscious green trees and impressive, although I didn't think they were as majestic as Monte Alban near Oaxaca. In the temples are engravings said to be 1,300 years old. I was awestruck that they could be so old, and still so clear.

I cycled the six miles back to Palenque, past a number of unappealing campsites. It was more appealing to try my luck with a hotel in town. As I pedalled into town I found myself at the end of a procession. I tried to go round the block to get in front, but it was a long procession. I was back where I started, at the end of it. So I followed at the back. It was a political procession, in support of the PRD – Partido Revolucionario Democrático, whose candidate in the 2006 Presidential elections was speaking that night in Palenque. A group of men watching the procession gave me a big cheer as I passed. Maybe I was going to be elected President of Mexico!

The presidential elections were interesting. They take place every six years and a sitting president cannot stand for re-election. The incumbent, Vicente Fox was of the right of centre PAN (Partido Acción Nacional). He was elected in 2000 in a surprise vote, ahead of the candidate of the PRI (Partido Revolucionario Institucional), whose origins were in the 1910 revolution and had held power continuously for over forty years. People told me that Fox had been good for Mexico, in fighting corruption and attempting to modernise the country. Mexico had needed a change after forty years of control by the Institutional Revolutionaries – a contradiction in terms if ever there was one. The PRD, also a left of centre party, were hoping to capitalise on the disillusionment against the PRI which had in recent years been exposed as a party that held onto power by corruption, manipulation and favouritism.[3]

---

[3] In the July 2006 election, the PAN candidate Felipe Calderón narrowly beat the PRD candidate López Obrador, forcing the PRI candidate into third place.

At last I made it into the centre of town. It had a large square, a busy main street, and little else. There was PRD bunting everywhere, and assorted noise bellowing out of tannoys. Mexicans love hullabaloo, so who was I to complain. I found a satisfactory hotel in a side street, far from the madding crowd, and went out to explore on foot. I didn't get very far. My progress along the street was halted by the whiff of fresh coffee spiralling out of a small café. When I looked inside, there was football on television, so I was a lost cause. Coffee, football, Mexicans to talk to – perfect. I perched myself on a small chair and settled down to watch Monterrey play Toluca.

The other customers thought I was a gringo at first. They were surprised that I was interested in football and knew a bit about the game. By now my Spanish had improved to the extent that I could use football terms confidently. That pleased me, as language teaching at school hadn't prepared me for real life practical situations like saying the forwards aren't getting enough of the ball.

When the match finished I went to an internet café to catch up on my other social life that I was temporarily missing out on, in Britain. My pal Alan had sent me such a hilarious account of a match he had been to at Harrogate Town that I was rolling about on my chair in uncontrollable laughter. The American at the next terminal told me that he wished he received emails as funny as mine.

My night in Palenque was a distraction from my heady social life in San Cristóbal. I was missing it already. Enjoying a hearty breakfast in a restaurant on the main square, I decided to return on the first bus I could. Meanwhile, I remarked to the waiter that no matter how much poverty there was in Mexico, people always seemed to be well turned out in smart clean clothes.

"Not in the *cantina* round the corner." he said quietly before scurrying off for my scrambled eggs. I reflected on this as I went up to the bus station. We had both been guilty of generalising, and whilst generalisations may be true of some people, they are not the universal truths that folk like them to be.

The views from the bus window were equally spectacular as they had been the previous day. Approaching San Cristóbal, however, we experienced something I had not seen for some time. Heavy rain. It was lashing down. So far, I had cycled in the rain only once. Other times it had always rained on rest days. The sun shines on the righteous.

Righteousness was completely non-existent at San Cristóbal bus station. The rain had been so heavy that all the bus bays were about six inches deep in water. It was impossible to get off the bus without paddling. We huddled together on a raised platform while a barefoot porter with his trouser legs rolled up retrieved our luggage from the lockers under the bus. This was a nice gesture on behalf of the bus company, but once outside the bus station we were alone in the floods. Cars splashed us as they drove slowly past. People were marooned on shop doorsteps. I made it back to my hotel just in time to shower and change before meeting Rinaldo for coffee at The Usual Place.

Rinaldo was glad to see me. He wanted my help. He had been to the doctor about something, and needed my assistance as an interpreter. The doctor's surgery was on

Real de Guadalupe so we walked up there through the festival crowds. He needed an injection. He recalls how memorable the occasion was - him with his pants down having the injection, me sitting on a chair turned to face the wall to safeguard his dignity, and at the same time a brass band marching past outside with the festival crowds. A scene to treasure for the rest of his life!

San Cristóbal was identified early on by the Spanish as having something special. Whether it was the mountain air, the green scenery, or the friendly indigenous people, who knows. Probably the right combination of all three. The Spanish settled there in a serious way building cathedrals, convents, and a distinctive style of urban colonial architecture that survives largely unaltered to this day. Today, the town is popular with foreign tourists looking for a flavour of traditional Mexico mixed with the Spanish influence. The exotic tamed by the familiarity of something European. They love to while away hours looking at the artisan crafts for sale on the steps of the sixteenth century cathedrals. This blending of two cultures is what makes Latin America so compulsive for many people.

The Spanish did something the British, Dutch, and French colonialists were reluctant to get into. They mixed with the natives, had children with them, and married them. Now, the vast majority of Mexicans are *mestizo*, or mixed. Pure whites and pure Indians are both very small minorities. This is common in much (though not all) of the Spanish new world. Contrast this to India, for example, where white British people lived quite separate lives from the people of India; or even – dare I say it – South Africa, where under the system of apartheid whites were prohibited by law from fornicating with blacks.

Why was this? There seem to be two reasons. The first is that after centuries of occupation by Greeks, Romans and Moors, the Spanish were accustomed to inter-marriage. The dark features we associate with the classic Spanish look stem from this. The second reason is that (according to the consensus amongst historians) the Spanish method of colonisation was distinct from the other European nations. It was driven largely by the need to plunder the riches of the Americas to finance the Spanish monarchy. The colonisers sent from Spain were mainly soldiers, i.e. men. When they walked off the ships, after weeks at sea without women, it was not long before they started breeding with the friendly accommodating locals they found ashore. There was not the same thoughtfulness of planning that the British pursued in Australia, for instance.

In her challengingly-entitled book "The Floating Brothel" Sian Rees describes the way the British identified a need to bring what is today called 'gender balance' to the small white population of the embryonic colonies in New South Wales. "They need more women" was the problem. The solution – ships full of female convicts were despatched by the British authorities, desperate to discourage the men already sent there from forming relationships with the native population.

The Spanish didn't have these hang-ups. They built San Cristóbal, married the locals, and introduced Christianity.

The city prospered as the administrative centre of Chiapas, which was then part of the Guatemalan Territories.

🚲

San Cristóbal today is a favourite haunt of the Mexican middle classes. Yes, they do exist, albeit in small numbers, refugees in a small no-man's-land that seeks to exist between the rich and the poor. In San Cristóbal the evidence of their existence is in the small number of trendy bars with late night licences, where musicians gather to play their instruments and sing. You could go to a bar to hear live music every night of the week. Small bands play in the squares and plazas late into the evening, and people gather round to listen appreciatively. Rinaldo and I went to some these venues, and added to our social circle in the process.

Another aspect of the middle classes is that they are able to articulate political grievances. One afternoon, I was walking across the Plaza 31 Mayo and spotted a woman behind a table collecting signatures for a campaign to provide relief to indigenous mountain people in the harsh winter weather. Exposing my western naivety, I said

> "Are you campaigning for heating systems in people's houses?"

> "No," she said, "Blankets."

🚲

I had been keeping in touch with an Austrian cyclist I met in Creel, back in September. He was now touring

Guatemala and Chiapas and by frantic emailing and logistical planning I was able to arrange to meet him in San Cristóbal. I returned to the hotel during the afternoon to find him standing in reception, looking a little bemused. He wasn't expecting the hotel to be full, and the prices to have doubled, because of the Festival of the Virgen of Guadalupe!

Luckily, I was paying the normal rate as I was a regular customer. Also, my room had two single beds, so Christoph was saved. We caught up over a meal and a couple of beers, then went to a bar where there was a concert. I knew Rinaldo would be there, he always knew where there was live music. It was like a sixth sense to him.

The bar was not ideal for live music, as it was long and narrow, with the bar all the way along one side. The band had been placed at one end, so although we could hear them, very few people could see them. People got round this by standing on bar furniture, standing on wall mountings, and even standing on the bar. The bar served large glasses of Chilean wine, which were going down very well, as wine does with live music. The band was called Amparanoia and was similar to Manu Chao. They sang one of my favourite songs, Welcome To Tijuana, the first time I have actually heard it in Mexico. An Australian girl standing next to us had never left Melbourne before, and certainly knew how to use the F word! (She was drunk). (No Australian stereotypes please!).

The Bohemian types who live in San Cristóbal were out in force for this concert. Some were Mexican, some were foreigners. It was interesting to see the foreigners who lived there being accepted amongst the Mexican bohemians. The foreigners maybe fitted in so easily because living in San Cristóbal is a 'lifestyle' move rather than a career move to make money and enhance one's social position, whatever that may be.

One of the foreigners who had made the lifestyle decision and was happy was Dana, the American lady I got to know who ran a bookshop called *La Pared* on Avenida Miguel Hidalgo. She had lived in San Cristóbal for many years, explaining that she always wanted to live in Mexico. She had travelled around looking at many towns, trying to weigh up where to live. One day, she arrived in San Cristóbal and decided within an hour of arriving that it was the place for her. That was about twelve years ago. The first time we met, she very quickly made the point that she was not by any means a supporter of George W Bush or the Republicans. I commented that I had met many Americans, none of whom had owned up to having voted for Bush. "That's because Bush-voters never go anywhere," she said, "They all spend their entire lives in places like Peoria, Illinois." I made a mental note never to go there myself. I may get lynched for being a non-believer in - whatever they believe in.

The following day was the day of the Virgen de Guadalupe. The climax of endless days and nights of music, fireworks and, well - din. Shortly before mid-day I was walking along the road that passed the Templo de San Francisco. Men were laying a trail of gunpowder and fireworks down the centre of the street. I stopped in a shop doorway to watch. They encircled the church. The shopkeeper said it was due to go off at twelve noon.

Some blond-haired backpackers accidentally kicked a few fireworks out of line, looking a bit startled. Sure enough at twelve o'clock sharp, someone lit the line of gunpowder at the end of the street. The whole scene was filled with the noise and smoke of an arsenal exploding, as the fire made its way along each of the four streets surrounding the church. Guy Fawkes would have been proud of them. A fire appliance followed slowly, just in case.

I had been in Mexico for almost three months. I had grown to love it so much, it felt like home. I was slightly anxious about the prospect of going to Guatemala and being in a different country. I had another worry. When I entered Mexico I was given a ninety day visa. It was now getting close to expiry and the last thing I wanted was to be technically deported from a country I was so fond of, due to overstaying my visa. Rinaldo had visa problems too. When he arrived from Belgium he was only given thirty days. Why he was only given thirty days compared with my ninety was a puzzle, as we were both European Union citizens and therefore Equal. Perhaps the Immigration official thought that Belgian beer was so wonderful that nobody would want to leave for more than thirty days.

Rinaldo went to the Immigration Office in San Cristóbal to enquire about getting an extension. The staff were very unhelpful and the process was long, bureaucratic and expensive. I met a Mexican who worked for the government and told me not to worry as the fine for minor visa infringements was small. I decided to risk it. It was time to go.

I had a last coffee with Rinaldo in The Usual Place. I reminded him he was supposed to be touring the world, but had so far only seen San Cristóbal. I left a larger than usual tip for the waiters who had never once failed to be cheerful and welcoming. I went back to the Hotel San Martin, assembled the manager and staff and gave them each a tip, plus extra for the manager to give the night staff. It was the first time in my life I had tipped an entire hotel, but it was also he first time I had ever stayed in a hotel for seventeen nights. The staff had been wonderful to me and deserved it. They waved goodbye from the front step as I pedalled down the street. It was the morning my visa expired, and it was a two day run to the Guatemalan frontier, mostly downhill. I felt sad at leaving, like so many others I had found that San Cristóbal possessed a bosomy embrace you were reluctant to pull yourself away from.

I took the road to Comitán and was looking forward to the mobility afforded by cycling, and to smelling the country air again. It was hard work after such a long break, and I stopped for a *refresco* at a shop run by the army next to an army base. While I was there, a car was stopped by some traffic police who happened to be passing. I wasn't sure what was going on, so I hung around waiting for the form filling to finish, so I could interview the driver myself.

He had been stopped because he had overtaken a bus on a *tope*, the famous speed humps I have already warned you about, dear reader. It is tempting to overtake busses on topes as they go so slowly, but it is illegal. I asked him if he had bribed the police to avoid getting a fine. "Of course not" he retorted "I paid the fine like everyone else". That challenged my guide-book inspired view that Mexican police are all corrupt.

I passed through more autonomous villages with bright murals depicting the fight to achieve their status. In one, an election meeting was in progress by the side of the road. I bought some grapes from a man selling them from a wheelbarrow which had a small set of weighing scales on it. Grapes are often sold from wheelbarrows, fastidious hygiene regulations are a preserve of rich western countries. A woman chatting to the grape seller told me it was another twenty kilometres to Comitán. I believed her and showed a look of dismay. Her husband then burst into laughter and explained it was only seven; she had been pulling my leg. *Un chiste.*

Comitán had an unusual Parque Central built on sloping ground with terraces. There was plenty of activity – stalls, music equipment being set up for an evening concert, and the ever present bootblack boys. I went for a meal at a restaurant that had three sets of doors opening onto the Parque and sat inside with groups of Mexican families. The room was lit by thirteen white paper lanterns of different sizes, hanging at slightly different heights. Potted plants were arranged at random and display cabinets showed clothes, tool kits, jars of produce, and Mayan ornaments. In the corner a cashier waited patiently behind her desk for customers to finish and pay. She never gave a receipt, the printed till roll flopped over her desk and touched the ground. A notice on the wall informed of a house for sale in Colonia Infonavit. There were fifteen framed certificates of one sort or another on the walls. The restaurant would pass as a museum. It was also overstaffed – you could tell wages are low in Mexico.

I sat amongst this eating a pizza and reflected on the things I like about Mexico. The list is long. I should be excited about going to Guatemala tomorrow, but I am sad at leaving Mexico. I return to my cosy little hotel room for my last night's rest before heading for a strange country.

The sadness was made worse in the morning, as I pedalled down to Guatemala. Entering a village, I could tell there had been an accident as cars had pulled off the road and there were people standing around, looking serious. Tree branches had been laid on the road as a warning. Slow down. Then I saw the body of a boy, lying motionless. As I approached a blanket was laid over him. He was dead. I didn't know whether to stop and take off my crash helmet or just continue past. Each seemed disrespectful. As I passed I heard a woman say "He was only a young boy". Judging by the lack of hysteria, neither his parents nor the driver was present.

I was thankful that I could cry under the privacy of my sunglasses.

My last day in Mexico was scarred by a death on the road, and the blow was made harder because it was a child. The death of children is the most distressing of all. I freewheeled into the border town of Ciudad Cuauhtémoc gazing up at the wild sierras of Guatemala in front of me. I was about to leave one of the finest countries in the world, and had to put what I had just seen behind me, and prepare for my first border crossing.

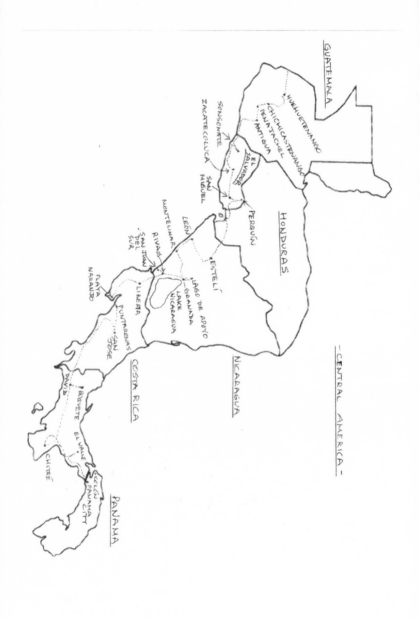

CHAPTER SEVEN

UP AND DOWN IN GUATEMALA

The border town of Ciudad Cuauhtémoc is rather grandly named for what is little more than a filling station, a bus office and a café. I stopped at the café for a last drink in Mexico and asked the man in the bus office for advice on changing money. He was a man of few words and pointed up the hill towards Guatemala. Two Canadian backpackers spoke to me in French, so my mind went into overdrive thinking in three languages at once. I'm glad I never worked as an interpreter at the European Union; I would have burst fuses galore. When I speak French in a Spanish speaking country, I sprinkle Spanish words all over the place.

Cycling from the village up to the frontier, the mountains became intimately spectacular. Rough peaks, wooded with deciduous trees and with occasional outcrops of white rock. A picture postcard welcome to Guatemala, but I knew I was in for a bit of hard pedalling. I went round a bend and suddenly the roadside shops and stalls started. You could buy anything, from washing up bowls to frilly knickers.

The place was called La Mesilla and it reminded me of Le Perthus, on the frontier between Spain and France. Frontiers are where different price levels hit each other face to face, and people from one country come to get bargains from the other. In Le Perthus, the French buy bottles of Ricard at Spanish prices. At La Mesilla Mexicans buy t-shirts and carving knives at Guatemalan prices. A woman asked me what I wanted to buy. I smiled at her and passed on. I am a walking disaster for shopkeepers, as I only buy things when I need them. There was so much activity that it was hard to push the bike through. Then I saw an office labelled *Migración* and someone pointed for me to go in. As I entered the two Canadians come out clutching their passports like trophies.

There were two smart men wearing uniforms behind a high counter. Filing cabinets lined the back wall. Stamps and forms were kept out of sight under the counter. Nervous of being two days over my visa for Mexico, I approached the desk and launched into a well prepared speech about how lovely a country Mexico was, and that I had enjoyed myself there so much that I couldn't help overstaying my visa. It was such a pity to have to leave what had to be the best country in the world.

Then my eyes fell on the Guatemalan flag stitched to the man's shoulder. Oh my god! I had delivered my speech to the wrong person. What would he do? Where was the Mexican frontier post?

He smiled and asked me for 30 pesos, the standard visa fee for foreigners. Stamping my passport, he suggested I change the rest of my Mexican money with the moneychanger waiting outside. Welcome to Guatemala.

Somehow, in the chaos of all the people, shops and stalls, I had missed the Mexican exit post. Now I was safely inside Guatemala, with a thirty day visa as my prize. I put all my anxieties behind me and used the services of the moneychanger. I asked him about hotels too. He said there were none in La Mesilla, but if I went on a few kilometres to El Reposo I would find one there next to a *gasolinera*. I dodged through a pair of lifting barriers which seemed to mark the frontier, and tried to press on through the crowds. It felt good to be legal again.

It was getting a bit late and I didn't want to go far if I could help it. The *gasolinera* at El Reposo sounded like a landmark I was unlikely to miss, so I pedalled on uphill through the rest of La Mesilla. I saw numerous little three-wheeled taxis based on motor scooters. They had small two stroke engines and were called *tuc-tucs* because of the engine noise. They went tuc tuc tuc tuc …... all through the town. They were bright red.

Once out of the town, I noticed that people by the roadside tended to look away as I approached. If I said *buenos tardes* I was ignored. It was a little un-nerving after three months in Mexico. I stopped where a man was working outside his house, to ask about hotels.

> "Pass on" he said.
>
> "You want me to pass on?"
>
> "Yes."

So I did. In a country recently devastated by guerrilla war I had to respect people's nervousness. The trouble was, it made me nervous too. I no longer had the cosy blanket of familiarity round me that I had in Mexico for three months.

The guerrilla war lasted for ten years and ended with the signing of peace accords in 1996. Countless thousands were killed in this period. Whole villages were massacred. Families became fatherless. Children were orphaned. Well meaning Americans arrived looking for orphans to give good homes to. Some were stolen. This added to an already suspicious regard for foreigners.

The theft of babies and children did not end with the peace accords. Guatemala has a liberal adoption law making it easy for foreigners – particularly Americans – to adopt Guatemalan children who are orphans. The market created by rich Americans who want a baby at any price is fed by poor Guatemalans who see a baby as an economic burden. Middle men step in as usual to cream off the profits. Some are dishonest and see this as easy money. Babies have been stolen, papers forged, lawyers have got rich.

It may explain the suspicious attitude I encountered in rural areas. Some people might have wondered if I were a potential child kidnapper in spite of being handicapped by travelling on a bike. As recently as September 2007 the Sunday Telegraph investigated the phenomenon and reported that foreign tourists had been attacked in rural areas because they were taking pictures of children. It is a sad reflection on the development of the human race when rich people buy children from poor countries. A modern day version of the slave trade.

I got to a shop where two jovial men stood behind the counter joking about something. I went in and asked about hotels. They told me I looked tired. Stressed might have been a better word, but I didn't quibble over linguistics. They re-affirmed the money changer's advice about a hotel next to a filling station. I had learned by now to get information and directions corroborated in this part of the world, as people were not always reliable.

Sure enough, round the next bend I saw the Hotel Reposo nestling under the green mountains, just behind a filling station. The rooms were in single storey blocks arranged haphazardly around the gardens. One of them was an office, and I went cautiously in, not knowing what to expect. A lady appeared and took me to a clean and airy room for which she wanted seventy-five Quetzals – under six pounds. It was charming to be in a country where the currency is named after a large feathery bird that looked more like a ladies' hat from the Edwardian era. I settled into my first night in Guatemala.

I had a shower and went straight out for a meal as I was ravenous. There was a general shop next door with a restaurant upstairs on the first floor. It had a giant balcony with chairs and tables, so I went up and picked the seat with the best view of the village. I ordered some chicken and the waitress asked me which beer I wanted, Gallo or Brahva. I had no idea, so I asked if I could see the bottles. That was a bit silly, as the bottles gave me no idea of the taste. I settled on a Brahva.

I sat back and surveyed the village from my vantage point, as I waited for my chicken to conclude its journey from yard to plate. There were people waiting on the main street, and a lot of passing traffic. This was the main road from the provincial capital of Huehuetenango to the frontier. Busses and *colectivos* were passing all the time, each filled to the brim with passengers. The *colectivos* had people hanging out of all the openings too, maybe thirty or more people on each one. The amount of baggage was striking too; each bus had a mountain of baggage strapped to the roof. When a bus stopped, *muchachos* jumped out of the back, climbed onto the roof, and sorted out the baggage that was to be chucked off. It was chaotic, but well organised. Well organised chaos is an art form, and these bus *muchachos* did it to perfection.

After dinner I walked round the village. A group of young men stopped me for a chat. One of them worked in Missouri, and had come home for Christmas. He worked there planting trees. He reckoned about 1,000 people from this area worked in the United States He drove a large new *camioneta* and wore noticeably fashionable clothes. By now it was dark and the shops had all closed. This took me a little by surprise. Three months in Mexico had made me take certain things for granted, such as the shops staying open till eight or nine o'clock. In El Reposo the shops were all closed by six.

At bedtime I gave the bike a superficial check-over. I thought the rear tyre was more worn than the front, so decided to swap them over. That was a daring move, given my hopeless ability at doing bike maintenance jobs. Maybe the two bottles of Brahva had given me Dutch courage. In no time two tyres were lying on the bedroom floor and two wheels were propped up against the wall. My confidence waned and I panicked in case I couldn't get them together again. Whoever said that bikes are easy to maintain hasn't met me. It is a myth that long distance cyclists know how to maintain their machines. I was walking proof of that. Well, cycling proof! I swore then made myself calm down. Breathe slowly, count to ten. I started again and managed to get the tyres back all right. Just. Then it was time for bed.

In the morning I set off early for the uphill ride to Huehuetenango, known locally as "way-way". Deep V-shaped valleys cut through the high mountains that boxed in my view as I laboured up the hills. There were people everywhere, I was never really alone. They grow coffee here, and many people were drying their beans in the sun, on plastic sheets, before selling them to a dealer.

The endless climb made me thirsty. Gasping for a drink, I pulled up at a roadside shop for a grapefruit juice. A man came out of the kitchen to serve me, obviously in the middle of his dinner. He gave me a Margarita, a large biscuit with a dollop of jam in the middle. "*Un regalo*" he said. As I was eating it, a van pulled up. The passenger door opened slightly and a pair of shoes fell out. I wondered what was going to happen next. Then the door opened a bit more, and a woman slid out of the van straight into the shoes. It was so graceful. She saw me watching, and burst out laughing. I laughed too. Then she opened the rear door of the van, and eight men jumped out looking for refreshments. Their eyes fell on my bike which became the centre of attraction. I told them I was going to Costa Rica (the story had changed a bit!), and the van driver bought me an energy drink as he said I would need it.

After my earlier anxieties, I was now beginning to relax in Guatemala.

As we stood there a platoon of soldiers walked past. We all looked equally surprised. The shop-keeper said it was unusual. Five minutes later, the soldiers came back to buy lemonade, and I asked the officer in charge what was going on. "Just practice" he assured me. He added that there was hardly a need for an army in Guatemala now and the numbers are being reduced. I broached the subject of the recent 'civil war' and he said the country was now safe and tranquil. I didn't push the subject of the civil war too much, as I recalled reading of tourists having their heads blown off twenty years ago for asking the wrong questions.

I continued my uphill plod to Huehue. By now I was used to steady uphill climbs and didn't really mind the work, as I was always rewarded with views. I kept going, minimising the stops, through fear of running out of time. A couple of the villages I passed through had basic looking hotels, but I didn't like the look of them. I was determined to make it to the bright lights of Huehue.

On the edge of town I saw a bank with a cash machine. This was my first test of the Guatemalan banking system. Would they recognise my bits of plastic as evidence of money? I went in and nervously teased the machine with my PIN number. It worked! I withdrew an outrageously large pile of Quetzal notes, in case this miracle of technology was going to be a one-off. I was now in funds and could paint the town red!

The locals were already doing a good job of painting it red. In the main *plaza*, a stage was being erected for a live concert. Behind the *plaza* was the busiest market I had seen since leaving Chihuahua, stretching along several streets and reminding me of the bazaars in Jerusalem, it was so busy. Some stalls were piled high with Christmas decorations and I bought some tinsel to bring some seasonal cheer to my handlebars. The *plaza* was packed with people. Children, sweet sellers, groups of men joking, women gossiping. It was all happening. I watched a circle of people gambling over cards. I wasn't tempted to join in – I had learnt that lesson years ago in Dresden, where I had once been hoodwinked into losing a hundred marks.

The Hotel Zaculeu had large rooms surrounding a leafy courtyard, and a slightly eccentric owner who seemed to expect me to haggle over the price. I knew right away I wanted to stay there.

In the pizzeria next door the waiters were busy putting up decorations. The Christmas tree kept disappearing and re-appearing, I couldn't quite work out what was going on. Whatever it was, it made the service very erratic. I was in one of those no-mans-land situations where I wasn't sure which waiter had been allocated to my table. After ordering three times, I was brought a bottle of Guatemalan wine, which my diary entry describes as "very sweet, but drinkable with food". I never tried it again.

Meanwhile the concert was getting under way in the *plaza*. I didn't need to go out as I could hear it perfectly well in my bedroom. However, the atmosphere there wasn't quite right so I went out and mingled with the Guatemalans. The concert was sponsored by Gallo, the brewery, so there were plenty of kiosks selling beer. I didn't see any drunkenness though. Binge-drinking seems to be a very British pastime.

The following day I needed a rest day. I had in my usual way discovered the hotel roof, so I sat up there reading and looking at the mountains. Huehue is 2,000 metres above sea level, but still manages to be surrounded by great mountains. Villages were dotted over the hillsides, and my eye picked out a road that I knew was my route for the following day. It was a high one.

Needing an Internet café, or at least thinking I did, I wandered out into the town, only to discover that everywhere was shut. I looked around in disbelief - in Mexico Sundays are virtually indistinguishable from other days; such is the Mexican devotion to retailing. Guatemalans are more observant of their religious devotion, for want of a better word. I asked two policemen if they knew an Internet café open on Sundays. They did, and walked me most of the way there to make sure I found it.

When I got back to my hotel, the doors were locked. This was crazy, I couldn't believe it. I knocked and knocked and knocked. Some passers by thought they knew where the doorbell was, but pushing it made no difference. In Santiago Astata I had been locked in my room. Now I was locked out. With my bike and belongings within. I walked round the block trying to figure out what to do.

Fifteen minutes later, still lacking an action plan, I went back to the hotel to check I hadn't missed a hidden doorbell. The door was wide open, the eccentric owner calmly sitting behind reception as if nothing had happened. When I told him my tale, he looked at me and said he always locks up in the afternoon, so he can have a sleep. I should have known that, of course. In my room I turned the TV on for the second half of the Mexican League final between Toluca and Monterrey. In Mexico, everyone was convinced that Monterrey would win and be champions. When I tuned in, Toluca were 1-0 up. The game was very entertaining. Toluca scored twice in injury time, finishing the game 3-0 to be champions. The cameras scanned the stunned faces of the Monterrey supporters, deprived of their certain victory. I turned off and went out for a coffee.

In the café a young man was dating his girl. She was hanging onto every word he said. I noticed the jewellery. Not hers, his. He was affluent and wanted the rest of the café to know it. Affluence like that is an unusual sight in Guatemala. He paid the bill with a flurry of banknotes and they left.

🚲

The road out of Huehue climbs through tranquil pine clad mountains, winding over narrow bridges crossing babbling water. It was reminiscent of Galloway. On higher ground the trees gave way to pasture. Sheep and goats were being driven along the road by whole families, making slow headway but maybe not in a hurry anyway. The families had dogs too. I had already noticed that some of the rural Indians were more nervous of strangers than was the case in Mexico. It was the rural Indians who suffered most in the civil war here. Solitary cows grazed in small fields.

In a village called Aguacatán I grazed my way along the long main street – a cake here, a banana there, finally a poke of chips from a man with a small metal stand and a real fire under his pan. People watched my slow progress along the street with mild curiosity. Many of the shops had pictograms painted on the front wall indicating what they sold. The hardware shop had pictures of tools around the door. The bike repair shop was decorated with a splendid racer embellished with go-faster stripes. The Aguateca language is still spoken here. The shop symbols were a practical way of dealing with what some people regarded as rural illiteracy, which might have been nothing more than an inability to understand the language of the invader. Gold and silver were mined here by the Spanish, but evidence of that has long since gone.

Past the village, the road was watched over by hilltops brooding under cloud. The slopes bore a mixture of small fields and trees, a real patchwork of different shades of green. Houses were dotted here and there, some roofed with the red tiles associated with Southern France or the North York Moors. It looked familiar, yet different. What made it look different were the people. Indigenous women dressed in dark blue woven skirts and *huipiles* hanging loose and decorated with colourful ribbons. Children wrapped in blankets clung to their backs, nervously eying up the foreigner passing on a bike.

The road swept sharply round a series of hairpin bends to a valley where families were working in the fields. I passed by quietly, raising a hand as a greeting. They returned the gesture and carried on working. I coasted into a village called Rio Negro – the black river. There was a dancing tournament in the *plaza* in front of the church. A man with a camcorder interviewed me about my journey and what I thought of Guatemala. You have to think quickly in these situations, making sure you are neither patronising nor moaning about some trivial complaint. I told him I was aiming for Sacapulas which he said was six kilometres along the road. He mentioned a steep hill, but I had been in his country long enough to take steep hills as given.

Salt was produced at Sacapulas, along the banks of the Rio Negro. People migrated here to work from areas to the north. The town was originally called Tajus, but renamed Sacapulas by the Spanish.

Just before the town, the tarmac turned to dust and rock. This often happened in Central America, as if the national budget for road surfacing didn't include towns. Perhaps they had voted for the wrong party. A metal bridge took me over a gushing river into the town. To the left was a *hospedaje* with a terrace overlooking the river. A woman came out of the kitchen and said there were no rooms. Pity, I thought. On the other side of the bridge was the Hospedaje Rio Negro. I entered through a bar where a slightly drunken man reclined in a seat. The owner took me up a spiral staircase to a room which was grubby and only contained two beds. There were no bedclothes at all. She said the beds cost twenty-five Quetzals each and as there are two I may have to share the room unless I pay for both beds. I didn't like it at all. I am not always fussy – I have camped in many strange and inhospitable places – but there was something about this place I didn't like.

Her husband could obviously see my nose turning up, so he pointed out that the room had a view of the river.

That was true, but I still didn't like it. He reluctantly told me there was another *hospedaje* at the top of the village, so off I went. After asking five people for directions, I eventually found it. At first I spoke to the owner through a window. She seemed a bit reluctant to deal with me. Then a boy opened the side door and said *"Pase"*. Come in. The side door was very narrow and led into a lean-to at the side of the house piled high with firewood and baskets of tomatoes. I struggled to carry my loaded bike through the doorway and into the lean-to. I left it there while the boy took me up four flights of stairs to a very light room at the top of the building. It had a bed and a table, and just enough room to put my bike.

"The room is thirty Quetzals"

"Fine."

"OK, pay me then." I do.

"Can I have they key please?"

"I want a twenty Quetzal deposit" he says, blandly and efficiently.

He tells me he is ten. I want to tell his mother he is a good businessman, but she already knows. She has disappeared, leaving him to it. I have to unload my bike in the lean-to, so I can carry everything up to my light, airy bedroom. It takes several journeys. I go for a wash and quickly deduce that although there is a mains water supply, nothing is actually plumbed into it. There is a stand pipe with a tap, over a large concrete contraption that has two tanks and an array of plastic bowls around it. I fill the toilet cistern to flush it, then realise it is easier just to tip a bowl of water down the toilet. There is a shower cubicle, but the plumbing system consists of the user holding bowls of water aloft and tipping the water over themselves. I am confused by the number of bowls, so I go down stairs and ask the woman for advice. My question causes much hilarity – you just use any bowl and pour the used water away.

I went to the restaurant by the river for a meal. There is a sign on the wall saying "No more than three beers per person." I had noticed this before, a quirky aspect of the Guatemalan drink laws. I asked the woman about it when ordering my third beer. "It's the law" she said, "but if you want a fourth beer that won't matter." It seems quite a flexible law. Perhaps a similar rule would help do something about the problem of binge-drinking in Britain.

After dinner I wandered down to look at the river. A pool had been built with stones, and a number of people were down there in their underwear having a good wash. As I stood looking a woman tipped a bucket of rubbish into the river close to where the people were washing, cheerily saying '*buenos tardes*' to me at the same time. Central America has a growing rubbish problem but the river had solved it for her.

In the *plaza* a brand-new four-storey office block looked completely out of place. Most of it was unoccupied. I asked some women standing in the *plaza* what the building was.

"It's the *alcalde*'s office"

"It's a pity all the money spent building it couldn't have been spent helping poor people"

"Yes, you're right, but that's what happens in Guatemala."

⚲

I was woken up at four o'clock by a loud mechanical noise like an engine of some sort, followed by lots of banging, as if they were doing some pile driving. I was already sleeping fitfully due to the absence of curtains at the window and the amount of light coming in. I resigned myself to a sleepless night and just lay there resting.

In the morning, fifteen steep uphill miles out of Sacapulas gave me sweeping views over the Rio Negro valley towards the Sierra Los Cuchumatanes, a solid block of rock with little feature. I could see a road going up onto the Sierra. It looked even steeper than the one I was on, and I was glad I wasn't on it. I sat outside a shop having a drink and was surrounded by a group of boys. They shouted "gringo" at me, but I told them that wasn't very original. They scampered off inside the shop for a while, and then re-appeared, clearing their throats. I cleared mine too. I noticed one of them was holding an English school book. I tried to encourage them with a few words of English, but they were overcome with shyness. Two of them said "Goodbye. Goodbye," then they disappeared again.

More miles, more hills, more stops for drinks and cakes. A plus for Guatemala is the wide availability of fresh cakes in shops and cafés. I have a soft spot for cakes which is well concealed in my slender figure. I wasn't rushing as I had a choice of towns to aim for that night.

The first was Santa Cruz del Quiché, which lived up to its rather grand name. A cathedral and town hall stood side by side at the top end of the *plaza*. The cathedral had a broad flight of steps up to the front door, which were filled with people meeting, waiting, chatting. The *plaza* was crowded too, and numerous shoe shine boys plied their trade, looking less opulent than their surroundings. Pablo was ten, didn't go to school, and charged one Quetzal for a shine. He said he usually had about twenty customers a day. He would earn just over ten pounds a week at that rate. I gave him two Quetzals to take his photo, and his friends teased him about being a film star. He wasn't very bright, and I caught myself wondering whether schooling would actually achieve anything for him. I was falling into the trap of justifying my surroundings.

According to my map it was nine kilometres to Chichicastenango. After an hour loafing about in the *plaza* I set off, thinking I would be there in no time. A couple of miles out of town the road ran steeply downhill into a gorge. I was careering round three-dimensional hairpin bends like a space cadet. Then it climbed equally steeply up the other side. I was pushing the bike along, thinking it can't be far now. Along came another gorge with steeper roller coaster bends and a tranquil river at the bottom surrounded by deciduous trees. An ideal dell for a picnic. Two men were standing by a white van and I asked them how far it was to Chichicastenango. Twenty minutes on foot, was their estimation.

I plodded on uphill. I had never experienced such steep hills and bends in my life. Pushing the bike uphill was giving me backache and I wondered where on earth Chichicastenango had got to. I had to change sides of the road to be more visible on the outside of each curve. I was getting annoyed. Another gorge, another bend, and then Chichicastenango appeared in the distance. It wasn't nine kilometres, it was nineteen! There had been a misprint on the map.

Something was on in town. I passed a funfair with all the lively trappings of frivolity. Rides, stalls, kiosks, and hundreds of people. I made my way into the town centre. Policemen were patrolling on foot in pairs. In Mexico I had only ever seen policemen in the backs of *camionetas*, sitting in groups pointing their guns up to the sky. I would go for several days without seeing any – a worry when you have the anxieties of a tourist. In Guatemala they were everywhere and I always found them helpful when asking for directions or advice.

The first hotel I tried was full. I stood there in disbelief as this hadn't happened to me before. "It's the Festival of St. Thomas tomorrow" he told me, suggesting the Hotel Giron round the corner. They had one room left. It had no bathroom, but the *muchacho* said I could share a cold shower. "Share with whom?" I enquired, trying to gauge if I needed to allow for queuing time. "The staff" he said. A cold shower is better than no shower, so I decided to stay put and not waste any more time searching for rooms as I wanted to see the Festival.

The Festival of St. Thomas happens every year in Chichicastenango, on 21st December. The town becomes a mecca for indigenous people from all over the country. It is a cacophony of music, fire-crackers, smoke and dancing.

Incense is everywhere, even seeping out of the church. Sleep is out of the question because the festival is one gigantic party with fireworks music and fun. I wondered how this had all survived the civil war. Maybe it had survived to spite the civil war.

Early in the morning the market square was filled with people, and there were groups of dancers performing traditional dance. They were using a form of maypole, on which the performers gradually unwind themselves from the top in a grand display of colour. There was singing, but the fireworks and crackers were so loud that the songs became merged into a single wall of sound, as if you were listening to a four-sided football match between Celtic, Rangers, AC Milan, and Inter Milan. Squeezed into the midst of all this were the market stalls, where traders were selling rugs, textiles and candles. Behind the stalls were huddled rows of little cafes, where women made stews in huge pans, their customers sitting in lines on wooden benches like at school.

After a couple of hours I needed a coffee.

Three months on the road had given me a hunter's instinct for cafes selling real coffee. I quickly found one in the main street and settled at a table next to the pavement for a late breakfast. As I sit there, a parade comes past carrying figures of saints on wooden platforms above their shoulders. There is smoke and incense; people carry candles. Most, but not all, are in traditional dress. A group comes by wearing face masks, wide brim hats and costumes of brown and gold, their great coats trailing along the ground in a sweeping presence. A band follows. More fireworks and bangers so loud I thought a volcano had popped. Now a group of women parade past wearing brightly coloured feathers on their heads. Three Dutch women stride past like giraffes, dwarfing the rather short Guatemalans. Three men walk along playing a marimba as it is carried sideways along the street by two other men. That needed some co-ordination to say the least.

A marimba is a wooden xylophone traditional to Guatemala and parts of Mexico. The Guatemalans regard it as their national instrument. It has a very distinctive happy-go-lucky sort of sound. They are normally played by three men standing in a row, each responsible for a specific part of the keyboard. It is the ultimate team sport musical instrument.

I recognised the woman at the next table as she was staying at the Hotel Giron. She was María from Guatemala City, spending a few days holiday in Chichicastenango for the festival. We spoke about the civil war which she described as a clash of ideologies with the indigenous mountain people being the pawns in the middle, not connected particularly with either side. The war was between wealthy families who owned and controlled virtually the whole country, and reformers who wanted to distribute power and wealth more fairly and equitably. As civil wars go, the motives were hardly original. What differed in Guatemala was the way the indigenous people suffered wholesale slaughter, intimidation and displacement as if the whole shooting match was their fault. Agrarian reform was part of the agenda, as were indigenous rights, but they were not the whole picture.

As we talked, street children came in to sell things, reminding us of the pervasive poverty of this country. It could have been tempting to brush them off like flies, but children don't deserve that. They were selling authentic looking woven craft, although nowadays there was no certainty that they hadn't been flown in from China. María agreed that they should be at school, but the system whereby families have to partially support their children at school made it hard. María said that until five years ago most teachers were intolerant of village people who couldn't speak Spanish. For many this was a disincentive to go to school.

We talked about my impression that most politicians in Guatemala were white, rather than *mestizo*, as were most television presenters and even the actors in adverts. María said that one of the reasons was that there had been immigration of wealthy Europeans in the 20th Century, some of whom were given land to grow coffee. They easily fell into the ruling classes and became part of the political hierarchy. White skin and blonde hair featured in TV adverts as they were regarded as superior to dark looks. María said that in Guatemala City wealthy people spend a lot of money trying to change their appearance, to make themselves whiter and purer than other Guatemalans. We agreed that people who do that must have problems with their self-esteem.

🚲

It rained for much of the day. It dampened my spirits a bit, but the locals carried on with the Festival regardless. Sitting in an internet café, I was pleasantly surprised when María popped her head round the door to invite me to go for some soup with her. She had been photographing people in traditional costumes at the Festival.

I left Chichicastenango the following morning in chilly, cloudy, but dry weather. I could have done with another day there, but two sleepless nights listening to music and fireworks were enough. It was a steep climb for the first ten miles to the junction at Los Encuentros. The junction was lined with shops and cafes. Every bus for miles around converged here to disgorge its passengers into the hands of the traders, before they sped off to their destination in another bus. I bought some grapes from a lady stall-holder, while an American tourist looked on, listening to my Spanish.

From the junction a refreshing downhill run took me to Solalá. I caught glimpses of a volcano. Lake Atitlan came into view. A second volcano followed. They all glimmered in the sun and I was excited. The road skipped along at a high level, giving me first class views. Some men working in a workshop let me to go in to take a photograph from the terrace at the back. One of them was wearing a Barcelona top so we had a humorous exchange about Henrik Larsson and of course Ronaldinho. In Solalá it was market day and I had to pick my way round the side streets as the main street was wall to wall with stalls. I wanted to linger but I needed to be sure of having enough time to check out the hotels in my destination, Panajachel.

Between Solalá and Panajachel the road skirts along a couple of hundred feet above the lake. I stopped at a viewpoint where a minibus halted to give its passengers the obligatory two minutes look. The driver sat on the bonnet looking bored. By now I had cycled 2,200 miles so was beginning to tell an impressive story to those who asked about my bike. Some New Zealanders looked at it in disbelief. They said I would be better off with a mountain bike. I don't understand the trendiness of mountain bikes; almost all tourers use a touring bike. Mountain bikes are fine for mountains but on long road stretches they are tiring as it is hard to maintain a decent momentum. It's an image thing. Mountain bikes are trendy, so everything else is "dull". My Dawes Horizon is the most comfortable bike I have ever owned.

Panajachel is idyllic. The views of lake and volcano must be one of the best in Central America. For this reason it is popular with Americans who want to live there, either to run businesses or retire. As a result it has earned the nickname of "Gringotenango". A street lined with tourist businesses runs from the centre of town down to the lake shore. After inspecting several hotel rooms I decided to push the boat out and go for a large room with a balcony overlooking the lake, costing about twenty pounds. It was Christmas, I wanted a rest for a few days, and I was going to do it in style.

Relaxing on the balcony, I watched the evening sky. The clouds were making magical light formations on the lake. Dusk at five thirty was a rich canvas of blues, greys and yellows. It was like an unseen Monet – different yet familiar. Finally the sky turned pastel orange, looking more like a Sisley. I was in my own private art gallery.

🚲

In the morning I found a restaurant owned by a Uruguayan man. He sat with his family eating breakfast leaving a very competent and friendly manager in charge. A little boy appeared at the side of my table and muttered something to me. I didn't quite make out what he said. Before I could ask him to repeat, the manager came over and told him to go away. I was going to protest, but the boy made his way to another table where a man in his twenties was eating pancakes. He passed his plate across the table to the boy so he could eat the pancakes and ordered him a large glass of orange juice. The boy became totally absorbed in putting maple syrup on his pancakes, eating them, and drinking the orange juice which the waitress had brought. The waitress brought him a clean knife and fork. I was filled with emotion because of the kindness of the man, and the reaction of the boy. It made me angry at the lost childhood of a small boy, who knows no love except the scraps of kindness he can tease out of people in a restaurant. The manager told me he is there every morning. I wanted to take him away and give him a good future – but no! He is best in his own environment. You can't compensate for lost love by material things. I could not solve the problems of Central America single-handed.

The incident made me recall the case of Elías Gonzales, which gripped Cuba in 2000. Elías and his mother were amongst a group of people escaping from Cuba to Miami for a better life. Their small boat capsized in a storm, killing some of the adults including Elías' mother. Elías was rescued and taken to the United States. His father had separated from his mother sometime before, and was still living in Cuba. Elías had some relatives in Miami who agreed to look after him after his rescue. Then the economic politics began. His father wanted him back, in Cuba. His relatives wanted to keep him, in Miami. He appeared on television decorated with the material trappings of life in the United States, to show people in Cuba how much better off he was. It was claimed that he liked MacDonald's and Coke, not widely available in Cuba at the time. The Cuban government supported his father's claim to have him back, as it was their right to be together as a family. The relatives in Miami refused to let him go, on the grounds that he was materially better off in the United States. He was being kidnapped for his own material benefit as if his own opinions or family needs didn't count.

The case became a major diplomatic issue between two countries seldom short of ideas to fight over. It went through the United States courts, who eventually ruled that Elias's best interests were better served by being with his natural father. The case dragged on for months; it was sad that the thing most wanted and needed by a child – love – was disregarded in a fight over how much better off he would be if he could be smothered with jewellery, tee-shirts, and burgers. Such is the value placed by society on love.

While in Panajachel I went for a boat trip across the lake to Santiago Atitlan. Walking ashore I was targeted as usual by sellers and taxi drivers. Ignoring all of them, I made my way up into the town. It was market day, and I was in the thick of it, the tall gringo surrounded by local people pushing, shoving, trying to get some bargains. I could only get through by pushing too, it was quite intimidating. There were sheets tied across the street to provide shelter from the sun, and they were level with my eyes. Guatemalans are noticeably short compared to Europeans, and I was on their turf so I had to duck.

At the top the street opened up into a small *plaza* where boys played football and *muchachos* looked on. A gate led through to a much larger *plaza*, dominated by a church and some buildings associated with it. The church was built in the 16th century and has been rebuilt a number of times due to earthquakes. It was a scene of strife in the civil war. Troops were garrisoned in the neighbourhood, and for a period villagers slept in the church to be safe from them. In the 1980's several hundred villagers were abducted, tortured, murdered. The area was plagued by death threats and disappearances. On 28th July 1981 the priest – who was really sticking his neck out to help the villagers – was murdered in the church. His name was Father Stanley Alpas Rother, from Oklahoma. There is a monument to him in the church, containing his blood and heart, put there at the villagers' request. At each side of the monument is a battery of crosses, arranged in lines, each commemorating the name of a villager who died or was made to disappear. There are about 250 crosses in all, touching the emotions.

In the *plaza* a man was selling small model bicycles made out of wire. He was a keen cyclist. I bought a little bike to stick on my crossbar, and asked him for route advice out of Panajachel. He recommended a route through the mountains to Patzún and Patzicia. I told him that the tourist information office in Panajachel had advised me not to take this route as I was almost certain to get robbed. He was surprised at this advice, as he had ridden it many times. The tourist information man, on the other hand, had been adamant that robbers would be waiting for me at almost every bend. I found this unlikely, given that no-one knew I was coming. Who would waste their time waiting on the off-chance that a tourist would be disregarding advice and cycling innocently through? It seemed so unlikely that I decided to chance it. I was getting a little tired of warnings that I was perpetually in danger.

The road out of Panajachel climbed steeply. It went up the side of a deep valley, and I could see effects of Hurricane Stan. Buildings had been washed away and there was dried mud still on the road. A café, closed for business, looked marooned in the middle of a river. Painted on the gable end were the words "Thank you Stan". I asked some people by the side of the road if Stan had been bad. "Yes" they said, "It affected everyone". Further on, the mud had been piled up on either side of the road by excavators, like when it snows hard in the Highlands, and the snowploughs make deep cuts through the duvet of snow. The road was steep because the hillsides were steep. They didn't "engineer" the road into the landscape; it was stuck on, like a newspaper picture blue-tacked to the kitchen wall. Above me were scars where the hillside had slipped away in the heavy rain that marked the hurricane. I wouldn't have liked to have been there then.

There was a hole in the road. About fifty feet of carriageway had disappeared into the river below, leaving a serrated edge of tarmac against the skyline. A dusty by-pass had been constructed around the hole, but there was nothing to stop me walking to the edge and peering over.

Anyone on the road when it fell would have met certain death.

The road continued to go up, down, left, right. I was walking more than cycling. Two teenagers passed me on bikes. I was taken by surprise, as I hadn't seen any recreational cyclists yet in Guatemala. I put on a spurt to catch up with them, so I could talk to them.

They were both seventeen, and enjoyed cycling on the quiet roads. They had done this route about forty times, they reckoned, so they knew all the bends and hills well. We talked about politics as well as the hurricane. The relative richness of my country compared to theirs was quickly on the agenda. Their bikes were called Maya Tour and had cost 900 Quetzals each – around seventy-five pounds. By Guatemalan standards these teenagers were from affluent families. I commented that they weren't wearing crash helmets and they said most people in Guatemala couldn't afford them. I said it was sufficient to be able to afford bikes!

In Patzún they took a different turning and we said good-bye. The town looked scruffy as it suffered badly in the 1976 earthquake and it was hard to believe that thirty years had passed since then. I bought some grapes in the market and contemplated my immediate future as I munched through them. The hills had been so severe that although it was two o'clock I had only done twenty miles. I wasn't sure if I could make it to Antigua, my planned destination for the night. I pressed on regardless, stopping only for a quick drink in a roadside café where I was the only customer. The waiter told me the distances to Chimaltenango and Antigua, and added that it was downhill nearly all the way. That last snippet was a bonus making me set off at a brisk pace.

The road swept down through open farmland, with people working in the fields. The old American school-busses growled their way uphill in the opposite direction, laden with people and baggage. The capacity to strap things onto the roofs was limitless. Maybe you could even move house by bus. I glided into Chimaltenango like a plane making it safely onto the runway. This was another town that had been damaged in the 1976 earthquake, and you could tell it had been rebuilt very quickly, with little regard to planning or aesthetics. When you need to rebuild your life after a disaster, you do what you need to. As I pedalled my way through Central America it was always a source of amazement to me how resilient human beings are at hanging on in parts of the world where you wouldn't logically want to live.

There was no getting away from it, Chimaltenango looked a mess and I made a decision to carry on to Antigua, even though it would be dark in an hour and a half. I was not carrying any lights so cycling in the dark would have been dangerous. When planning the trip I decided I wouldn't cycle at night, so I had left out lights to save weight. If the worst came to the worst, I would walk along the road in the dark facing the oncoming traffic.

A short way out of Chimaltenango was a lake with boats on it and children playing. The place was jolly and it would have been a good place to stop, had there been somewhere to stay. I reluctantly urged myself on.

Dusk was falling as I reached a place where each side of the road was lined with old single storey adobe buildings. There were no signs and the place had an air of gloomy anonymity. I wasn't quite sure where I was. The traffic was heavier and there were little *tuc-tucs* everywhere like bees around a hive. I stopped outside a large church and asked a woman how far it was to Antigua.

"This is it" she said, pointing down at the road as if to emphasise. I asked her where the hotels were. She waved her arms in the general direction of the next parallel street. The first one I looked in had pokey claustrophobic rooms. At the next, the wide-boy on reception looked at my bike and told me I could leave it for safe keeping in his bedroom for twenty Quetzals! A double win – he gets my money and my bike! I laughed at him and moved on. At the next hotel, the Hotel Cristal, the owner said *"bienvenidos"* the moment I walked in. It was good to be made welcome, the rooms were arranged around an internal courtyard, and my budget enabled me to treat myself to the best one. I had arrived in Antigua.

CHAPTER EIGHT

LA ANTIGUA GUATEMALA

La Antigua Guatemala, to give the town its full name, was the original capital built by the Spanish for the Viceroy of Guatemala in the sixteenth century. In those days the Guatemalan territories included Chiapas in Mexico and extended all the way to what is now Costa Rica. It was an important centre and the Spanish confidently set about building substantial cathedrals, administrative buildings, and spacious plazas to consolidate their hold on the Central American isthmus.

Then disaster struck. Earthquakes in 1583, 1689, 1717 and 1773 damaged or destroyed many of these buildings, which the determined colonisers then rebuilt. Finally the penny dropped, either that God was not pleased or more probably that the site was geologically unstable, and the capital was moved twenty miles away to Guatemala City in 1776.

It was the equivalent of moving round the corner to get away from a neighbourhood bully. Guatemala City was itself completely destroyed by another earthquake in 1917. This susceptibility to earthquakes may by now have become ingrained into the Guatemalan psyche. In his classic book about his journey through the Americas "The Old Patagonian Express", Paul Theroux describes Guatemalans as "sullen at the best of times, displaying a scolded resignation - bordering at times on guiltiness – when the subject of earthquakes is raised." It was true that I had found Guatemalans a bit on the sullen side; I had put this down to the decades of oppression and murder. Paul Theroux made his epic journey in the 1970's and saw the sullenness from a different perspective. They are people who have been terrorised by nature and terrorised by struggles between the Establishment and reformers.

Theroux paints a gloomy picture of Guatemala in the 1970's. A country where democracy had not existed since a coup in 1954 had replaced an elected socialist government with military rule. It was a feudal system where everything was controlled by a handful of families who were paranoid about communism. The army was dominated by them, the press was under their control, and they held onto everything. It wasn't surprising that revolution, communism, or just a good old fight, should seem an attractive idea to peasants with nothing to hope for. Guerrilla movements grew up and were matched by right wing death squads, determined to "identify" and "eliminate" anyone who threatened their hold.

The violence and death peaked in the 1980's and 1990's, if twenty years of misery can be described as a 'peak'. Finally sense began to prevail – or the protagonists ran out of steam – and peace accords were signed in 1996, marking a turning point, or at least a slowing down of violence. The Peace accords did not stop the violence completely. It takes time for a boiling pot to cool down to room temperature. In 1998 Bishop Juan Gerradi was murdered after publishing a controversial report. As recently as September 2005 the Legal Advisor of Casa Alianza, the charity that helps street children, was murdered in Guatemala City. He had been advising Casa Alianza on cases involving irregular adoptions, murders, sexual exploitation, trafficking and other human rights violations concerning children. Orphans, poor children, the most vulnerable people in society are so easy to exploit, and people with a vested interest in such exploitation will stop at nothing to remove obstacles from their path. Working against such odds takes a lot of bravery. Unfortunately Casa Alianza can only touch the tip of a huge iceberg.

Guatemala is still a violent country. Selective murders take place regularly. On my second day in Antigua the newspapers carried a cover story on the murder of a young *tuctuquero* in Guatemala City. The next day, bus drivers in the capital went on strike to protest against the murder of several bus drivers. Guatemala City was a place not to go to, I was told, and I had no plans to go there. That there is still violence is not in doubt. What seems to have shifted is the motivation. Politics has gone out of the window. Now people are warring over drugs and organised crime. Terrorism, oil, drugs, commercialised sex, religion. The world still has plenty to fight over.

After my hilly ride from Panajachel, I slept soundly my first night in Antigua. I awoke to discover that the other bike locked up in the hotel courtyard belonged to another international traveller. When I met him he was wearing a well worn cloth cap, from which protruded grey hair and whiskers in all directions. He looked as if he would have been equally comfortable touring the world in a rowing boat. I wanted to hear about his travels so I suggested going for breakfast together so we could have a good talk about travel, and cycling in particular.

His name was Peter, originally from Oregon and now living in Washington DC. He had left Texas six weeks previously, travelling by a mixture of bike and bus. Like me, he had no rules against that. He was about sixty, and told me it was the first time in his life he had ever left the United States. His plan was to see as much of the Americas as he could, and discover whether the good things and bad things he thought about the United States were true. He was impressed with the countryside, different people, and differences in culture that he experienced. That is the essence of travel! He had read that El Salvador was unsafe, and was planning to take the bus through to Nicaragua. I made a mental note to email Leo and Gavin for advice on that one before committing myself.

As we ate we got on to American politics. Peter told me how disenfranchised he felt from a system where two large identical parties are in control. Rich, ideologically the same, and only interested in the businesses that finance them, not in people. Listening to this was depressing. His country is one that controls the world, preaches democracy, and yet does not have real democracy at home. What hope is there for the rest of the world?

We wandered around town for a couple of hours looking at the colourful adobe buildings, and then discovered a small café where we could get decent coffee. The café had small wooden tables, and at one side was a counter where you could order coffee. Next to the counter was a glass display cabinet brimming with cakes. We tried the blackberry cheesecake, which was – according to Peter – better than any you could get in Manhattan! I took his word for that one. It was certainly worth going to Guatemala for!

Antigua has many language schools. There are two reasons for this – the Guatemalan accent is very clear, and the schools are relatively cheap due to the low wages. I decided I needed to brush up on my Spanish so visited a few to see what was what. I have spent many years learning both French and Spanish. This means that not only am I passably fluent in three languages (if you include English!), but I also have a good idea about what I am looking for in a language school as I have used many.

The lady at the first one I went to was more interested in showing me the programme of social activities than telling me about their teaching styles. I wasn't impressed. At the next one, the manager immediately set about giving me a level test to determine my strengths and weaknesses. In language teaching, a level test is a structured conversation which is used by the teacher to listen to the language you use so he can judge your level of competence. For example the teacher will test the correct use of phrases such as "I went to Madrid" compared with "I have been to Madrid".

He told me I needed to work on improving my use of past tenses. I enrolled for nine hours one to one tuition over the next few days. I arrived for my class the following morning and climbed the narrow staircase to the roof of the building, where some partitions had been made to create small informal classrooms. The view of the volcanoes and the surrounding rooftops was amazing. I was a bit apprehensive as I might not like the teacher. However, the proprietor of the school had matched us well. My teacher, Roberto, was a lawyer with good political awareness, and our temperaments and interests contained much common ground. We got on like the proverbial house on fire, although I never found a Spanish equivalent to that phrase!

On the first morning we discussed the class system in Guatemala where everything is owned by seventeen families. There is very little competition or scope for people to compete. He said that the same family owned the franchises for both Coca-cola and Pepsi, as well as Gallo beer and the largest bottled water brand, Salvavidas. Roberto told me the scandal about cement. If you want a bag of cement, there is only one company that sells it and they charge thirty-five Quetzals per bag. The Mexican company Cruz Azul tried to import cement and sell it at twenty-two Quetzals a bag, but the government blocked the import on quality grounds. I wonder who influenced the government to do that!

Roberto told me he thought the few middle class people in Guatemala were pre-occupied by the need to study and get qualifications, so they could stay in the middle classes and cling on to what they had. He felt isolated from politics as the politicians, once elected, simply continued to use the corruption system to feather their nests. I showed him an advert I had seen in the morning newspaper, describing a government scheme to help older people. It promised to set up a fund to give older people a better quality of life. The advert glorified in being non-specific, and also talked about the fund being dependent on overseas aid and donations. Taxing the rich did not seem to be on the agenda. Roberto said it was really only a promise made in advance of the elections next year, and it probably would never happen as the electorate was accustomed to unfulfilled promises. He concluded that with the eternal Latin American problem of corruption in power, improving the lot of the poor was insurmountable. This depressing realism is what led Che Guevara to conclude that the only solution was revolution.

As I cycled through Central America I spent much time mulling over the question of why the English-speaking world is generally economically successful, whereas Spanish Latin America tends to be an economic disaster. Corruption was often cited as the cause. Corruption is selfishness, getting what I can for myself irrespective of the wider consequences. While living in Spain I had noticed a selfish streak in Spanish men, but to be fair selfishness is not uniquely Spanish, people of all races have selfish streaks. It is part of human nature. I tended to come back to the same conclusion that the Spanish colonial system of land ownership had facilitated the lack of wider economic progress.

Roberto had a part time job working for a government funded project to give advocacy assistance to indigenous people who had land ownership problems. He found it very fulfilling, although not well paid. A lawyer who needs to supplement his income by teaching must be following a vocation he enjoys.

We spoke about the minimum wage. The legal minimum in Guatemala is 1,256 Quetzals per month – about a hundred pounds – and that is what most people get. Bank clerks get more, about 1,700 Quetzals per month, as they have to look smart. Minimum wage legislation is a catch twenty-two situation. One the one hand, workers need legal protection from exploitation, on the other hand many employers interpret it as a maximum wage. If a high proportion of workers earn the minimum wage, there is less disposable income floating around the economy. Disposable income makes the world go round.

One evening I went to see some Guatemalan disposable income in action. The owner of my hotel had a part-time job as a swimming instructor at a luxury tourist hotel on the edge of town. He offered to take me there as a guest, so I could have a swim and use the health club. We arrived at a plush oasis of luxury that looked completely out of place in a poor country. Manicured trees lined the entrance. Doormen saluted as we walked into the foyer. We went to the bar where I was signed in as a visitor. I daren't ask the barman for a beer in case my credit card limit didn't cover it. We walked past a children's pool where some kids were frolicking around with plastic dolphins. We went to the health spa, where an efficient looking woman in a tight maroon skirt-suit issued me with my towel and locker key. She didn't actually say it, but I could hear her thinking "Don't even contemplate stealing the towel. You will be shot." Affluent overweight Guatemalans rolled about like hippos in the bubbling water, smugly aware of their privileged status. In many British cities the local councils subsidise swimming pools to give wider access for all. Such a concept hadn't arrived here yet.

The following morning Roberto asked me about the British National Health Service. I am proud of it, in spite of the warts, especially when I am in a country that doesn't have one. He asked me if I had noticed that many Guatemalans have teeth missing. I had, of course. He said it was a question of economics. A dentist would charge between a hundred and two hundred Quetzals for a filling, whereas an extraction is only twenty Quetzals. Furthermore, an extraction prevents the problem re-occurring. What splendid value for money!

"Have you noticed that hardly anyone wears glasses?" He asked.

"Yes.

"Do you think that's because Guatemalans have good eyesight?"

"Maybe the carrots here are extra good."

"A pair of glasses costs at least a third of a month's wages."

"That's a lot when you need 100% of a month's wages for food."

I clearly needed glasses too, as I had overlooked that it was almost New Year, and the owner of my hotel had re-let my room to a couple from Guatemala City who were coming to Antigua for the celebrations. I hadn't been specific enough about my plans when I arrived – it was entirely my fault. I had to rush back after my Spanish class to change hotels. I found another hotel round the corner where the rooms on the first floor looked onto the central courtyard. Each had a wide balcony where you could sit looking down into the courtyard, up at the volcanoes, or simply sit chatting to other residents. There were a number of long-term residents there, which was a good sign. One of them, a French Canadian lady doing voluntary work with children, sat sipping a glass of red wine as if she were in Nice.

Another room was occupied by a German couple, whom I took to be man and wife. Until Heinrich told me the highly amusing story of how his wife had run off to Spain one Saturday with his car, his computer, his son, and another man. It wasn't clear to me which of them he missed most, but he tracked them down by checking credit card transactions and phoning dozens of hotel receptionists. After all this detective work he intercepted his son in a street in Benidorm. His son coolly said "Hi Dad" as if they were doing their Saturday morning shopping in Heidelberg, and led Heinrich to his wife's love-den, where he was happily re-united with his car and computer.

Antigua is close to several volcanoes. They dominate the view and puffs of smoke often punctuate the clear air surrounding the town. I wanted to climb one, but everyone spoke of the risk of robbery and pointed me in the direction of various guides. The stories of robberies did not convince me, I thought it was simply a ploy to instil fear in tourists and increase the business of guides and their agents. Aside from the fear factor, the guides have route knowledge, a considerable asset in a country where mapping is poor to non-existent. The prices included transport to and from the start of the walk, another advantage. I settled on a trip up Volcan del Agua, paying my money to an agent. I had to be outside the agent's office the following morning at six, to get the best of the weather, as it often clouds over during the day.

I arrived alone on the deserted cobbled street, outside the crumbling and firmly closed office, at six o'clock on the dot, and waited. And waited. It was a pain to be up so early, as I had been kept awake late in the hotel by the owner talking loudly with a friend who had just returned from the United States, and had a lot to tell. This put me in a grumpy mood as I waited for my guide. A gruff man in a shabby anorak and an even shabbier car arrived twenty minutes late without saying a word. I was worried he might be my guide, and felt uncomfortable as I got into the car.

He whisked me off to the village of Santa María de Jesús where another man was standing in the village, waiting for us. He was wearing a woolly hat, was called Fidel, and had an engaging smile. I liked him straight away. The driver returned to Antigua and Fidel led me along a village street to his house, where he popped in to collect his rucksack and a dog named Bobby, and then we walked up through the village. It was quarter to seven. As we climbed above the village the soft rays of the rising sun lit up the early morning mist and the fronts of the colourful buildings, like a magic painting.

The track was narrow, hemmed in on both sides by a rich variety of verdant trees and bushes. At one point we had to step aside to let two men with horses past. The horses were laden with freshly harvested maize and neatly chopped firewood. Fidel said the farmers lived down in the village, and owned land higher up on the volcano. Most of the land was owned by small farmers, rather than absentee landlords, the farms passing from father to son. If there were more than one son, one had to buy out the shares of the others to prevent sub-division into uneconomic units.

We talked about their horses. According to Fidel you could buy a horse for about seventy-five pounds. A good, strong one could cost four times as much. A lot of money for a Guatemalan hill farmer. Horse rustling was common enough for people to keep their horses in the house if they could. Nice for the children to play with! Apart from the working horses, I saw no animals grazing, only crops. The soil looked remarkably rich and it supported a great variety of flowers, plants and birds. After two hours we stopped at a clearing for a rest and a look at the view. We could see the summit, looking deceptively close. It was hard not to be fooled by wishful thinking. A steady stream of people was coming down, and some told me they had slept overnight on the summit to get the clearest views as the sun comes up.

Two hours and a lot of effort later, Fidel, Bobby and I reached the crater at the top. It is funny to arrive at the top of a mountain and then look down into a small crater. It had a flat grassy bottom the size of a football pitch. I say that because some makeshift goalposts had been erected. There was a chapel too, as well as a small bothy and some wooden frames on which people could erect plastic tents. A well organised crater.

It was encircled by its perimeter ring, most of which was the same height apart from the stretch next to the chapel, which had been blown away by an eruption a few hundred years ago. We wandered along the narrow path that followed the rim looking through the clouds at the views, waiting for the neighbouring volcanoes to come into view. They did from time to time, due to the ever-changing pattern of the clouds. We sat down leaning against a brick telecoms hut to eat a snack. Fidel repeated the story to me that there are so many robberies on the path that you are only safe with a guide. I was still sceptical as I had seen plenty of independent walkers without guides, and little evidence of the sort of people whom I thought might commit robberies. The probability was blown up out of all proportion, I think. Fidel was carrying a radio, which he used from time to time to report our progress to his wife.

We belted down from the summit at a cracking pace. It was hard on the knees and I knew I would pay for it the following day. Having the radio meant that my transport back to Antigua was waiting for me when we got back to the village. I said goodbye and thank you to Fidel, and twenty minutes later was back in the centre of Antigua indulging in coffee and cheesecake in the Café Condesa, feeling smug with my achievement.

In the evening I went into town to see the New Year celebrations. The streets were bright and lively with people, some carrying sparklers. Restaurants were full, the sound of laughter mixing with the chinking of cutlery and the popping of wine corks. I wandered around watching the commotion. Voices, fireworks, marimba music. In one street boys wore circular wooden frames on their backs carrying fireworks. The fireworks were lit, and the boys did cartwheels down the street, flames and sparks flying everywhere. It was spectacular, and probably illegal under European Health and Safety rules.

As expected I was stiff in the morning. I had breakfast on the hotel terrace, looking up with a feeling of satisfaction at the volcano I had climbed, listening to more of Heinrich's funny stories. I went out for a coffee at the cheesecake café. Once before when I had been there, I noticed three retired American men sitting at the table in the open window. They were there again, but a delivery lorry had parked immediately in front of the window blocking the view. To my amazement, one of them went to ask the delivery man to move the lorry, so they could look out onto the street. To my even greater amazement, he did!

The following morning I left, after a big hug from Heinrich and a lengthy photo session in the street outside the corner café where we had breakfast together. The maroon wall of the old building made a good background for the pictures. After a week in Antigua I was sad leaving, but I reminded myself I had a few more miles to do to get to Panama.

The altitude of Antigua meant it was downhill all the way to Escuintla, twenty-five miles away. I coasted down enjoying the views of the volcanoes, one of which was pushing out great puffs of smoke as a farewell gesture. Escuintla had a dual carriageway ring road which was well-engineered but had no signposts at the roundabouts. Route finding was a mixture of guesswork, one wrong turning, and some advice from a police patrol car waiting for speeding motorists. At a filling station I stopped for my first drink after leaving Antigua. I had done twenty-five miles and it was unprecedented for me to do such a distance without needing to stop for a drink.

From Escuintla the road was flat with few undulations. It was a change from the mountains and volcanoes I had passed through. Indeed, I did not know flat roads existed in Guatemala! The landscape was home to brown cattle with humped shoulders.

At Taxisco I took a turning to the right, which led down to the coast. There was hardly anyone around, it felt eerie, and I tried not to be intimidated by the loneliness. The road ended at a slipway next to the river. A pontoon, containing a four-by-four car and four ladies, was waiting to leave. The boatman waited for me as I gingerly carried the bike on board, the pontoon wobbling from side to side with my movements. The ladies were catching up on village gossip and tried to include me in the conversation, although I didn't know anyone they were talking about. The boat made its way through weed infested water. From time to time the 'captain' had to slow down and lift the outboard motor out of the water to avoid it being clogged with weeds. Herons and egrets watched us from the safety of side creeks we couldn't go up. Smaller boats were being punted about in the shallow river. We passed other pontoon ferries, and after half an hour arrived at the *embarcadero*, a rather grand pier, at Monterrica. It was like Rothesay – a jolly beach town with all the razzmatazz of people on holiday.

I hadn't seen the Pacific for six weeks, or 600 miles, since I climbed up from Tapanatepec into the fierce headwind that welcomed me to Chiapas. I went straight to the beach to look at the sea again, glad to be re-united with it. I found a hotel that had two rows of small modern chalets around a circular swimming pool. It was cheap, cheerful, and popular with Guatemalans. After a swim in the pool I walked along a dusty track to Johnny's place, which was listed in all the guide books, and had a fair smattering of travellers laying back on the reclining seats. I settled down on the terrace fronting the beach for a few beers with which to drink in views of the Pacific Ocean.

The evening sun shining on the sea gave everything a warm glow. Young men were playing volleyball on the beach, directly in front of the café. I sat watching, envying their lithe bodies, and for a moment I lost my concentration. The ball sensed this, and came whizzing past my face, knocking my glass of beer to the floor. The player whose service had been so lousy immediately shouted to the bar staff to bring me a new beer! I was happy. As any coach would say – never take your eye off the ball! After bringing me my replacement beer, the girl working the bar put on my favourite music by Manu Chao, as if by personal demand. A magic way to watch the sun go down.

⚦

I was awakened by the sound of the Guatemalan children splashing in the pool. It felt homely and welcoming, so

I decided to stay another night. An Austrian girl I had met in Panajachel two weeks earlier arrived, surprised to see me after all this time. We walked along to the turtle sanctuary, which had many crocodiles and iguanas, but only one turtle. The crocodiles wallowed in circular concrete pens about a metre high, and I idly speculated whether the crocodiles could jump a metre. They seemed too lethargic, but you never know with crocodiles.

I wandered down to the *embarcadero* to watch the activity there. Boatmen were sitting in a circle chatting. Passengers were sitting in one boat patiently awaiting its departure. A woman was cooking chicken to sell to waiting and arriving passengers. She gave me a newspaper to read, then sat with me asking about my star sign so she could read my horoscope from the paper. I don't really believe in that stuff, but I played along. She was keen to make sure the boatmen didn't leave with too few passengers. Each time a boat left, she would spot some more passengers coming along the road, and then call the boat back. One boat made three attempts to leave before finally getting away, much to the annoyance of two backpackers who seemed to be in a hurry to go somewhere. Maybe they had a connecting train to fret about.

The following morning I returned to the *embarcadero* to take a pontoon back up the river. It was quiet and I had to look around for a boatman willing to take me. He wanted twenty-five Quetzals for the journey, whereas I had only paid ten to come down river. I offered him ten which he accepted. The weeds were again a problem, if not worse, and progress was slow. I felt guilty about only giving him ten Quetzals. When we reached the slipway next to the road he tied up at the far end of the row of pontoons, and I had to carry my heavy bike over all the other pontoons to reach the road. Maybe he got his own back on me.

Soon I was pedalling along the quiet road past cattle, chickens and pigs. People working in the fields waved as I passed. I reflected on how industrialisation and mechanisation had stripped the British countryside of its people. Stopping in a roadside café I was joined by some policemen, so I figured the food must be OK.

I went to Chiquimullila, where there was a hotel. The town was a hive of activity, with *tuc-tucs* buzzing around like demented wasps. This was going to be my last night in Guatemala and I was excited about the prospect of being in El Salvador. I checked in at a hotel proudly standing at the top of the town. After a bit of dithering about which room I wanted, I made my way down to the Comedor Primavera, an unlikely name for a Chinese restaurant. I ordered a chicken curry and sat listening to the two Salvadorean men at the next table discussing business on the road. I was brimming with anticipation.

The chicken curry was a bad decision. I woke up in the early hours needing a toilet. Once more, as light dawned, I realised I was in no fit state to move on. So much for my last night in Guatemala! The only words I could utter to the lady in charge were "Where's the pharmacy?" She could tell from my colour what my predicament was and turned on the sympathy taps, telling me to lie down, take plenty of water, and stay in my room as long as I wanted. It's always re-assuring to hear calm advice from a sympathetic lady when you are low.

In the evening I felt fit enough to eat again – this time I hit the Italian joint and settled for a pizza. Wandering back afterwards through the darkened streets, some children shouted "Gringo" at me then disappeared when I turned round. The unwitting cultural racism in children bothered me. I felt it was no different to me shouting "Nigger" every time I saw a black man walking through my own city. I'm sure the children doing this mean no harm and almost certainly don't see it as racism. Are we over-sensitive when we take exception to certain language? Elderly, poof, spastic, chinky, gringo. What's in a name? Old geyser, me, just a boring old fart!

Later, in my hotel room, I became aware of some activity outside. It wasn't loud, just consistent noise as if something was going on. My room was on the ground floor, next to the parking area. I opened the door and was surprised to see two men sorting day-old chicks at the back of a pick-up truck. They were putting the chicks into crates of a hundred to sell at the market in the morning. They had a couple of thousand chicks altogether, and expected to get a hundred Quetzals for each crate. It was clearly worth their while coming into town and paying for a hotel room before going to the market early in the morning. I was worried the chicks might be cheeping all night outside my room, but after sorting them, the men drove them off somewhere else.

The ride down to the frontier was quiet and uneventful. Farewell Chiquimulilla, farewell Guatemala. The Guatemalan frontier post was a row of huts with a number of different queues. I was ushered to a window where the official asked me for my entry form. I could not

185

leave without a ticket to say that I had arrived. Fortunately I found the scrap of paper and the official was happy. I pedalled into no-man's land looking for the Salvadorean frontier post which was a kilometre down the road. No-man's land was full of *tuc-tucs* buzzing around, determined to replace the quetzal as the national bird. Then I saw the immigration office and became excited about entering another new country. My milometer read 2399 miles in total, of which 340 had been in Guatemala. I felt that at least 300 of them had been uphill. Guatemala is that sort of country.

CHAPTER NINE

EL SALVADOR IS ON ITS FEET

The name El Salvador conjures up many images, most of which are not very positive. I was encouraged by the "Welcome to El Salvador" sign at the frontier. It looked fresh and new, as if they meant it.

Where do you begin when writing about El Salvador? Well, it is a small country, the smallest in Central America. The population is four million and it is said that a further one million live and work in the United States. They have a reputation for honesty and hard work, although the people of neighbouring states may dispute this out of jealousy.

From 1980 to 1992 there was a shocking civil war, with thousands of deaths and regular atrocities committed by both sides. What were the two sides? Haves and have-nots, rich and poor, has to be the usual answer. Travelling through the country the stark contrast between the beauty of the landscape and the humiliating poverty is everywhere. On the roads, lorries carry cargoes of people to and from work. Young men standing, shoulder to shoulder, chest to back, in the rear of a gravel lorry, being taken to a job that pays a few dollars. When these lorries passed me, I wondered whether the lorry driver simply pressed a lever to tip them out onto the ground like a pile of rubble. That was how the owners saw their workers – rubble to make money on. As the lorries passed me, the human cargoes looked down on me and my bike without any facial expression. Perhaps they couldn't understand why a rich gringo had to resort to using a poor man's machine for transport.

In the nineteenth century El Salvador cashed in on the growing popularity of coffee in Europe and North America, and developed a strong coffee growing industry. This was done at the expense of the *campesinos*, who saw their rights to common land taken away so that the land could be given over to the commercial interests of the controlling elite. Small farmers had difficulty coping with the demands of a world coffee market, playing further into the hands of the elite. The seeds of division, exploitation, repression and revolution were sown with the humble coffee bean.

The twentieth century saw further polarisation. The Wall Street crash of 1929 had a catastrophic effect on the world coffee market, which devastated El Salvador's coffee-dependent economy. A military coup saw off an elected liberal government. Repression then rebellion followed each other in a predictable cycle, going round and round and achieving little. The rich are well cushioned from the effects of this, the poor just suffer.

In 1932 thousands of Indians were slaughtered in a campaign that would today be called ethnic cleansing.

Bizarre, in a country where the population is almost entirely *mestizo*. Perhaps the Indians weren't considered to be *mestizo* enough! "We want pure *mestizos*" you can hear them demanding.

In the 1971 census, 64% of agricultural land was owned by four per cent of the population, while 66% of rural families either had no land, or insufficient means to feed themselves. Housing was poor too. In his book "El Salvador" (1973), Alistair White wrote of the social and economic situation the country. He describes the housing situation as "worsening annually through the growth of population, the gradual deterioration of existing dwellings, the low purchasing power of the population, and the lack of adequate finance to build new houses in sufficient quantities". Sixty percent of families lived in a single room. Clean water and sanitation were a luxury.

The 1977 elections produced another rigged result and a right wing President. He wasn't far enough to the right for some people's liking. A military coup followed in January 1980. The country descended into chaos, with right wing death squads touring the country meting out instant justice, and left wing guerrillas mobilising and advocating social change.

The assassination of Archbishop Oscar Romero in March 1980 signalled the inevitable slide into civil war. Left wing guerrilla groups merged themselves into a coherent organisation called the Frente Faribundo Martí de Liberación Nacional, or FMLN. It is named after Agustín Faribundo Martí who was the leader of the Salvadorean Communist Party in 1932, when the coffee plantation owners lowered the already minuscule wages, causing a revolt. The government quashed the revolt by executing the leaders, including Faribundo Martí. The FMLN bears his name in honour of his enforced sacrifice.

1980 also saw the election of Ronald Reagan as President of the United States. He wasn't prepared to sit idly by and watch the spread of the dreaded communism on his doorstep. So the United States helped the Salvadorean government. The aid was largely through the supply of arms and training. This had the effect of prolonging the civil war into a stalemate that was only ended in 1992 with the signing of peace accords. The involvement of the United States, and the effect this had in prolonging the war, has caused much resentment among modern Salvadoreans.

I remembered also our good friend Bartolomé de las Casas – whom I had encountered in San Cristóbal - mentioning El Salvador in his "Short Account of the Destruction of the Indies", recalling a particular incident of barbarity committed by the Spanish against the Indians at a location close to what is now San Salvador.

El Salvador is a country used to bloodshed.

🚲

It was against this backdrop that I stood nervously but expectantly in the queue at *migración* at the frontier. The hall was modern and well organised, and busy. Some Canadians were in front of me, and to my right in the other queue a group of Costa Rican men in their twenties were trying to steal a look at my passport. I was flattered as my passport mug is no better than anyone else's. I was more interested in watching my bike, which was propped up against the inside wall of the immigration hall.

I reached the counter and was served by a pleasant young woman in a smart blue and white uniform, who questioned me about my intentions. When I told her I was cycling through her country, she said "I'll give you a sixty day visa then, just in case". This generosity was a bit over the top really, as El Salvador is a bit smaller than Wales.

I had to change my remaining Guatemalan money into dollars, and received a reasonable rate from the second money changer I asked. Well, he heard the quote given to me by the first one, and simply undercut him. We each thumbed through the other's notes, as forgeries are said to be common, although personally I have never had a problem with money changers. This one had a thick bundle of notes, bound together with elastic bands. Quetzals on one side and dollars on the other. As business grew, so would his brick of notes. I wondered what might have happened had I tried to grab it from him and run off. If I had I tried, I doubt some how whether I would be writing this now.

With my sixty day visa and wad of banknotes, I pedalled smugly into El Salvador. I was pleased with myself at making it into my third country since arriving in Mexico, in spite of all my misgivings about having warped wheels back in Creel. People had warned me that a lot of Salvadoreans carry guns, a relic from the civil war. A lady by the side of the road had a huge pile of melons she was trying to sell. A large tarpaulin was suspended over them to keep the sun off. As I stopped to buy one, I noticed a man getting out of his car to buy some put a revolver down the front of his trousers. I made a mental note not to pick a quarrel with anyone over the way they parked.

It was getting late and I didn't want to travel too far in case it got dark. I had received an email from Leo and Gavin recommending a beach called Barra de Santiago, which was only about twenty kilometres away. It was along a branch off the main road and there were places to stay there. After asking several people for directions, I eventually located the turn-off. It was a stony, dusty road with giant pot-holes big enough to hold a ceilidh in. *Camionetas* waited at the junction to ferry people off busses on the main road down to the village. As I cycled through the dust I was passed by a *camioneta* with four back-packing surfers in the back. They looked American or Australian, but they didn't smile or acknowledge me as they went past. I never saw them again.

The sign at the junction had said it was seven kilometres to Barra de Santiago, but according to my little distance measuring device it was nearer seven miles. The beach was beautiful. Yellow sand, palm trees, surf, and a row of *palapas* waiting for people to serve. A *palapa* lady showed me where there were rooms available to rent but they were dark, dingy, and the sort of place you would only stay at if you wanted to play on the bad image of El Salvador. I found a place next door run by a man in his sixties with better rooms at half the price, so I went for it. The room I was given contained a bed and a chair. The bed only had a stiff mattress, so I needed to use my sleeping bag. I opened the wooden window shutter to let in some air and light, and saw that the room was very dusty. I solved this problem by borrowing a broom from the man and giving the place a good sweep out. This seemed to encourage him into a frenzy of cleaning activity, as he started vigorously brushing, sweeping, and washing everything in sight. Pity he hadn't done that before I arrived.

I needed a bit of a wash after the stress of cycling over an international frontier and the dust of the road to Barra de Santiago, so I trotted down to the beach for a swim. The white waves were high and rough, sending loud booming sounds along the beach. There was a strong current, so I didn't go in far. There were small groups of Salvadoreans on the beach. Being in a new country always feels strange, but I felt comfortable in El Salvador. The beach wasn't very crowded even though it was weekend. After my swim I went over to the row of *palapas* and decided to eat at one where I could sit and watch the sun setting over the sea as I sipped my lager, waiting for my fish to be cooked. A constant source of pleasure travelling down the Pacific coast was the serene moments at sundown.

The beer was called Pilsener. It seemed odd that I should be sitting in the tropics drinking a beer named after a town in the Czech Republic. After my sunset dinner, I walked along the dark main street of the village and had another beer at a small shop. I sat at a wooden table in front, next to the dirt road, noticing the iron grilles at the door and window, which prevented customers from actually entering the shop. You had to ask at the counter for what you wanted. It gave the impression of a country under siege. I looked at my maps that I had brought with me. Some girls, who looked about eight, came over to sit with me so they could look at them too. They had never seen maps before. I showed them where we were, and where I had come from. Modesty prevented me from saying I was going to Panama. Well, perhaps I still didn't quite believe it myself. El Salvador to Panama seemed a long way.

There were no street lights, only the lights from shops. The relative darkness of the village seemed ghostly. It made me think of the curfews enforced during the civil war. Life during the war was graphically illustrated in the film "Innocent voices" directed by Luis Mandoki, and made in Mexico in 2004. The film is based on the life of co-writer Oscar Torres, a Salvadorean who was a child during the civil war.

The film is a powerful reminder of lost childhood. The central character is Chava, aged eleven, is who is suddenly cast into the role of the man of the house because his father flees to the United States. Chava is left behind with early experiences of death and barbarity. There is a nightly curfew, ostensibly to protect people, but in fact used by the military to terrorise people. His mother struggles to get the children home from playing in time for the curfew. During the curfew they are engulfed in fear as the house is sprayed with bullets from one side or other. We don't know which side, it doesn't matter – they are bullets. The film vividly portrays fear and bewilderment.

In El Salvador at this time children were conscripted into the army when they were twelve. The army calls at Chava's school one day to collect the twelve year old boys, calling out their names from the school register. There is an emotional scene of a classmate wetting his pants when the officer called out his name. He is taken away, wondering whether he will ever see Chava and his other friends again.

Later in the film, Chava's family is preparing a party for his own twelfth birthday. Some friends arrive as the candles are being circled on the cake. His mother realises the significance of the twelfth candle and holds it back. The cake has eleven candles and a gap.

Chava comes home and is surprised by the birthday party. The surprise turns to dismay as his eyes fall on the cake and the gap where the twelfth candle should be. He turns and runs, runs away from his lost childhood.

In a subsequent scene, Chava has by now joined the guerrillas and during a skirmish with the army he seizes a gun. He aims it at a soldier who hasn't seen him in the undergrowth. The soldier moves his cap and Chava sees his former school friend who had wetted himself with terror. Chava could not kill him; he drops the gun and flees. War is brutal, yes, but a civil war has the twist of the knife in that friend fights friend, brother fights brother.

Eventually Chava's mother finds a safe route for him to join his father in the United States. She cries as he says goodbye. It is a film without a happy ending; you can't leave the cinema without a tear in the eye.

I thought about the civil war as I sat looking at the wooden houses in Barra de Santiago, and the people I could see moving about. I wondered how they had fared during the war. It was not something I could lightly ask people; besides, it has been well documented.

Back at my lodgings, the owner's wife had now appeared. She was a large woman with a very accommodating dress, and she had no difficulty talking about life in El Salvador today. "Thieves and robbers everywhere" she told me. That day, she had been to Sonsonate on the bus, and had been completely taken aback when somebody had robbed her as she sat on the bus. The thief had managed to get her purse, and, given the large number of folds in her dress, I had to admire the thief's dexterity. He had got away with forty dollars. She was gob-smacked, although that didn't seem to stop her telling me about it. Her conclusion was that I shouldn't go to Sonsonate as I would be robbed too.

I didn't have the heart to tell her that I was indeed planning to go there the next day. I regretted that I hadn't asked her directly about the civil war as I felt she had a story to tell, somewhere in her commodious dress. The problem was that she talked almost non-stop, and I felt a bit reluctant to encourage her further.

I left fairly early after a breakfast of sausage and egg at one of the beach *palapas*. Pedalling in the sunshine along the bumpy track back to the main road I was happy to be in El Salvador, and wondered what all the fuss was about. I stopped at a small shed by the side of the road where a man and his daughter were selling Coca-cola. I gave the girl my one remaining Guatemalan coin, and she was thrilled to bits with it.

Joining the main road, I found the going increasingly more difficult. My stomach was churning, only two days after my extended stay in Guatemala for the same reason. The sausage and egg at the beach *palapa* had to be the culprit. Culinary mistakes become more evident when squatting against a tree beside the road, pretending to be invisible to passing traffic but failing miserably.

At a crossroads I turned left and followed the dual carriageway into Sonsonate. My eye was fixed on Volcan Izalco which seemed to be marking the position of the town. It was perfectly conical, still and solid-looking. The clear blue sky gave it a sparkle. Lorry loads of farm workers kept passing me, their passengers staring at me with fixed gazes.

I approached Sonsonate past a modern shopping area. Fast food, banks, sportswear shops all conspired to make me think I had wandered into the United States by mistake. It looked out of place after the chaos of Guatemala. It was a contrast from the poverty I had seen all around me. I began to wonder where the money was to support these businesses. I went down towards the bus station but the area looked rougher than rough, wilder than wild, and so I didn't bother to ask which of the anonymous buildings might be hotels. I returned past the fast food zone and took the other road that went into the centre of town. It was mayhem – market stalls lined either side of the road, selling fruits, vegetables, DVD's, tools, everything but the kitchen sink. There were so many people walking about it was difficult to make progress through them with a bike. I felt really in the way.

A policeman stood on the corner of the plaza, his uniform looking crisp in the sunshine. I had a list of hotels I had written down from a guide book and showed them to him. This was his conundrum for the day. He took off his cap, scratched his head and pondered. He had no idea where any of them were. "Was I sure" he seemed to be asking me. I wasn't sure at all. I left him and pedalled round each of the streets, looking for somewhere to stay. They were lined with terraces of single story stone buildings, painted in a range of colours that would outshine a rainbow. In a decaying street I found a place calling itself a hotel, where I was shown a dirt infested room with nothing in it but a filthy mattress, and no lock on the door. The residents already staying there, all men, stood around eyeing me up. My chances of survival were debateable but I didn't even start the debate.

Going round the block a few more times I came to the conclusion I didn't like Sonsonate. It had one good point - a bank that had a cash machine in a room which was large enough for me to take my bike in with me. Furthermore, the machine seemed happy to dispense me a hundred dollars without any fuss. So, rather than being robbed, I managed to pedal out of Sonsonate with more money than I had when I arrived. Bingo!

According to my map, there was a town down on the coast about twenty kilometres away called Acajutla. I couldn't tell whether it was a port or a holiday resort, but figured that either way it would have hotels. I left Sonsonate by the same dual carriageway that had taken me there. This time, I noticed a rather decrepit railway line following the side of the road. I had seen the railway station in Sonsonate, chained closed and full of decaying railway carriages, stuck in a cob-webbed time warp, as if waiting for Dr Beeching to come along and sweep it all away. I was surprised to see that the railway tracks looked as if they still might be used.

There was a ramshackle wooden bar under some trees sheltering some skinny cattle, next to the railway line. Curiosity about railways always gets the better of me so I crossed the railway line and went in for a drink. I didn't feel comfortable. As soon as I walked in everyone stopped talking and looked at me. I am used to that happening in the Highlands of Scotland, but in El Salvador it seemed a bit more threatening. I decided the best tactic was to break the ice, so I asked a man standing at the bar about the railway. "Yes," he said "A train comes by about once a week. A freight train".

The barman assured me that the best hotel in Acajutla was the first one I would see, on the main road and called El Kilo Dos as it was exactly two kilometres from Acajutla.

I saw El Kilo Dos from a distance of a hundred metres. It had an enormous roadside sign, and was on the other side of the road next to a filling station. It was a modern hotel and as I walked in saw that it had a swimming pool which people were sitting round. A group of *muchachos* were drinking bottles of beer and having a good laugh about something. A family was playing around in the water. The atmosphere was happy and relaxed, and I wanted to be part of it. A room was twenty-two dollars which I thought a bit pricey, but I didn't want to waste more time looking round Acajutla for somewhere better, so I checked in and joined the crowds round the swimming pool.

My stomach was still giving me trouble. The receptionist offered me an alka-seltzer, which went down very well. I drank some water. Then a bit more water. The relaxed atmosphere beside the pool made me feel better and I eventually ventured into the hotel restaurant for dinner.

There was a sticker on the door saying "El Salvador Esta De Pie" – El Salvador Is On Its Feet. I asked the waiter about it but he hadn't noticed it before, so he went to ask the lady in charge. She came out and told me that it simply means that El Salvador is getting better, and can stand up for itself after years of oppression and American interference. The waiter added that it must be getting better, as foreign tourists have started to come, unlike ten years ago when there were none. The sticker and the conversation took my mind off my stomach and the disappointment I felt about Sonsonate, so I began to feel cheerful again. The waiter even brought me a bottle of British made Worcester sauce with my meal.

The alka-seltzer hadn't completely cured my stomach as I spent much of the night migrating between bed and toilet. In the morning I wasn't sure whether to stay another night or move on. Sitting by the pool in a state of deep contemplation, the receptionist brought me another alka-seltzer and two bottles of water. I eventually persuaded myself to move on. I didn't want to spend a whole day sitting next to a swimming pool beside the dual carriageway.

The coastal plain of El Salvador is relatively flat. A ribbon of green palm trees and grass, perched between the volcanoes to my left, and the sea to my right. Cattle were grazing as if grass were a delicacy. I covered the first twenty-five miles in an hour and a half, which seemed to justify my decision to leave. My target for the night was a dot on the map called Zunzal, about forty-five miles away, and I felt confident about getting there as I sped along the flat coastal plain.

Flat? Well, as all touring cyclists know, flat terrain never lasts for long. Some cliffs got in the way. Worse, the road makers decided to make a few short cuts by building some tunnels.

Tunnels and cyclists do not go well together. Tunnels are dark, they can be wet, and if there is a bend, you cannot see the other end so they can be a bit disorientating. Another problem is that you cannot always be certain whether the tunnel wall is smooth and flat, or has jagged rocks protruding from it. The temptation is to cycle as close to the centre as you dare, to minimise the effect of disorientation and reduce the danger of striking anything.

To add to all this, I was travelling without any lights!

The first tunnel was straight, short, and downhill in my direction of travel. I waited at the entrance for there to be no traffic, and then belted through as quickly as I could. I repeated this tactic for tunnels two and three. Then came Tunnel Four. According to the sign at the entrance it was 570 meters long, so I knew it would take several minutes to get through. The chances of there being no traffic in that time were slim. Even writing about it now is making me nervous; such is the fear cyclists have of tunnels.

I was half way through when a lorry entered the tunnel behind me. The roar of the engine and the glare of the main-beam headlights were terrifying. I quickly decided to press myself into the tunnel wall and wait for it to pass. In my haste to reach it I tripped and fell over, dropping the bike on the road. That could be disastrous in darkness as I had no idea if something had fallen off. I panicked as the lorry was bearing down on me. Would he see me? I got up and grabbed the bike, pulling it with me into the tunnel wall. Just in time, the lorry passed me and I was still alive.

The fifth and last tunnel was a breeze in comparison. After passing through, I looked over the bike and saw that one of the panniers was covered in mud. As far as I could see, nothing was missing. I had a lucky escape and was thankful. Soon after, I collapsed into a cliff-top restaurant with breathtaking views of blue sea, blue sky, white waves, and green coffee plantations. I ordered a beer and a chicken sandwich. I needed some comfort food.

It was four o'clock and I started to feel relaxed again. The waiter brought me back to my senses by telling me that Zunzal was still twenty-three kilometres away.

I arrived in Zunzal as the sun was going down. Six surfers, all in their twenties, were walking along the road in flip-flops carrying their surf-boards. I stopped them to ask about hotels and to my amazement they were all English. They asked me numerous questions about my journey, and took photographs of me and my bike. They asked so many questions that I forgot to ask them why on earth they had come to El Salvador, of all places. Surfing can be a very image-centred macho sport, but I think I out-macho'd them by coolly looking at my milometer and saying I had just done 2,500 miles.

I found a surfers' hotel on the beach. I felt the rooms were a bit over-priced at forty dollars but reminded myself it was still a good deal compared with anywhere in Europe. I asked for a first floor room, which had a balcony overlooking the swimming pool, behind which were the restaurant and the beach. The room itself was a bit spartan, but clean. The balcony had a hammock. There was a shop on the lane next to the hotel that led down to the beach, and it had a fridge full of beer. No prizes for guessing what I did next.

Whether it was a good idea to drink beer on a bad stomach, I don't know. What I do know is that another night was punctuated by visits to the toilet. When day broke, I knew I needed a day of rest. The swimming pool was very inviting. I spent much of the day in and around it chatting to other tourists, mainly from Europe. An Austrian man had been mountaineering in Guatemala, near Huehuetenango, and told me about the difficulties he had had with altitude sickness. A Belgian couple had taken a year's unpaid leave to travel the world. Travel continues to be the pursuit of the rich, going to countries whose inhabitants can't afford food, let alone a round-the-world air ticket.

I chatted to the man who owned the hotel, a Salvadorean who had worked in the United States, where he learned to speak English and earned enough money to come home to El Salvador and build a hotel. His story was a good illustration of the rationale behind the Salvadorean government's decision a few years ago to abandon the Salvadorean currency and switch to the US dollar as the general currency of circulation. A large number of Salvadoreans work in the United States and send money home to their families. They also visit when they can, bringing money with them. Others return home after earning enough in the United States to establish financial security for themselves.

The problem was that much of this money was hoarded as US Dollars, and not used to benefit the local economy. The government decided to switch to dollars in order to free up this vast pool of money and stimulate investment. The ploy seemed to be working. The owner of the hotel probably wouldn't have invested so much in this venture – if at all – if he had had to convert his savings into Salvadorean currency to do so. That would have been too risky. At least he could now invest in a business where the return would be in US dollars, rather than a currency which may have doubtful value in the future.

It sounded remarkably like Fidel Castro's stunt a few years ago. In Cuba, it had been illegal to own dollars, but many people possessed them and hoarded them. If they spent them, it was on the black market. This was no good for the state economy, so Castro simply legalised dollars. He set a realistic exchange rate equivalent to the black market rate, and opened scores of dollar-only shops where people could spend their money on food and consumer goods not available for Cuban Pesos. It worked. People spent their money, and the state shops boomed.

The losers were people without access to dollars, as they found that a range of things were suddenly not available to them. They then had to queue at exchange kiosks to buy some with their relatively worthless Cuban Pesos. A dual currency system was the result.

It was different in El Salvador. The previous currency, the Lempira, was completely abandoned and substituted by the dollar, at an official exchange rate which was the same for all. They seemed to have learned from the Cuban experience.

The downside was that some Salvadoreans complained to me that the switch to dollars had caused inflation. I am never sure about this argument. The same was said when Britain switched from pounds, shillings and pence to pounds and new pence, and when Spain, France, etc., switched to the Euro. That might be true of café prices and taxi fares, but the main costs of living – housing costs and supermarket prices – would tend to be converted on a strictly accurate basis. In overall terms, the effect on inflation would be fairly marginal.

In the evening I went to the hotel restaurant where I couldn't help listening to some surfers at the next table talking without interruption for an hour about waves and surf. One of them even had a wooden board mounted onto a ball, which he could stand on and waggle his hips from side to side as if he were actually surfing. They never talked about anything else, and I wondered why the girl-friends found them so interesting. Perhaps their previous boy-friends had been accountants.

With two and a half thousand miles under my belt, I began to take it for granted that cycling was easy. I looked at the map and decided I would try to get to the town of Usulután, about sixty-five miles away. At seven in the morning I felt surprisingly bright, considering I hadn't had much sleep, and was on the road by eight thirty. I breezed through La Libertad without stopping, swerving at the last minute to narrowly avoid a manhole with no cover. La Libertad had seen better days and didn't look inviting. It was hard to believe it was the seaside resort favoured by people from San Salvador. Rows of faded, crumbling buildings looked as if the next high tide would wash them away, like sandcastles on the beach. Men sat on park benches, and shouted as I went by. I usually took these shouts as encouragement, but in La Libertad I couldn't be sure. I wasn't even tempted to stop and look for an ice cream.

After sixteen miles cycling, La Libertad safely behind me, I stopped for a drink. I had great difficulty motivating myself to set off again. Each mile got harder and harder, and I took every opportunity to stop for a drink. My persistent stomach upset over the last few days had made me debilitated, and I was struggling to go on. I just wanted more and more fluid, all the time telling myself I had another fifty miles to do. It didn't help that the temperature was over thirty centigrade, and the sun relentless. So much for timing my ride in the dry season.

At a popular café they were serving a lunch of stewed beef and vegetables to shouting, argumentative building workers. I perched on the corner of a long bench table and ordered three drinks in rapid succession. Setting off, I quickly needed a tree to squat behind. The next ten miles were an ordeal. I began to accept that I wouldn't make it to Usulután and would have to settle for Zacatecoluca instead. It would mean spending an extra night in El Salvador, but I was actually beginning to like the place, in spite of my constant stomach upsets.

Volcan de San Vicente began to dominate the view. It had twin peaks, like a camel. According to my map it lay just behind Zacatecoluca. I fixed my stare on the volcano, as a way of willing myself on. My diary notes that "at the moment cycling is a bit of an endurance test, however, I do want to carry on. Stopping isn't an option until I or the bike have to. I told the Belgians I met yesterday that even if someone stole my bike now, they couldn't take away the 4,000 kilometres I had already cycled."

Finally, Zacatecoluca. A chaotic higgledy-piggledy place that lies just off the main road, hugging either side of a turning that climbs up towards the volcano. The streets were narrow and thronged with market stalls under tarpaulin sheets, stretched between lamp-posts. The main road junction was a natural place for busses to stop, avoiding the need to negotiate their way into the town. This created another mini-metropolis as numerous businesses had sprung up to serve the waiting bus passengers. Some of the busses were going to Usulután, so I revived my original plan to go there and tried to hitch a lift. The busses were all too crowded for me to even contemplate asking about taking a bike, so I finally laid to rest my ambition of getting there that night. My diarrhoea was getting so ridiculous that within the space of ten minutes I visited the same filling station twice to ask for the key to the toilets. I reluctantly accepted the inevitable, and went into a pharmacy for advice.

The pharmacist was very helpful, and sold me some tablets I recognised the name of which she assured me would stop the diarrhoea. I felt instantly relieved, until she delivered the punch-line. No alcohol.

I checked in at a brightly painted modern hotel along the main road, which had a swimming pool, and of course a toilet in my bed-room. The only other guests were nine Salvadorean surveyors, all men. The Salvadorean government is re-mapping the whole country, and they had reached this area. One of them had a birthday, so they were having a party, to which I was invited. I regretted that I was under medication, and although the first two tablets had already made me feel better (psychological tablets!) I didn't want to risk a further upset. So I watched with slight envy as someone chopped up a variety of fresh fruit and put the pieces in a large jug, to be followed by a bottle of vodka. It looked really delicious. Isn't that typical of sod's law. The one time on my trip that I was invited to a party, I was under medication and couldn't get drunk like everyone else.

That may have been just as well, as the subject of politics came up. I referred to the abbreviation used for the right-wing Alianza Republicana Nacionalista party - ARENA, jesting that as *Arena* is also the Spanish word for sand, the party is like a house built on sand. One of the surveyors took this as a prompt for a long tirade about how ARENA had saved the country from the ridiculous revolutionary forces of the left, and that he couldn't understand why anybody would want to support the FMLN. His colleagues mainly supported him, a couple keeping quiet. For me, it was a good illustration of how polarised politics still are in this country, even though peace has in theory reigned for more than ten years.

Another vivid indicator of polarised political divisions was the kerb-stones. Cycling along I was constantly reminded of Northern Ireland, where the kerbstones are painted red-white-and-blue, or green and white, according to the predilections of the local residents. In El Salvador, many stretches of road had red and white (i.e. FMLN) or blue and white (ARENA) kerbs. There were even odd stretches where one colour had been painted over the other. Middle ground didn't exist.

The following morning my tablets seemed to have done the trick and I felt fit enough to continue to Usulután. I went to a swish new bank on the edge of town to use a cash machine. A guard with a large machine gun came out of the bank to supervise the transaction. It felt mildly comforting to know that if anyone tried to run off with my card, they would get sprayed with bullets. Then I realised that I would probably be caught in the cross-fire, so my comfort melted away. I vanished with my cash as quickly as I could.

Outside Zacatecoluca the road spanned a wide river, with a dis-used railway bridge next to it. The road bridge was decorated in FMLN colours. I stopped to admire the clear views of the volcanoes, and a car pulled up beside me. The driver got out to take some pictures too. He was a Salvadorean who lived in Colorado and was back home for a holiday. He wanted some pictures to show the beauty of El Salvador to his friends in the United States. He said how wonderful he thought the United States was. Standing on an FMLN bridge I felt secure enough to tell him I didn't quite agree with United States foreign policy, but he blanked that one out.

I was still debilitated from the diarrhoea so my progress was slow. On a bend, several lorries were parked on either side of the road. It was a roadside restaurant, and I reckoned if it were popular with lorry drivers it must be all right. I needed nourishment and decided to risk a meal. Neat little wooden tables and chairs were arranged outside the kitchen, under the shelter of a tin roof. Food was being cooked in large pots in the open over several fires. A large plastic bowser contained home made fruit juice which was liberally scooped out for customers. There was one table left free so I went over to nab it. I took off my crash helmet to reveal that my newly acquired sun-hat was emblazoned with the name of a Salvadorean football team (Firpo), which made everyone laugh. It was a good ice breaker.

The man running the restaurant brought me an excellent plate of pork and onion in tomato sauce, with courgettes and rice. He later came over to chat to me as I sipped my coffee. He told me he thought El Salvador was generally safe now, though he regretted the large number of guns around as they were ending up in the hands of criminal gangs, or *pandilleros*, mainly in San Salvador.

The food went down well but I was still weak so I used any excuse to stop. After a few miles there was a small roadside shop in a village composed of entirely new houses. They were small uniform little boxes, made of concrete with tin roofs. They reminded me of the rows and rows of houses I had seen in Cape Town, hastily built in an attempt to remedy black homelessness. I got off my bike and went over to the shop. The couple who owned it were just sitting down to their lunch, but were pleased to interrupt their feast to chat with me. In 2001 an earthquake had destroyed the whole village. They had lived in tents for four years while the village was re-built by the government and an aid agency. They had moved into the new house in April 2005. They said camping was horrible in winter. Just then their ten year old son arrived. He was a shy boy, but he loved trying on my crash helmet. I realised that he had spent almost half his life living in a tent. The family was happy with the new house, and laughed when I remarked that having a tin roof, there was less weight to fall on their heads in the next earthquake.

Pedalling on, it wasn't long before I was stopped at a police checkpoint. There were three officers. One of them asked me about my journey, where I was cycling from and to. I noticed he was fingering his gun as if he was treating it to a little foreplay. He may have been doing it unconsciously, but I noticed it. Another one asked me if I was carrying much money.

Alarm bells sounded. The moment had, I thought, finally arrived when I was going to be robbed by Latin American policemen. Calmly I said "No, only plastic money plus enough cash for two or three days."

"That's good" he said "be careful with it, you don't want to be robbed."

With relief, I asked them what they were looking for in their checkpoint. "Contraband" they said. They didn't bother to search my panniers.

I finally reached Usulután after a few more stops. In my delicate state I had managed to cycle thirty-six miles, but they had taken all day. The actual pedalling time, according to my little machine, was just over three hours, so I must have been sitting around eating and chatting a hell of a lot.

The streets of Usulután were lined with solid stone buildings, many of them shops, fronted by equally solid looking pavements which rose a foot or two above the level of the road. The pavements were a torture to walk along because of frequent steps to cope with the changes in level between one shop and the next. El Salvador is not a country for the disabled. The shops were busy, but people still looked up as I cycled past, picking my way through the narrow streets. A large colourful board above the pavement announced the Hotel Florida. Looking through the iron gates I saw an inviting tree-lined courtyard, but couldn't get in as the gates were locked. Ringing the bell a few times managed to summon a very matronly woman who showed me the rooms upstairs, all to one side of a veranda that overlooked the trees and the courtyard. There were hammocks in the courtyard, one outside every room. Bliss. I gave the lady her money and immediately settled into a hammock for a good swing, looking out to the leafy branches of the trees. After a few minutes of this, I went down to ask her about getting a beer, and she sold me a couple of bottles out of her fridge. I took them back up to my swinging hammock and drifted into peaceful alcohol-assisted inactivity. I felt I had deserved it after days of feeling weakened.

Later, I went out to an internet café. It was full of young men all playing music loudly on the computers. As soon as one turned up his music to out-noise the others, the others turned theirs up too. The selfish determination of young Latin men never ceases to amaze me. I told the guy running the place it was unpleasant. He shrugged his shoulders and I left. Emails can always wait. I wondered if the civil war years had inculcated a fear of confrontation, explaining the shop manager's indifference to the behaviour of the young men.

The following day – more volcanoes and another filling roadside lunch at a lorry drivers' café. I continued to the town of San Miguel. The name made me think of beer and Spain for some reason.

On the way into town I saw a bike repair shop so I popped in to buy a pair of pedals, as one of mine was still creaking slightly. It had been doing this since I was in Mexico, but an American had told me that bike shops were very poor in Nicaragua, and as I was nearly in Nicaragua I decided to minimise the risks and carry some spare pedals.

The bike shop was a large square room with a concrete floor. It was a mess. Bikes, wheels, bike components, and frantically working bare-chested boys filled the space with little room for manoeuvre. Sweat and bike grease mixed together to produce a fragrance that even Yves St Laurent would struggle to market. The owner was friendly and impressed with my journey. I was the first customer to have cycled to his shop all the way from Mexico. He gave the cables a good check-over, and asked one of his boys to thoroughly clean the chain and gears. As if that weren't enough, as I was leaving, he pressed into my hands a tee-shirt with the name and phone number of the bike shop printed on the back. Just for the record, the shop was called the Bici Taller Romero, and the phone number San Miguel 667-5058. The pedals are still in use as I write this, albeit on a different bike.

Feeling much better, I settled into a comfortable hotel to plan my next moves in El Salvador. I was planning to cycle into the mountains to visit the headquarters of the guerrillas.

CHAPTER TEN

GUERRILLAS IN THE MOUNTAINS

During the civil war the FMLN broadcast Radio Venceremos – we shall overcome –from a hidden bunker, high up in the mountains over a thousand meters above sea level. Its purpose was to portray events in the view of the guerrillas, to counter government propaganda. It also played Latin American music for popular appeal. The studio was in the village of Perquín, the headquarters of FMLN. It was a good location, as the only way in from San Miguel climbs eternally, mile after mile of relentless gradients and bends, rendering any attack slow, and far from being a surprise. It was a hard climb on the bike, in the sweltering heat and unstoppable sun. Beyond the village lays Honduras, over a frontier of inhospitable mountains. Cycling into a dead end added to the thrill.

The film "Innocent Voices" portrays the hope given by the sporadic broadcasts of Radio Venceremos. In one scene, Chava and his friends are playing a transistor radio when they pass a group of soldiers on patrol. The signature tune of the radio station comes on, and the soldiers tell them to turn it off. The boys don't want to. The priest sees this, and rather than see the boys get into further trouble, plays the tune over the church tannoy, deafening the whole plaza with it. The soldiers shoot down the tannoy, and in the meantime the boys run off.

The former broadcasting studio is now open to the public as part of the Museum of the Salvadorean Revolution. I was shown round by a guide who was formerly a guerrilla. The room had been lined with egg boxes as makeshift but effective sound insulation. The generator had been dug in deeply, to avoid noise detection. My guide told me the museum had been set up as part of the Peace Accords deal in the nineteen-nineties and was, he asserted, free from political funding or interference. Looking at the wording of some of the exhibits, I would doubt that somehow. I think he meant it hadn't been censored by opposition viewpoints. There were a number of posters on display from other cities and countries giving support to "the struggle". There was one from Valencia in Spain, my home for over a year. The rest of the museum contained exhibits of guns and a large number of photographs and hand written accounts of atrocities.

One atrocity happened in the village of Mozote, a few miles away. On 11th December 1981 government troops entered the village and rounded everyone up. Even people who had been friendly towards the army were included. An account of what happens is narrated candidly by Joan Didion in "Salvador", published in 1983. She describes how the men were blindfolded and shot in the centre of the village. The women were taken outside the village, raped, killed, and their bodies burned. The soldiers then discussed what to do with the children, according to Didion, who interviewed the sole survivor. They choked them to death. Around a thousand people perished, although there are no official figures as the massacre was largely ignored until peace came much later. The mass graves were exhumed in 1992. There is now a large memorial to the dead in the village, which is being re-populated. It is a sombre place to visit.

In 1984 the FLMN shot down a helicopter carrying Domingo Monterrosa, who orchestrated the Mozote massacre. The wrecked helicopter is on display in the museum – a war trophy that survived the Peace Accords.

Perquín now sees enough tourists to boast three places where guests can stay. I hesitate to use the word "hotel" as this paints a rosy picture of tea-making facilities, plumped up duvets, and constant hot water. On my first night I stayed at The Gigante, and it was definitely not the rosy picture I have just painted. It was approached down a leafy track through the woods; like going to the teddy bears' picnic. There were no signs, I had to repeatedly ask the way from villagers who were foraging around with their shopping, perhaps also looking for a picnic spot. I asked two ladies sitting outside what looked like a giant sawmill constructed of timber, where the Gigante was.

"Here" one of them said, pointing into the slightly ajar door of the rambling building. I went in. It had a high ceiling with a dried earth floor sloping to the right. A small TV adorned one of the corners, looking insignificant in the dark cavern of a place. As my eyes were still adjusting to the poor light, one of the ladies came in and told me the bedrooms were down some steps at the end of the slope.

Carrying my bike I went down to a long grey partition wall which didn't quite make it up to the ceiling. Its monotony was broken by bedroom doors. My room had a bed, a chair and a table with some tourist information leaflets fanned out on it. The washroom was at the end of the corridor.

As I was showering, the lady brought sheets for the bed. I returned to my bedroom cubicle and devoured a whole fresh pineapple I had bought from a roadside seller on my sweaty climb up to Perquín. It was unbelievably invigorating.

The hotel where I spent my second night was quite a contrast. An American from Delaware has built some Swiss-style chalets on the hillside just outside the village, and named it the Perquín Lenca.

The Perquín Lenca is well located for hill-walking, and as the civil war was far enough in the past I felt completely safe going for a trek along the tracks at the back of the hotel. My nose led me to the summit of a hill, with a clearing on top and a refuge for hill-walkers. The view was breathtaking, long sierras stretched in front of me into the distance as the sun went down, in a streaky watercolour sky.

I returned to my cosy chalet, which had a veranda and a hammock. Swinging lazily in the hammock with a bottle of beer, looking at the dusky mountains, was as close to perfection as I could imagine.

Over dinner I spoke to the hotel owner. He was enthusiastic about El Salvador and its prospects for the future. He had been there for many years, including the civil war period which hadn't fazed him at all. He enthused about how hard working and honest Salvadoreans are, making it a good country to invest in a business. His mother was visiting, and she sat nodding as she listened to our conversation.

Word got around the hotel that I was Irish, which is a bit of a puzzle as I am not. From such a distance, European countries probably all fade into one another. In the restaurant a Salvadorean sat at the next table. He was eighty-two. He was very curious about Northern Ireland and asked me a lot of questions about it. He asked me if it was really true that people there were fighting each other over religion, rather than political ideology as is more normal. I agreed it's bizarre. I could really only rationalise it by saying I thought the root of it was Protestant paranoia over being controlled by Catholic rules.

The Salvadorean civil war was characterised by periods of quiet interspersed with acts or barbarism and atrocity. Twelve years is a long time for a small country to sustain a civil war with continuous fighting. From what people told me, there was superficial normality, with an undercurrent of fear and suspicion leading to aggressive moves by one side or the other. Many people agreed with my analysis that it had been rather like the Troubles of Northern Ireland. Even the painted kerbstones agreed with my theory.

ڶ

It was a shame to leave the tranquillity of the mountains, but the log cabins were fully booked the following night so I had little choice. I was a little nervous about free-wheeling mile after mile round all the bends down to the coastal plain, so before setting off I changed the front brake blocks for the first time. With added confidence I coasted easily down to the blisteringly hot town of Santa Rosa de Lima.

It was a shock to leave the mountains and be back in the midst of people. El Salvador is densely populated, especially along the relatively flat fertile coastal plain. People are everywhere, almost to the point of intrusion – where do you go for a pee? The positive aspect of this is the frequent number of shops and cafés at my disposal. I even passed an open air cycle repair shop. Calling it a shop is stretching things a bit. The sole building was a small square garden shed, barely large enough to stand in. All around it were wheels and tyres festooned to trees. It would have done in an emergency.

Santa Rosa bustled with activity. The streets were lined with women squatting in front of the old adobe houses beside piles of fruit and vegetables they were selling. It was very colourful. Policemen struggled to control the noisy, smelly traffic. In the midst of all this my bike was becoming an obstruction, but I didn't allow myself to feel intimidated. It was going to be my last night in El Salvador, and I was sad about leaving such a surprisingly lovely country. I found a room at a cheap but clean family-run hotel, and went for a walk around town. The centre was dominated by a large Parque Central with fountains and miniature waterfalls built into it. Several people struck up conversations with me as I floated around looking at the shops and fruit stalls. I heard children saying "Alo" to me, mimicking the trade name of a phone card being marketed.

The roof of my hotel had generous views of the town and surrounding hills, a good place to have a couple of beers under the starlight. I left it a bit late as the shops still maintained the 'curfew' hour of 6 pm. I had to find a *cantina* where I could buy some bottles to take away. I have mentioned before my trepidation about wandering into *cantinas*. As soon as I walked in I was accosted by a man, slightly worse for wear, who asked me for money so he could buy cigarettes. He said "It's not my fault if I have no money, but it is my country." This was probably a reference to the United States involvement in the civil war, which still causes anti-American feeling. "It's not my fault either" I replied as the unflappable barmaid put my bottles into a bag. The man followed me up the street, he was determined either to get some money or prove a point. I managed to lose him by mingling with a large group of people crossing the Parque Central. I harboured no grudge; there are drunks everywhere, not just in El Salvador.

Later, from my rooftop vantage point, I watched some bin-men find a batch of brand new white shirts in the refuse bins belonging to the fast food chain nearby. The shirts were calmly inspected, folded up, and put in the drivers cab. All in a night's work.

🚲

I had managed to cycle over 300 miles in El Salvador, in spite of its small size. I approached my next frontier feeling a bit blasé; this was my third frontier, and my fourth country. Honduras. I cycled past the lorry checkpoint, getting a wave from the customs officials. Then came the Salvadorean *Migración* offices. There were several queues, a bus had just arrived. I got into a queue and held my bicycle at my side. A pair of money changers, the Likely Lads, offered me thirteen Honduran Lempira per dollar. I laughed. Some Hondurans in the queue told me not to accept less than eighteen. The Likely Lads came back and offered me a better rate, but I had decided out of principle that I would use a different money changer. I noticed that none of the Central Americans were giving them any business. Wide boys look the same everywhere.

The office had two adjacent windows, one for the El Salvador exit stamp, the other for a Honduran entry stamp. Stamp, shuffle, stamp. All over in seconds. Then I pedalled over a bridge across a river, no-man's land. Most of the other traffic over the bridge was on bikes. On the other side were two rows of bright blue buildings with a large curved roof covering the space between them, like a Victorian railway station. This was the Honduran customs post. It also contained a small bank, so I went in to change some money. The bank clerk told me to use the money changer outside. A bank refusing business is rare. Outside were two moneychangers, each with the now familiar brick of bank-notes held together with rubber bands, offering me eighteen Lempira to the dollar.

A deal was done. I had my passport stamps and Lempira, there were no further formalities, so I pedalled along looking at Honduras. It was hot, dry and parched. It was also noticeably poorer. I saw houses of dismal quality, people herding skinny cattle along the road, and children walking about bare-foot. There was less traffic than in El Salvador, and many people were getting about on horseback. Bareback, no saddles. As I passed, people shouted 'Hello' and other welcomes. I felt privileged to be in Honduras.

I stopped for lunch in Nacaome. I timed it right as about a dozen people were eating in the restaurant. It looked like a large garage with a cooking range in the corner. There was a choice of pork or chicken, served with rice, beans, and a variety of stewed vegetables. Compared with the poverty I had already seen, the meal was a feast and I tucked in with gusto. When I asked about the toilet, the woman pointed to a cabin in the back yard, and gave me a small plastic bowl and a little piece of soap. There was a stand tap outside the toilet cabin.

I started to wonder how much time I would spend in Honduras. It is a big country, and I had heard there were plenty of places to stay. I still had my faithful tent, last used in Mexico, so camping was an option. I sat in the cavernous restaurant studying my map, and suddenly realised that the prospect of reaching Panama, only three countries away, looked realistic. This was a turning point in my attitude, as I became more focussed on a destination, the Panama Canal, rather than simply meandering about. I had passed through Guatemala by a fairly circuitous route, and had taken a few detours in El Salvador. I considered my options regarding Honduras.

To go north, further into Honduras, would involve going to the capital Tegucigalpa. I had so far managed to avoid all capital cities, for the main reason that cycling through cities is unpleasant and not particularly safe. I had not cycled in any major city since Guadalajara, three months earlier. I decided that I didn't need to go to Tegucigalpa, and didn't want to. This meant that I would simply pass through a corner of Honduras, on my way to Nicaragua.

This strategy suited me for another reason. Having sampled El Salvador and got a real sense of the recent history of the place, I was impatient to get to Nicaragua. As a young man I had watched television coverage of the Sandinista revolution and subsequent civil war with the Contras. I was captivated by the place and had wanted to go there for the last twenty-five years. I couldn't wait.

Mulling this over, my eyes fell on a small island at the bottom of the map, in the Gulf of Fonseca. The island was called Isla el Tigre, Tiger Island, and it had a small town called Amapala marked in confident capital letters, as if shouting at me to go there. It would be a short detour from the direct road to Nicaragua. A minor road led to the small port of Coyolito directly opposite the island. The exact distance wasn't shown on the map, but I judged, literally by rule of thumb, that I would be able to make it that day. I had read that it was possible to get boats from there over to the island.

The turning to Coyolito was just before San Lorenzo. The road was hot and dusty, with children scampering about barefoot looking for some fun. Shouting "Gringo gringo" at me as I passed was their buzz of the day. It became so persistent and annoying that at a small wooden shop, where I had stopped for a drink, I walked over to two such boys and shouted "Hondureño Hondureño" at them, to even the score. They scurried away as quickly as they could; leaving me wondering if the exercise had been worthwhile. I had got it off my chest, which was enough.

Very little grass grew in this part of Honduras, what had grown was quickly torn up and devoured by the walking skeletons which passed for cattle. Stopping for another drink at a house with a large Coca-cola sign on the wall, I was invited in to shelter from the sun. The whole family lived in the large single room which had a row of beds at one end. They seemed to accept lack of privacy as normal. All the men supported Real Madrid. I was already learning that Honduras was like Scotland – people supported one or other of two big teams. In Honduras they were called "Real Madrid" and "Barcelona". As I got up to leave a herd of cattle came past on the road, the sun shining brightly on their brown hides.

Coyolito is a sleepy little town. I got there as it was approaching five o'clock and went directly to the pier, where a naval boat was tied up. Pipes and cables feeding it were straddled over the ground, making it hard to approach the knot of small passenger boats waiting hopefully at the end of the pier. The first boatman I approached offered to take me over for thirty Lempira. I decided to shop around before committing myself. The next man wanted 140 Lempira. At first I thought I had mis-heard him. "No," he said, "140 Lempira". I went back to the first man before he changed his mind.

His little boat rocked from side to side as he manhandled my bike onto it. It was nothing more than a rowing boat with a motor attached. I sat next to my bike as we pushed off into the choppy sea, watching the little waves smacking the front of the boat. I was anxious about the bike. If the boat capsized I would be able to swim for it but my bike would sink without trace. A cyclist without a bike is like a fish out of water. The crossing took about fifteen minutes and I was plonked on a slipway next to a small house in the middle of nowhere. You get what you pay for – I had taken the cheapest boat and had been taken to the point on the island closest to our starting point.

As I gave him his thirty Lempira, the boatman said I would be able to cycle into Amapala in no time. He was right. The complete absence of signposts was little hindrance; I turned right, followed my nose, and kept going. Some women chatting on a street corner pointed me in the direction of a hotel. It was modern and built onto the hillside like a lop-sided layer-cake. Balconies, staircases, trees and bushes combined to give the place the feel of a conference centre, except that it had been accidentally built in the wrong place and was empty. Empty except for two ladies from Philadelphia who were sitting in reception as I arrived casually pushing my bike, as if I had just been along the promenade and back before breakfast.

Susan and Peggy had just come from Tegucigalpa and were pleased to have an English speaker to talk to, especially as I was travelling somewhat unconventionally. We went for dinner together, to a restaurant on the sea shore where could sit on a wooden terrace at the back, the waves slopping about beneath us. There, the women startled me by saying that not only had they voted for

George W Bush, but they were proud of it. This was a remarkably honest confession I hadn't often heard. They told me they voted for Bush because they thought he was so honest. At this, I had to bite my tongue, not easy when you have a mouthful of fish that had until recently been in the sea below. To give credit where due though, after I mentioned that I had mislaid my torch a few days earlier, Peggy reached into her bag and gave me her little torch as a present. Spontaneous gifts which are useful are the best, however small, and I still have it.

The hotel owner spoke good English. He was in his late thirties, maybe forty, dark and handsome with wavy hair and a broad charming smile. He had been to Madrid, unusual for a Honduran. He was from one of the families who controlled much of the businesses in the country. Building the hotel was his contribution to the family empire. He employed local people and family members. I commented that his teenage son badly needed to go to charm school - when taking my order for breakfast, he couldn't hold back saying "You want coffee <u>and</u> orange juice!" The owner showed me the conference room, with sweeping views of the mountainous coastline – reminding me of the Firth of Clyde – where he had hosted meetings of government ministers and officials.

As a town, Amapala was in sharp decline. The paint on the old single storey houses had peeled so much that it was difficult to deduce what colour it had been when applied all those decades ago. Shop owners stood expectantly in their doorways, thankful for my custom when buying a handful of bananas for a handful of pennies. It was hard to believe the town had once been the official port of Honduras, and had been busy with the trans-shipment of imports and exports between sea going ships and smaller vessels plying the estuary. One day I cycled round the island, a distance of sixteen kilometres on a road made entirely out of what looked like patio blocks. They interlaced well, and made a re-assuring humming noise as I encircled the island. It struck me as being remarkably like Millport, except that it lacked the ice cream shop half way round to serve the hundreds of day-trippers from Glasgow. I felt at home, nonetheless. And like Millport, cars were outnumbered by bicycles here.

Signs of poverty were all around me. Small houses, scruffy barefoot children, inactivity. Even the dogs looked depressed. "What keeps Honduras going?" I wondered. The main economy is fruit-growing. It was developed in the early decades of the twentieth century in an attempt to introduce foreign investment. The investment arrived in the shape of United States fruit companies, paying low wages in order to provide cheap food for relatively affluent consumers at home. Successive Honduran governments accepted low-wage investment as they were reaping the benefits of a limited amount of infrastructure development carried out by the fruit companies. A little bit of corruption helped, of course. Thus developed Honduras as a 'banana republic'.

The producers are always the ones who suffer in these situations. Low wages, cheap food, and large profits for the companies in the middle. There is an analogy in modern

---

[4] Source – www.tesco.com Directors' remuneration report, financial year 2004/5.

Britain where a small number of dominant supermarkets keep selective prices low to remain competitive. "Forcing prices down" boasts one of them. How do they "force" prices down? They squeeze their suppliers. Many food producers have seen their incomes decline because of the thirst for lower prices. In the meantime, the salaries of directors and managers are not squeezed, they get absurdly high.

According to the annual accounts of the supermarket chain Tesco, for example, the salaries and 'emoluments' paid to the Executive Directors in 2004/5 ranged from £1.2m to £3.2m – each.[4] They are all listed individually, together with the comparable figure for the previous year. Between the two years their salaries and emoluments had all increased by between seven and nine percent – well above the rate of inflation. At the same time, their suppliers, particularly the small ones with less clout, were seeing their income reduced in pursuit of the holy grail of lower prices.

It is over-simplistic to blame the supermarkets alone for this. Many of their customers are poor and want cheap food, irrespective of the consequences for the producer. Poor people in rich countries are at least on the right side of the economic divide, as they benefit from the supermarkets' policies. Honduras has been on the wrong end of this syndrome for almost a century, leading to overwhelming poverty while a fantastically small elite band of people control 95% of the country's resources. Food for thought.

The following day I climbed to the top of the island. The track started opposite the entrance to the navy base, and given the proximity of El Salvador and Nicaragua it didn't surprise me that there was a base here. Honduras and El Salvador were once at war over a game of football, of all things (a bit like Glasgow on a rainy Saturday night after an Old Firm game). It was 1969, the game in question was a World Cup Qualifying match. Since neither country actually qualified for the tournament, let alone won it, the whole thing may look futile with hindsight. However, the war was not caused by the match itself, it was sparked off by tensions over the large number of Salvadorian people living and working in Honduras, due to the poor economic conditions in El Salvador at the time. Some of the Salvadorians were squatting illegally in border areas in Honduras. There was violence at the match in San Salvador, which Honduras won. In a classic example of cascading over-reactions, El Salvador bombed the Honduran capital. The ensuing war lasted four days and cost over 3,000 lives. The Liverpool manager Bill Shankly once said "Some people believe football is a matter of life and death. I'm very disappointed by that attitude. I can assure you it is much, much more important than that."

Football can never justify war; the problem is the amount of passion it brings out over things not connected with the ball itself. In 1995 Celtic fan Mark Scott was murdered on his way home from a match in Glasgow for purely sectarian motives. (His murderer was convicted.) This led to the establishment of Nil By Mouth, a charity dedicated to tackling the problem of sectarianism in Scotland. Initiatives like this must be applauded.

Bill Shankly may not have actually believed the words he said; he could have simply been reflecting a sad truth of society. We need to be more tolerant.

I started climbing the track, aware that in the absence of belligerent ships or football supporters the Honduran navy was probably whiling away their day by watching my progress through their binoculars. A woman, sitting strategically at a junction, prevented me from going the wrong way. Half way up the mountain, a battered and rattling 4x4 appeared. Two men were sitting in the front, the one in the passenger seat swigging a bottle of beer. The driver stopped and offered me a lift. At first I declined. He started telling me that he had lived and worked in the United States and every Central American country except Panama. He said that Honduras was best because it was 'home' although it was a close call with Guatemala, where the money was much better. He interrupted his talking to offer me a lift again, and this time – with the ice now thoroughly broken, I jumped in. The track was steep, rough and overgrown in places but the 4x4 made easy work of it, albeit noisily.

Rounding a corner two men were trying to manhandle a large boulder off the track. It was about a metre across and was clearly more than a match for the two of them. We stopped to help, five of us using sticks as levers. Between us, we managed to get it to the edge of the track, from where it was sent crashing into the forest below. It must have weighed a ton, and I hoped there was no-one below. The work done, we all piled into the 4x4 and continued to the summit which was surrounded by a fence. As we got there a security guard opened a gate to let us through. The driver explained who I was, and he welcomed me in. I jumped out and wasted no time in seeking out the best viewpoint. I sat in the sun eating my tinned fish and bananas, looking down at the deep blue sea, and further to the hills of Nicaragua, where I was looking forward to going.

The security guard came over and lent me his binoculars, pointing out various landmarks. He liked the job as it enabled him to spend much of his time up in the cool mountain air rather than the sweltering heat that bakes most of Honduras. He said island life was a little boring, although for him the only realistic alternative was trying to migrate to the United States. He didn't want to do that, as it wasn't home. They worked in forty-eight hour shifts – two days on, two days off, and had a small hostel at the summit. I noticed he was carrying a gun. He seemed mildly surprised when I asked if it really was necessary for armed guards to live on hill-top radio masts.

When I returned to Amapala the villagers were playing bingo in the main square. They were sitting at small wooden tables, studying rows of cards with pictures of animals in squares on them. As the right call was made, they covered a card with a token – a metal bottle top. I considered joining in, but gambling is not one of my strong points.

After a third night in the deserted conference centre, I decided to leave my little haven of Millport-in-the-Tropics and asked the hotel owner to organise me a boat back to

Coyolite. At ten o'clock a small motor boat appeared and once again my nerves jangled as my bike and bags were carried over the sea into the little vessel. The hotelier came on the boat with me, as he needed to go to Tegucigalpa for some building materials. He kept his *camioneta* in Coyolito, to save taking it to and fro on the boat.

I battled against a headwind all the way to Choluteca where disaster struck. The nightmare of all travellers. A cash machine swallowed my card.

At first I thought I had imagined it. I stood there patiently waiting for something to happen, and then checked my wallet to make sure that I had actually put the thing in the machine in the first place. My heart sank deeper and deeper.

I tried to get into the office which the cash machine was attached to. After much knocking and pushing on my part, a man reluctantly came to the door and explained that the cash machine was nothing to do with them. He gave me the address and some directions to the company that refilled it every day, and off I went.

When I got there, I could tell it was a cash security company. Armoured cars lined the pavement, and the office looked like Fort Knox. I rang a buzzer a few times, and a cheeky looking face appeared at a small peep-hole door, behind an iron gate, about a metre off the ground. When I told him what had happened, cheeky-face said simply *"Lunes"* – Monday. This was Friday. I was aghast at the thought of having to spend three nights in Choluteca, with hardly any cash. I certainly wasn't going to risk using a card again until this had been sorted out. I pushed the buzzer again, and once more cheeky-face appeared and said *"Lunes"* at me, almost as if it were his joke punch-line. I could have punched him in the face – no doubt that's why they have to have a security door on the place.

I told him I was only passing through Choluteca and couldn't wait until Monday. He said that maybe the man who had the keys to the machine would come back that night. Well, maybe or maybe not – he was frustratingly vague. I said that if I needed to I would wait there on the pavement until somebody with a key to the machine arrived. *"Lunes"* he said again, as if tempting fate.

I went off to find a hotel, still having enough cash on me to make such a commitment, and bought some fruit. I was preparing for a siege. I returned to the office, and pressed the buzzer again. I told Lunes the lunatic that I was here again and I meant it. Then, another face appeared at the office window. He asked me my name, and when I told him he looked through a pile of bank cards he had, to see if mine was among them. It wasn't as they were all yesterday's cards. The machine had a fault, but nobody had thought to put a notice on it telling people not to use it. Meanwhile, a well dressed Honduran woman turned up with the same story. Initially Lunes gave her his well worn one-word treatment. She said "It's Friday, how can I get through the weekend without any money?" Then someone else arrived. With three of us on the pavement, me armed with a bag of fruit, they obviously felt they had to do something.

A third face appeared at the peep-hole. It was called Franklin and its owner said he would phone me at my hotel if they got the card sooner than Monday. A van driver with the keys had gone to another town to fill a cash machine, and maybe he would return to the office. I nipped back to my hotel to get the phone number, and then nipped back again to give it to Franklin. He was more helpful than Lunes, and said that he had ascertained that I would be able to collect my card at eight the following morning. I tested him with a range of Spanish words all meaning "sure?" each having varying degrees of certainty. He confirmed *seguro*, the most certain of them all. I could do nothing more than retreat from the front line to wait and see what happened in the morning.

Conscious of the fact that I would soon be down to my emergency cache of dollars, I tried to use another card at another bank. The machine "refused the transaction on the instructions of my bank" which baffled me. This card had been issued by a small bank in the Yorkshire market town of Knaresborough, and I struggled to believe – given the seven hour time difference – that someone in Knaresborough was sending instructions to Honduras. I went back to my hotel room to brood, and decided that if I was going to have money problems in Honduras, I wasn't going to stay long. I was only a day's ride from Nicaragua, and the temptation of getting there as soon as I could was too great for me. As soon as I got my card, I would be offski.

I was back at Fort Knox the following morning promptly at eight. Lunes opened the peephole and I immediately asked for Franklin. I wasn't putting up with any more nonsense from Lunes. Franklin looked at me, then passed a blue bank card through the opening. It was mine! I was united with my plastic money at last. The feeling of relief was indescribable. I went straight back to my hotel to pack as I wasn't going to risk losing my cards in any more Honduran banks.

This episode was a shock to the system. Since starting my ride, I had relied entirely on cash machines. They were accessible in sizeable towns of all countries I passed through, all accepting debit cards of one brand or the other. I had travellers cheques as well, and a number of dollars in cash for emergencies. I found the increasingly pervasive acceptance of plastic debit cards made travellers cheques pointless, and I eventually had to cash most of them for the sake of it, simply to avoid carrying them. Internet access to bank accounts enabled me to monitor transactions regularly at internet cafés.

🚲

From Choluteca there are two routes into Nicaragua. The direct route goes across the coastal plain towards Chinandega and then León. Going this way, the frontier was thirty miles away. The road would be busy with commercial traffic. The alternative route goes inland through the mountains, crossing into Nicaragua near Somoto. It would be a lot quieter. The distance to the frontier this way was over forty miles, mostly uphill. It will be no surprise to readers that I chose the latter route. I wanted to see the mountains.

Not only was it uphill, there was a headwind and it was raining. It was like cycling up Glencoe. After fifteen miles of cycling hell, I approached a small *camioneta* that had stopped by the side of the road. The driver was filling his water bottle from a mountain stream. In the back sat four men in their twenties, each wearing a baseball cap and carrying a small bag. I stopped to fill my bottle, and the driver asked me if I wanted a lift. "Five dollars" he said, a little hopefully.

I dithered, then a gust of wind decided for me. I remembered that I had no rules – and it was several weeks since my last bus ride in Mexico. I offered the driver three dollars to take me to the frontier. He accepted, and I pushed my bike into the already crowded back of the *camioneta* and sat next to it on the hard metal floor. The other men in the back were Nicaraguans who worked in El Salvador, on their way home for a visit. No doubt with their pockets stuffed with much-needed US dollars. The youngest asked me if I would give him the beads I was wearing around my neck as a present. When he tried them on they suited him, so I let him keep them.

Climbing into the border mountains, I was aware that this was the territory used in the 1980's by the Nicaraguan Contras and their United States "advisors" to train and launch raids across the border into Nicaragua. I tried in vain to see evidence of past skirmishes, but the jungle quickly obliterates everything. It all looked peaceful and innocent.

We stopped a hundred yards short of the border in the drizzle. We got out and slowly walked to the frontier post. I presented myself to the authorities sporting a waterproof jacket seldom seen in Central America. It was useful though, as I needed all the pockets for the forms, ball-point pens, and more forms, needed to get into Nicaragua. I was almost there.

CHAPTER ELEVEN

NICARAGUA AND POLITICS

The immigration offices were sleepy in the rain. There were hardly any other travellers, and I dealt with the formalities efficiently in a few minutes. Or so I thought. I freewheeled down to a chain dangling across the road, guarding the entrance to Nicaragua. A policeman asked to see my passport. Then he asked for the "paper" for the bike. I thought he was joking at first, but he was quite firm. I had to go back to the offices and get someone to sign in my bike.

Bureaucracy can be frustratingly irritating, but I knew I had to play the game their way. I went back up to the office compound and pedalled round it a couple of times looking for signs of activity. It must have been tea-break. There was no-one around apart from a handful of teenage boys, hoping to earn tips from people crossing the frontier by being helpful. They understood the frontier procedures perfectly – probably better than many frontier officials. I told them I needed a paper for the bike and they knew exactly which room I had to go into to get one. It was the Customs department.

I went in with my entourage of 'all-purpose boys' who were all doing their utmost to assist me. It felt good to be on the receiving end of competition. The customs official presided over a very old fashioned type-writer, one that went "clackety-clack" as he thumped the keys to make the metal letters stamp an imprint on the sheet of paper he had rolled into the machine. He had numerous questions, such a "value of bike". I lied that I had bought it for only a few dollars. He wanted to see the receipt and I lied again that it was second hand, therefore no receipt.

Then came his coup de grace. "Licence plate number" he asked. "None" I said. "All bikes in Nicaragua have number-plates." he retorted. I reminded him that it wasn't a Nicaraguan bike, but he was reluctant to accept my word. One of the Nicas (as Nicaraguans call themselves) suggested lifting the bike up to see if the number was stamped underneath. Perhaps they had seen other British tourists with their postcode embossed into their bike frame. So I lifted my bike into the air, and the boys (who were all known to the Customs man) confirmed rather grandly "None!". He believed them, thankfully, and issued me with my licence. The boys had all been very pleasant so I gave them a handful of money to share, and freewheeled back down to the chain. The policeman saw me coming and dropped the chain onto the road. I went over it, and finally after years of wanting to be there, I was in Nicaragua! An ambition had finally come true, and I was singing at the top of my voice.

A hundred yards along the road was a two-storey whitewashed house; one of its front rooms was a shop. On the gable end wall, in large proud letters, was painted "Welcome to Nicaragua". I went in and bought a celebratory drink and some bananas. The family fussed over me as if I were royalty. I felt welcome indeed.

The road continued to the small town of Somoto. There was hardly any traffic and I pedalled along looking at the scenery, enjoying my sense of exhilaration at the very thought of being in Nicaragua. The hills were lush green and steamy in the rain, heightening my sense of history. The tranquillity belied a violent past. I imagined Contra soldiers crawling about in the jungle, bringing fear to the small number of people living in this border area, as they tried to destabilise the revolutionary Sandinista government that had taken over the country in 1979. Revolution had come as a final, decisive end to forty years of cruel control and exploitation by the Somoza family.

Nicaragua's history since the start of the twentieth century involved much interference from the United States. This brought with it instability and suffering. At the turn of that century a nationalist liberal dictator, Zelaya, was in power, dithering over the desire of the United States to build a canal across the isthmus. Nicaragua was a favoured route because the size of Lake Nicaragua made a route through the country feasible. The United States was finding Zelaya difficult to deal with, as he was resisting their demands for sovereignty over large areas of land through which a canal would pass. In 1904 they chose Panama as their preferred route at the expense of Nicaragua. This was a catastrophic decision for Nicaragua as it would lose out financially compared with its southern competitor. There was much anger in Nicaragua over this, and the debacle precipitated a civil war. This prompted the United States to invade, to maintain stability, and US marines were stationed in the country from 1909 until 1932.

During this period there were a number of rebellions. Agusto Cesar Sandino rose out of this chaos in 1926, pledging to lead people in their struggle against the conservatives in power and the American occupation. He pledged to continue the fight until they left. The marines finally pulled out in 1933 and Sandino signed a peace deal with the conservative government. He was by now a very popular figure throughout the country. At the same time, Anastasio Garcia "Tacho" Somoza took command of the US trained National Guard. In 1934 he perceived Sandino to be a considerable threat in the next presidential elections and had him shot, to prevent him standing. The 1937 election was therefore fought free from the direct threat of Sandino, and Somoza took power by rigging the result.

In spite of political division fuelled by poverty, Tacho Somoza managed to hold onto control through oppression, facilitated by his dual role as President and head of the National Guard. He and his family amassed a fortune by funnelling whatever wealth they could lay their hands on into their own pockets. Companies were bought, monopolies created. Money was flowing like an unstoppable river into their coffers.

Tacho Somoza was assassinated in 1956 by an angry young poet called Rigoberto Lopez Perez, who himself was immediately shot as a result. Tacho's eldest son Luis Somoza took over, keeping a firm grip on the reins of power until he was deposed by a heart attack in 1967. Then the third Somoza – Luis' younger brother Anastasio Garcia "Tachito" Somoza – stepped into the hot seat.

Tachito Somoza continued the family tradition of greed and oppression. His greed was so gross that it eventually outraged even the other members of the wealthy elite, who had become frustrated at the way Somoza businesses and monopolies charged such high prices that their own businesses were jeopardised.

This anger helped germinate the seeds of revolution once again. Unrest grew in the 1970's. The Frente Sandinista de Liberación Nacional (FSLN), named after the late Sandino, became the main centre of gravity. It rapidly gained support during this decade, making it harder and harder to oppress. Freedom of the press was reinstated in 1977 enabling the newspaper La Prensa to openly criticise the government. In January 1978 its editor, Pedro Joaquin Chamorro, was assassinated. Although he was not a Sandinista, his death sparked off demonstrations and strikes. It was getting harder for Somoza to keep control.

In August 1978 the FSLN launched a spectacular attack on the National Palace. Somoza retaliated, the country slid into turmoil which ended in July 1979 with Somoza conceding defeat and fleeing to the United States. The FSLN installed a revolutionary government comprising both Sandinistas and representatives of the upper class, under the leadership of Daniel Ortega.

---

[5] "Nicaragua – The Threat of a Good Example" Published by Oxfam, 1985.

If Nicaraguans thought that was the end of their troubles, they were wrong. It was only the beginning.

The new government set about undoing the worst effects of the Somoza regime. The National Guard was disbanded; an ambitious education programme was implemented which saw more teachers appointed and the literacy rate improve from 25% to 80%; and health was given high priority, leading to a general improvement in the well-being of the population. An Oxfam report concluded that "Nicaragua was to prove exceptional in the strength of government commitment to meeting the basic needs of the poor majority."[5] A wave of optimism spread through the country, and the Sandinistas quickly became a popular, reforming government.

The reaction of the United States to all this was crucial. Initially the government of Jimmy Carter gave aid to the new government. In 1980 Ronald Reagan was elected as President. He was not impressed. He saw the Nicaraguan government as a left-wing threat. Aid was withdrawn, a trade embargo followed, and worse still, the Reagan administration funded and trained an army of former National Guardsmen – which became known as the Contras – to fight a terrorist campaign against the Sandinista government.

By now some of the moderates, including Violeta Chamorro (widow of the murdered newspaper editor) had withdrawn from the government. The Contra War, as their terrorist campaign was known, started to cause a great strain on the government, which reluctantly introduced conscription in 1983. In spite of this the Sandinistas won the 1984 elections, but electoral success did not stop the United States undermining the Nicaraguan government through terrorism. Finally in the 1990 elections, after being made war-weary and in an atmosphere of threats from the United States, Nicaraguans threw out the Sandinistas and elected Violeta Chamorro as their new president. The experiment with revolutionary socialism had ended.

During the Contra war many of the Contras were based over the border in Honduras, where they trained under US supervision in relative safety. The area through which I was now cycling was then the front-line for their cross border attacks against the Nicaraguan government.

Somoto is a quiet town lying just off the main road. It has a broad plaza with a vast cathedral on one side, and the rambling, slightly eccentric Hotel Panamericana along the adjacent side. I wandered into the hotel looking for a room but couldn't find anyone. Eventually a woman responded to my calls and took me through a sedate sitting room filled with potted plants, caged birds, and the odd cat or two, to a neat little row of rooms on the other side of a flower bed. I made myself comfortable and went out to explore the town.

The first thing that struck me was the number of protestant churches. The cathedral was very catholic right enough, but each street in the town had at least one if not two protestant churches of varying descriptions. I went into a small dark shop where I could smell fresh coffee.

The owner offered to make me a cup, even though it wasn't actually a café. Such spontaneous flexibility endeared me to my new country very easily. The coffee was indeed fresh, the man behind the counter said it was grown locally in the hills. I asked him about the protestant churches too, and he said that they had sprung up during the Sandinista years as the end of the dictatorship meant that many people had felt liberated from Catholicism, as well as Somocism, as the era under Somoza was sometimes known.

After a meal in a nondescript restaurant with a surly waiter I returned to the hotel to relax amongst the plants and birdcages. The owner came to chat to me. When I told him I had cycled here from the State of Chihuahua in Mexico he told me he had lived there. "Texas, too" he added, as if to impress. He told me he had gone there during the Sandinista era as a revolutionary country was no place to run a business. I suspect that being on the front line close to the Honduran border, he had probably done the right thing.

In the morning I breakfasted with a couple of Nicas who lived in Florida. They too had left in the Sandinista years, finding life too difficult, and had now settled in the United States. They were fond of Nicaragua, but had made a more secure life for themselves in Florida.

I left Somoto on a quiet road, surrounded by steep wooded hills with a great variety of trees. As I went on towards Estelí the vegetation became browner and there were neat little dry stone walls marking boundaries. Chickens ran around on the eternal hunt for a grain of something. I stopped at a roadside shop with a wooden roof along the front, covering a concrete forecourt which had wooden benches round the edge. I sat there for a while, sipping a soft drink and chatting to some teenage girls. A succession of locals came in for various things including bicycle components, which I found faintly re-assuring. The atmosphere was very relaxed. I reached the outskirts of Estelí mid-afternoon. The Pan American Highway by-passes the town, and many roadside businesses have been built along the main road so that traffic doesn't have to deviate into the town for necessities. I stopped at a filling station where someone had told me there would be a cash machine.

There wasn't, prompting fears that I may be in for another Honduran-style wild cash chase. A customer told me the cash machine had been moved to the Shell station up the road, so off I went. When I got there, the attendants looked at me as if they didn't even know what a cash machine was. Another customer told me there was another Shell station further up the road, on the other side. I found it, it had a cash machine, and to my great relief it had a new fangled card-reader where you didn't actually have to insert the whole card into the machine. You only had to put it in far enough for the chip to be read, meaning you could hang on to the rest of the card between thumb and forefinger. Relief! I took out a huge wad of banknotes – the maximum the machine would allow me - which made the security guard blink. I wasn't planning on running out of money just yet, thank you very much. Three American girls buying donuts asked me where I was going, and they were impressed with my journey.

Estelí looked downtrodden. It had obviously suffered through being a Sandinista stronghold and on the front line in the Contra war. Flower stalls in the main square gave a feeling of normality. Behind them it was still possible to see Sandinista murals depicting the achievements of the period. In other parts of Nicaragua they have been painted over, but Estelí remains a stronghold, so the murals remain. There were two or three small hotels to choose from – businesses which had flourished when foreign volunteers came here in the 1980's to help with the revolutionary cause. I decided to stay at the Hotel Miraflor which had friendly owners and an attractive bar and restaurant.

I was given a room with a window looking into the bar. I could see that Spanish football was on television and the family were gathered around watching. I sat on a settee with some of them to watch an absorbing game between Real Sociedad and Athletic Bilbao, ending 3-3.

A boy of about twelve was sitting on the settee next to me, and I assumed he was one of the family. At half time the hotel owner brought me some chicken and chips and I shared my chips with the boy. He told me he had been ridden into by a bike that morning, and showed me the wound on his leg. He asked me for twenty Córdobas so he could get some medicine. At first I thought it was a bit cheeky of him. Then I realised he didn't live there. He worked in the town as a boot black, his wooden box of brushes had been under the settee and I hadn't noticed it. He picked it up and limped around the restaurant trying to get some custom from the people eating there. No luck. He looked forlorn so I called him back over and gave him the twenty Córdobas he had wanted, annoyed with myself for appearing so mean at first. I noticed then that his clothes were in tatters. He was a street boy, and the family who ran the hotel often let him rest there while he worked his way around town.

After the football I went out for a wander around the town. On one side of the main square was an ice-cream parlour. My sweet tooth was demanding a dessert so I went in. It had a security guard which seemed a bit over the top for an ice-cream parlour. However, when his attention was distracted four street children came in and swiftly worked the tables for whatever money they could scrounge. When he realised he ushered them out as quickly as he could.

Estelí has a long main street going up a hill off one corner of the square. There are small shops on either side; some were doing a roaring trade, and some doing very little. Half way up a large advert hoarding covered a derelict site, on which was an advert encouraging people to reap the profits from the development of tourism, as Nicaragua needed the money. Looking around, that was overstating the obvious. The site was derelict because it had been shelled by the Somoza government in 1979. Estelí supported the Sandinistas, and in an attempt to quell revolutionary feelings Somoza had the town shelled to try to turn the population against the Sandinistas. There is still much evidence of this destruction in the town. If a government bombs its own people, what are they supposed to think of the government? How could the government expect to win? I found the Heroes and Martyrs Museum, which had closed for the day. There was a fire station on the opposite side of the road, and a couple of firemen told me when it would be open the following day. "They are all volunteers" I was told "Mothers of the dead. Some of them are getting a bit old now, so don't be surprised if they open late."

The following morning I was back at the Heroes and Martyrs Museum shortly after it opened. The museum is a very moving and emotional portrayal of the 1979 revolution and the Contra war, made more powerful with the numerous photos of people - mainly young men – killed in the area. It brought home to me the human cost of war. In 1979 I was twenty-five, the same age as some of the men in the photographs. I spoke to a woman who had lost her twenty-three year old son.

"We had to do something to end the dictatorship" she said. "Above all, it was worth the effort."

Sadly, she now regretted the rise in crime, drugs, and delinquency in the country. This is the price we pay for freedom – but is it freedom? She is not unique of course, but I felt pangs of sadness talking to a woman who had lost a son in a war. I asked myself if all wars were senseless. Nicaragua's was born out of desperation to get rid of a dictator. What was totally un-necessary was the way in which the United States encouraged violent opposition to the new government, especially after its power was legitimised in the 1984 elections which the Sandinistas won with 67% of the vote, in spite of the difficulties.

In the 1980's I was an Oxfam activist and had often taken part in campaigns to focus on the achievements of the Sandinista government. I had regularly bought Nicaraguan coffee at Oxfam shops, as another way of showing solidarity. Talking to the bereaved mother in the museum made it seem so much more real to me.

Nicaraguans still deeply resent the involvement of the United States. A note in the museum referred to the proposal to create CAFTA - a Free Trade Area for Central and North America as a threat. There is a fear that US firms will use their power to muscle in and destroy local businesses that can't compete.

In addition to the photos are weapons, clothing, and written accounts of various skirmishes and incidents. A display in the museum explained the significance of the Nicaraguan flag. The national flag is formed by two horizontal pale blue bands separated by a white band containing an emblem in a three sided equilateral triangle. The triangle represents the equality of all Nicaraguans. The emblem inside depicts five volcanoes representing the five Central American states that gained independence from Spain in 1821. In front of them is some water, representing the seas surrounding Central America. There is also a hat, the Gorro Frigio, representing freedom. The rays shining from the hat represent the strength of the sun. Finally, a rainbow shows the hope of Nicas for a better and prosperous country.

Underneath the flag was a simple statement. "*Las Madres Siempre De Frente Con El Frente*". The mothers are always in front, with the Front. Nicaragua has always had to struggle between polarised views.

In the afternoon I went for a bike ride to Salto Estanzuela, where there is a waterfall and a pool where it is good to swim. Taking the bike may not have been such a good idea as a rough and hilly track leads to it from the main road. I met two English lads in their twenties sauntering along the track clutching their Lonely Planet guidebook for safety. They were going to the pool too. They were touring Central America for three months. I asked them why they had chosen to see Central America. "Because it's cheap" they both said in unison, as if confirming each other. I was disappointed at what I saw as shallowness on their part, but perhaps I was wallowing in too much personal history. I was their age during the Sandinista Revolution – they had yet to be born. One of the disadvantages of growing older is that I find it frustrating that younger people can sometimes seem totally uninterested in events which to me only happened yesterday, and were part of my life.

In the evening I went to the White House Pizza a couple of blocks from the main square. It was furnished with wooden tables and bench seats. I had just ordered my pizza when the lights went out. A power cut! I sat tight for a while, and then fumbled my way to the counter, using my Mexican cigarette lighter as a beacon. The woman behind the counter gave me a candle and said the ovens were still functioning, so the pizza order was still progressing. I looked outside the front door and saw that the whole neighbourhood was in darkness. I grinned to myself at the thought of all the anger this would be causing in the Internet Cafes. The Nicas in the street seemed to be accepting this as normal, so I went back to my table with my candle, with which I could just about make out the names on my map of Nicaragua. The lights came on after fifteen minutes, and my tasty pizza soon followed.

Back at my hotel, a chess match was in progress. Almost every table in the bar was occupied by a couple of chess players, with a few spectators watching intently. I watched for a while, trying out a glass of Nicaraguan rum called Flor de Caña. Then I had another. It tasted good. After a third, I went to bed and immediately fell asleep. I never knew the outcome of the chess match.

In the morning I had a hearty breakfast at the Hotel Vuela Vuela, which had a restaurant with an attractive flowered courtyard at the back. The hotel rooms had recently been modernised and some Americans were wandering around slightly apprehensively. I too was a little apprehensive, as I knew that it was about a hundred miles to León and I would not be able to make it in a day. I sat there for a while considering my options. The road that went there was, according to the map, a minor cross-country road which branched off the main road to Managua at a place called San Isidro. There were no significant places marked between there and León. I was unsure what condition the road would be in, and unsure about whether I would find accommodation. On the bright side, I had been in Nicaragua long enough to feel comfortable at the thought of camping if I had to. I set off having decided to put off making a decision until I got to San Isidro.

The first five miles were uphill, effort rewarded with some really good mountain and valley views. In spite of the heat, the countryside was as green as anywhere you would see in the British Isles. I stopped in a pretty little village of adobe houses, called La Trinidad. A woman in a cavernous clothes shop which also sold cakes and soft drinks said she thought there was somewhere to stay at El Jicoral, half way to León. That encouraged me. I reached San Isidro at one-thirty having only done twenty-two miles. I felt it was too early to stop for the night, so I asked a taxi driver who was filling up at the petrol station for information. Sometimes I think taxi drivers know everything.

"Yes" he said "There is a *hospedaje* at El Jicoral."

"What is it called?"

"I don't know"

"How do you know there is one then?"

"People who have been in my taxi have told me. Oh, the road is very bad too.

Metalled, but with many, many potholes."

"On a bike you should be able to pedal round them." he added, seeing my slightly deflated look.

I considered his advice. I wanted to go to León. I didn't want to go via Managua as it was much further. I didn't fancy cycling in Managua, whereas the thought of cycling through a remote area was very appealing. I pedalled round San Isidro a couple of times, kicking up dust, while I decided what to do. San Isidro was small, poor, and uninviting. It wasn't difficult to remind myself that I was supposed to have a sense of adventure, so I set off down the road to León.

There were plenty of good omens. It was downhill, there was little traffic, and I had a tail wind. I could see from the lie of the land that I was going to get a lot of downhill cycling, as I was on a highland plateau, whereas León was on the coastal plain, and I could see the plain stretching out in front of me, miles away. Having a tail wind was the icing on the cake.

The road, however, was appalling. I was dancing around the biggest potholes I had ever seen. After five miles, I stopped and considered whether to turn back. I decided to carry on; I had managed five miles after all. To my relief the surface improved considerably. After twenty miles, going through a very small village I spotted a policeman, so I stopped to see what he knew. He said that El Jicoral was another six miles and I should ask at the police station there for information about lodgings. It was comforting to know that the place did at least have a police station. If I got desperate for accommodation, I could have a couple of beers, smash a window, and get myself arrested!

I enjoyed another downhill stretch, with views of distant volcanoes. Approaching a bridge over a river, there was a sign that said Puente El Jicoral. There were a handful of houses on the other side of the bridge. A woman told me the village was just round the corner, to the left of the road. I followed her directions and sure enough a narrow road branched off past a deserted restaurant, taking me to a small village with four neat rows of buildings round a large concreted square. At one side were a shop and a police station. I went into the police station, where two jovial looking officers looked as if they were arresting somebody. They were removing his trouser belt. They suggested I went to the restaurant for advice. When I got there I disturbed a group of girls in the kitchen who knew very little. One of them suggested I try the big house next to the bridge.

The first house I tried was the wrong one. The man told me I needed to cross over the bridge. On the other side was a large house set back from the road, with what looked like a giant concrete chicken house next to it. The entrance drive was protected by a barbed wire gate, which I managed to knock over as I unhitched it to pass through. At the back of the house was a large porch area with two women sitting outside, chatting. I asked about accommodation. Before committing herself, one of the women asked me a few questions, obviously weighing me up. She explained that a foreigner had once stayed there without paying. Oh, why are foreigners all so wicked, wherever you go! I tried to mollify her by offering to pay in advance. She took me over the yard to the chicken house, which turned out to be a building made up of very small, basic bedrooms. It wasn't particularly clean, but she only wanted twenty-five Córdobas, and it did at least have a bed. She had no key for the door, so I would have to rely on rural security.

I gave her the twenty-five Córdobas and prepared to go back to the village shop to get some provisions, which I wanted to do before it got dark. She promised to turn on the electricity at six o'clock.

At the village shop, a few villagers were sitting outside on the wooden veranda. A boy with a broad rimmed straw hat sat on a horse. The shop was jam packed full with so much stuff, there was barely room to walk. I waited at the doorway while the shopkeeper rummaged around for whatever I asked for. A tin of peas? Yes, of course. Some tuna? Indeed. Bread? Naturally. A few tomatoes? Why not. Whatever I asked for, he managed to conjure up, sometimes with a bit of swearing in the process. I was a bit conservative with my beer order, for some reason.

I went back to my luxury chicken house and sat on a chair outside to eat my feast. By now it was after six o'clock and getting dark, so I went over to ask the woman to switch on the electricity. She agreed a little reluctantly, as if doing me a massive favour. I don't think she trusted me at all. Then I noticed that my meal tin was missing. It had been stolen by the dog. The dog was watching me from a distance, licking his lips. I was furious – liking dogs is not one of my strong points. I had to find the tin as I used it a lot for mixing up meals and snacks. I couldn't ask the dog where he had put it, and it was almost dark. Miraculously, using the small torch given to me by Peggy in Honduras, I found it behind a tree. The dog was lucky to have survived the incident, I can tell you!

I decided to venture back to the village shop to get some more beer. By now the stars were shining like polished jewels, with no streetlight glare to tarnish them. When I got back to my room with the beer, an electric fan had appeared. As I opened a beer, a man I hadn't seen before came out of the house and invited me to use one of the hammocks hanging from the eaves. Suddenly I felt welcome. I lay there looking at the stars, reflecting on the day's ride. Yes, there had been millions of potholes, but I had cycled round almost all of them. The road had been manageable so far, and I estimated I was 45 miles from Leon, which I would be able to do the next day quite easily, regardless of the conditions. I was getting blasé.

---

[6] The Sandinistas, again led by Daniel Ortega, won the 2006 election. See later in chapter.

The man sat with me for a while. I asked him about the Contra War. Was the revolution worth the subsequent bloodshed and destruction caused by the Contra War? "Of course it was" he said "we had forty years of a dictatorship, with no freedom, only hunger. It was worth the pain because now we have freedom and are free from hunger too." He said the Sandinistas are still popular and people are no longer afraid of the United States when voting. He hoped the Sandinistas would do well in the 2006 elections.

I felt buoyant to hear such a positive view of things.

I woke up at six. I could hear the toilet cistern filling with water so I made use of the running water while it lasted. The family was already up and about when I emerged from the chicken shed ready to cycle off. It was good to get an early start. The morning views were bright and fresh. Men on horseback herded cattle. People walked or cycled along the road, going to work. Many carried machetes, the universal tool of the rural worker. By now I didn't find them intimidating. At a café a man sat next to me to talk. He had an injured leg, from a road accident. I told him about my journey and the fascination I had had for Nicaragua during the Sandinista years. "Things were better under the Sandinistas" he said, in a tone of voice that contained no doubt. "In spite of the Contra War?" I checked. "Yes" he said emphatically "in spite of the Contra War. Anyway, that was the United States, not Nicaraguans." He said that the Sandinistas had put an end to hunger and fought poverty. Now, the country had a right wing President which the United States approved of, and hunger was on the increase again. He too hoped the Sandinistas would win the 2006 election.[6] We spoke about CAFTA, and his view that the United States would gain the most by displacing local businesses.

I still had to concentrate on the road. A bad stretch contained many large, deep potholes that had been filled with sand. Great clouds of dust rose when cars drove over them. In the heat it was like cycling in the Sahara. I stopped for a rest at San Jacinto at a turning leading to some geothermal springs. On the corner was a large house where a man sold ice-creams. I went in and couldn't believe the contrast. He had an expensive modern chest freezer packed full of ice creams and desserts, at one end of an otherwise bare and spartan house. He sat on an old wooden chair in conversation with a friend. In Latin America such juxtapositions are normal. I gorged two ice lollies in rapid succession, which must have looked so decadent to them. I visited the boiling mud pools at the geothermal springs. Some local boys were playing baseball and they offered to show me round, hoping to earn some money. I managed without them, after giving a local woman four Córdobas to watch over my bike while I was looking around.

From here the road got better, passing through rice fields. Rice was introduced to the Americas by the Spanish. The terrain was lower and flatter. A few miles further on I came to the junction with the main Panamericana at Telica. The junction was busy with lorries and busses. Empty plastic bottles were being frantically unloaded from a lorry at a rambling old café on the corner. I looked forward to an improvement in road surface as I stood there drinking a bag of cold water. A boy asked me if I would sell my bike when I got to Panama. How could I, when we have been through so much together?

I whizzed along the main road and was in León in no time. It was surprisingly small – the country's second largest city, at one time the capital, but there were no skyscrapers anywhere. It was like stepping back into a time warp. Modernity had passed León by.

It took me a while to find lodgings; many places said they were full. Eventually I found a private house which had a number of rooms to let in the grounds. I was given a small room with a hammock outside.

Some of the other people staying there had been there for a while. A Canadian girl was working as an English teacher at the university. She had a Nicaraguan boyfriend and was living there to be near him. A Frenchman was working as a French teacher. A Dutch girl – no, she wasn't teaching Dutch. She worked for Utrecht city council in the town planning department. León is twinned with Utrecht and she was on a month's secondment giving León council some advice on town planning. I found it easy to slip into the social circle the three of them had already created.

León is compact and easy to explore on foot. It has virtually no modern buildings and the rows of colourful old adobe buildings reminded me of towns in Cuba. The Parque Central is dominated by a giant cathedral that certainly needs a coat of paint. It is the largest cathedral in Central America. It is possible to climb the steps inside one of the towers and walk around on the roof, enjoying good views over the town, surrounding countryside, and the row of volcanoes that dominate Nicaragua's skyline.

The city has a university, and it buzzes with student life – cafes, bars and restaurants abound. There is a large market hall in the centre, a rabbit warren of stalls presided over by matriarchal women, who observed everything that went on in their domain. There were a lot of street children too, and a group of stall holders had got together to form a support network for the street children. They provided food, advice, and support. They stood up for the children when they had conflicts with authority.

A café advertised guided hikes to the summit of Volcan Momotomba, to raise money for the market's street children support network. This sounded good so I went in to find out more. The hikes were run by volunteers who donated the profits to the market. I put my name down for an overnight hike in the full moon. Unfortunately the excursion was cancelled as they couldn't get permission to pass through the hydro-electric power station. I was dismayed at missing the trip, especially as it was for a worthwhile cause.

León has always had liberal traditions. It seems surprising therefore, that it was also a stronghold of the Somoza family, who often liked to stroll through its streets. It was here that the first Somoza was assassinated in 1956. As a Somoza stronghold the city saw much heavy fighting in 1979. There is a ruined fort called El Fortín about four miles out of town, where the Somoza forces were finally overcome in 1979. When it fell, the Sandinistas declared themselves the new provisional government. One afternoon I went there on my bike. Several people had told me it was dangerous because there were thieves on the road. However, I took a chance, reasoning that the thieves weren't expecting me. If they were on foot I could out-pace them on the bike anyway. By now I had heard so many stories about thieves on roads that I took it with a pinch of salt. As a precaution, I set off carrying virtually nothing of value except a few Córdobas to buy refreshments.

The ride was lamentably uneventful. First I had to go to the village of Sutiava, and then bear left along a dirt track. There were a couple of dodgy looking men on the track, but they took no notice of me. Reaching El Fortín I discovered that a man in his forties was squatting in one of the ruined rooms. He said he would keep an eye on my bike for me while I wandered around examining the ruins. It was possible to get onto the roof. The views towards the city and the volcanoes were superb. The line of volcanoes from this angle resembled the symbol of Nicaragua on the flag and on the coins. The building had also been used as a prison in the Somoza period, and I sat for a while absorbing the atmosphere and thinking through the history of the place.

After half an hour I pedalled back to Sutiava. On the outskirts of the village I bought a drink in a small shop which was well hidden behind a front garden full of giant bushes.

"Are you going to El Fortín?" I was asked.

"I've just been there"

"It's very dangerous"

Then as an afterthought he added "Well, mainly on Sundays".

I sat outside on a concrete ledge to drink my juice, and the man came out with his wife. They wanted to talk about the revolution, which didn't disappoint me.

> "Of course, the revolution was worth the effort. We got rid of oppression, of a dictator who killed people who spoke against him, who made people poor, who denied peasants land to grow food."

You couldn't argue with that.

> "There was no delinquency under the Sandinistas because there was almost full employment."

They regretted the current rise in delinquency and linked it to high unemployment. I was curious about the former National Guard. If the Somozas had become so unpopular because of oppression and poverty, I wondered what sort of people joined the National Guard, and why so many joined.

> "It was a lifestyle that some people found attractive. A better alternative to working on the land. Some people are happy to take orders all the time."

No doubt they were paid relatively well, too.

�🚲

León was founded in 1524, the same year as its rival city of Granada. The original site was a few miles to the east on the shore of Lake Managua. Known as León Viejo, it was destroyed by a volcanic eruption in 1609, and consequently rebuilt on the present site. It is possible to visit the site of León Viejo, and I did so by sharing a taxi with John, a rather talkative American from Rhode Island, who was staying at my lodgings. The owner of the lodging house also suggested we went to Volcan de Hoyo where we could swim in the crater lake called Laguna de Asosca.

The taxi driver, Roberto, took us to the entrance of León Viejo and said he would wait for as long as we wanted. A guide took us round, a girl of about twenty with a hilarious sense of humour who saw the funny side of virtually everything. She hoped there wouldn't be an eruption while we were there. Maybe just an earthquake or two. The ruins have been well excavated, with plenty of interpretive signs to assist the visitor.

After an hour or so we asked Roberto if he would show us Lake Managua. By now he had opened up a little. A young man – too young to remember the Sandinista Revolution personally – he was nonetheless interesting. Roberto deeply regretted Nicaragua's decline once again into poverty, and the related violence, especially in Managua. He felt that León was relatively safe and was pleased to be living there. Above all, it was evident from the way he talked about things that he was proud of Nicaragua and its recent past.

After Lake Managua we asked Roberto to take us to Laguna de Asosca. It was a good job we had negotiated this into the original deal, as the drive was quite an ordeal, especially for Roberto. He had to stop a couple of times to ask other drivers the way. We turned onto a narrow trail that expired in a thicket of bushes. He forced his way through the bushes onto another track. We finally stopped outside a ramshackle wooden farmhouse and Roberto asked the farmer the way to the lake. He wanted 20 Córdobas to show us the way. Having got so far, it seemed churlish to argue with poor people over a paltry some of money which wouldn't even buy a cup of coffee in Britain.

Twenty Córdobas richer, the farmer then delegated the task to his twelve year old son, who rode along a track on horseback as we followed on foot. The boy was quite dour, but he did tell us the horse's name – Pinto. At last we swam in the laguna, washing off the dust of León Viejo as Pinto and the boy watched us from a safe distance. After our swim, the boy took the opportunity to herd up some cattle, and we followed them along the track back to the taxi. Roberto was leaning against it, having a cigarette with the farmer. We returned to León feeling very satisfied – us having had a good day out, and Roberto thirty dollars richer.

León has several sites relating to the revolutionary period. There is of course a Heroes and Martyrs Museum, similar to the one in Estelí in that it is staffed almost entirely by mothers of the fallen. Again, the mainstay of the museum was row upon row of photographs of the victims.

The murals, on the other hand, were different. One, on a corner of the Parque Central occupies the site of a department store that was destroyed in 1979. It depicts the outline of Sandino, wearing his familiar hat. It also contains the words of the letter written by Rigoberto Lopez Perez shortly before he assassinated Somoza senior, precipitating his own demise. It is best to go and see the mural in the early evening as the sun is going down, the orangey-yellow rays of sunset adding special warmth to it.

Another museum worth seeing is the 1921 prison, where Somoza's National Guard had committed deeds of torture against opponents of the regime. There is a well in the courtyard where men were dropped on a rope, blindfolded and upside down. The rooms now contain many murals depicting man's cruelty to man, inspired by the events in the prison over a period of years. I was taken round by a guide, and I asked him what sort of people joined the National Guard. I couldn't elicit a direct answer out of him. Were they conscripted, were they paid well, or did they join simply because they liked Somoza? He seemed to infer that money was part of the answer – the need to have a paid job and not ask too many questions.

Afterwards, I went to my favourite *comedor* for lunch. As I sat eating, I saw a boy shining a customer's shoes in the doorway. The customer was reading a newspaper, and the boy was looking up trying to read the newspaper as he frantically rubbed at the shoes. Literate boot-black!

🚲

One morning we all got up to discover that a Colombian had arrived at the guest house. He was in his forties, had thinning hair and a black moustache, and wore light blue denim jeans and jacket. It was never clear why he was in Nicaragua – most people had a reason to be there. I had breakfast with him, and he depressed me by telling me how dangerous everywhere in the world was. Not just Colombia, but the whole of Latin America and even his adopted home city of Marseille in France. When he learned that I had cycled to Nicaragua from Northern Mexico he almost didn't believe me, saying frankly that I was lucky to be alive.

The following day two more cyclists appeared. Yann and Marie were from France. They were cycling from Mexico City to Chile, with a flyover from Panama to Ecuador already booked. I wasted no time in inviting them out to lunch so we could compare notes, bikes, equipment. It seemed such a bizarre coincidence that we should end up at the same guest house in León.

Over lunch, I asked them if they had spoken to the Colombian man. "Yes" said Yann "He told us we were lucky to be alive."

The poor Colombian man must have been so confused. Meeting not just one, but three cyclists who had made it from Mexico had completely demolished his theories. From then on, he kept a low profile, hardly leaving his room. No doubt he was afraid in case more lucky cyclists popped up from Mexico.

León is near enough to the sea to have its own beach resort, a little place called Poneloya, at the end of an undulating road about twelve miles from the city. There was a sporadic bus service, so I decided to give the bike a rest and experience a journey on a Nicaraguan chicken-bus. A bus was waiting silently at the bus stop when I got there. A man told me it would go in half an hour, so I went to buy some fruit. It was a Sunday and a lot of people were headed for the beach. The bus became fuller and fuller. By the time it left, there were more people standing in the aisle than there were sitting. People squeezed three or four together on the seats to make more room. Children were excited at going to the beach. Food was passed around. It was happy and chaotic. On the outskirts of Poneloya large houses with high fences bordered the road, which ran parallel to the sea making it difficult to actually see the sea. Some of the houses were crumbling, having been abandoned by their rich owners during the Sandinista years. At the end of the road, the bus pulled into a circle of dust and disgorged its passengers. Most seemed to know where to go – one or other of the *palapas* that lined the shore. Hardly anyone went onto the sand itself or down to the rough, noisy sea. I had a beer while I surveyed the scene, and then decided to walk along the shore.

There were more *palapas* further up the beach which were less busy, so I went to one for a fish lunch, then lay on the beach for a while listening to the Pacific waves. I strolled back for the last bus back into León at four thirty. It was packed. I just about managed to find six square inches of floor to stand on, and a strap to hang from. The bus didn't go all the way into León. It terminated outside a shop where most of us piled into a lorry for a bumpy ride shoulder to shoulder to the Parque Central. What a day.

I mentioned to Paco, the guest house owner that I had seen large houses on the beach that had been abandoned during the revolution. He said that was what had happened to their house. The previous owners had left the country when the house was ruined during the fighting in 1979. Paco had bought it in 1980 as a ruin, and rebuilt it. The previous owners now lived in the United States and had no interest in it now. I told him that when Germany had been re-united, some people who had fled East Germany ten or twenty years previously had gone back to reclaim their houses, making the new occupiers homeless. He said that had happened in Nicaragua too, at the end of the Sandinista period in 1990.

Paco opined that things had been better under the Somozas. Why? Because everyone had a job and things were more stable. A dollar cost seven Córdobas then, now it was seventeen. He thought the country was still just as poor, but worse off because of the problems of rising crime. I said "You can't beat a dictatorship for solving the problems of crime!" He thought the Sandinistas had tried to fight poverty but had ended up putting money in their own pockets – in the end, they were no better than other politicians. A negative view of politicians is, like football, a common bond between people throughout the world. I think it's worrying, but maybe the football is more satisfying than trying to change politicians.

One of the bars in León specialised in serving backpackers. It had a backpackers' hostel, and the menus were in English. The backpackers tended to specialise in talking to each other, rather than the locals. Conversation sometimes became competitive, each trying to out-do the other in how cheaply they could travel. For some people, travel is nothing more than an exercise in living cheaply. The problem is, cheap travel is achieved at the cost of exploiting low paid workers in other countries. Without low paid workers, cheap travel for people from rich countries would not be an option. If a pizza and a bottle of wine cost exactly the same throughout the world, many people would perhaps make do with a weekend in Brighton, rather than galloping round the world in search of cheapness.

After eight days in León, it was time to leave. Continuing my policy of avoiding capital cities, I devised a route that would take me down to the coast, avoiding Managua. It would take me out of León on the Old Managua Road to Santa Rita, from where a right turn led to the coastal town of Montelimar. The French-sounding name was tantalisingly exotic. I said good-bye to everyone at the guest house and was on the road at eight, as I calculated I had over sixty miles to do that day.

CHAPTER TWELVE

NO BOATS TODAY

The Old Managua Road was well named. Potholes were plentiful. In some places the tarmac had completely disappeared, as if someone had rolled it up and taken it away. It was dry and dusty, and it wasn't long before I was sitting on a wooden bench outside a *pulperia*, drinking a soda and watching the world go by. Most of the world went by on horseback, including a boy who tethered his horse to a post cowboy-style, then went into the *pulperia* to buy a two litre plastic bottle of Coca-cola. It was juxtaposition if ever there was one. You wouldn't have seen John Wayne do that.

A dot on my map called Santa Rita was no more than a junction, where a road diverged to the right. It was signposted to Montelimar so I swung onto it. Then, clack-clack, clack-clack. The road surface was made of small concrete paving stones laid like cobbles, shining white in the hot afternoon sun. At first I was pleased with them, but after a while I noticed there were holes where some were missing. I had to continually watch out for them as they were deep enough to be dangerous if you cycled into them.

I saw oxen pulling carts along the road. Irrigation supplied water to fields of maize. I hit the small town of El Carmen at the crazy hour, when a secondary school closed. Unlike in Mexico, where most teenagers wait at the roadside for a lift home, in Nicaragua many schoolchildren cycle home. I caught up with a group of boys pedalling along very slowly, having an animated discussion about something important to teenage boys. I knew what would happen as soon as I passed them, and I was right. The race was on.

They went faster to try to catch me. They thrilled in the race. Downhill I had the advantage of weight; they had the advantage of youth going uphill. We went on like this for a couple of miles, me passing them, them passing me, all the while I was watching for holes where paving slabs were missing. I chickened out approaching a bridge, as the deck wasn't the same level as the road. They didn't say much; my suggestion that they carry my bags met little response. I was glad to let them win the race. One more win for the macho culture.

Montelimar took me a little by surprise. Its exotic name was maybe a clue. It is a large rambling country estate built as the summer home of the Somoza family. During the Sandinista period it was confiscated and plans made to convert it into a luxury holiday resort, with golf courses and tennis courts. After the fall of the Sandinistas the new government continued with the development, but sold it to a Spanish resort company. I wouldn't feel comfortable hob-knobbing with the rich in such a poor country, so I went on to the next place, a small fishing port called Masachapa. I stayed at a hotel where my room was built on stilts on the beach. At high tide I could hear the sea lapping against the stilts. Had there been an earthquake, my room could have plopped down onto the water and floated away across the Pacific, into a dreamy distant sunset.

There was no earthquake, so in the morning I went down to the waters edge to watch the fishing boats come in. The beach was a place of fervent activity. There was no fish market as such, as you might find in Scottish towns like Peterhead. Instead, the local women waited on the beach in small groups straining their eyes to see which boats were coming in next, and where they might land. As soon as they worked out where a boat was going to beach, the women would charge over to try to beat each other to get the best fish. Everything the boats brought in was snapped up. Competition for the fish was fierce. I stood with them by the sides of each boat as it came in, watching the excitement and not feeling in the way at all. Some women bought only one or two fish, others bought whole bucketsful. Some were buying for hotels and restaurants.

When the boatmen had sold their catches, the boats were rolled ashore on a series of wooden rollers. They helped each other to do this, necessary co-operation as it took several men to roll a boat up the beach. Men on three-wheeled bikes took the engine batteries away for storage.

A group of conspicuously rich-looking Germans arrived on the beach. Conspicuous with their cameras, their fatness, their white skin. They were quickly surrounded by poor Nica children, either selling or just plain begging. They were also targeted by three-wheeled cycle-taxis looking for fares. The whole disparate group made its way en masse along the beach, like the Pied Pipers and their entourage.

A young man on the beach, Martín, told me he wanted to be a doctor, and was planning to go to Cuba for five years to study. He was able to get a grant from the Nicaraguan government to do so. Cuba has an excellent reputation throughout Latin America for its medical facilities and training. Martín wanted to be a doctor because he cared about people.

I decided to move up the coast a little to the neighbouring village of Pochomil, and in doing so recorded my lowest daily mileage of the trip – 1.71 miles! The Hotel Altamar was friendly and I had a room at the end of a timber-built block, with a small veranda at the front where I could sit and chat to the handyman. The hotel was at the top of a cliff overlooking the beach, and the open-air restaurant had good views of the beach. I treated myself to lobster, which tasted good in the cloudy sunset.

Pochomil lacks the fishing boat frenzy of Masachapa. It is simply a seaside resort for Managuans, at the end of the road. Pochomil's beach is lined with *palapas*, their ladies cooking fish purchased in the morning on the beach at Masachapa. There are bars and shops, and at weekends frequent busses to and from Managua. Unfortunately I was there on a Saturday, and the bars were as busy and noisy as the mosquitoes in my room.

A sleepless night was washed away by a morning swim, followed by a Gallo Pinto breakfast. Gallo Pinto literally means "painted rooster" and is a special blend of rice, beans, and spices which Nicas love for breakfast, usually with eggs. After breakfast I left, going north through fields of rice and sugar cane towards the mountains. I saw more irrigation systems, which impressed me, but at the same time I felt indignant that a country that could irrigate land should be so poor.

Sometimes in my mind I blamed the people around me for being so poor, for being so unsuccessful in the world. I cursed what I called the "Latin American mentality". I was of course being brutally unfair. They are victims of a history of oppression and foreign interference. They have never had the strength or collective mass to rise above it. Hugo Chavez, the president of Venezuela, is trying to, backed by the power of oil which he can dispense to chosen allies. That day I saw CNN news on television. Chavez had expelled some United States diplomats for spying. Donald Rumsfeld had responded by calling Chavez a communist threat, an easy way of whipping up domestic support.

The shop where I saw this contained little of material value other than the television. The woman who lived there had sliced up a melon to sell. I sat munching some while she told me how hard life was in Nicaragua, with so little to look forward to. These moments, stopping to talk to local people, are the essence of cycle travel. I should have pitied her for having so little. Instead she pitied me for having to cycle so far. It was beyond her comprehension that it was possible to cycle from Northern Mexico to her shop in Nicaragua. "You must be tired" she said. "That's why I'm resting here" I replied. I invariably want to sit down when I stop for refreshment.

The road climbed for twenty-two miles. It was a bit of a drag, and I sometimes walked for variety. At the top it was windy making the radio mast hum. The road joined the main Pan-American Highway, and there was a row of roadside cafés. I sat on a metal stool at one drinking a coca-cola, surrounded by boys waiting for something to happen. They weren't quite sure what to make of me. They looked at my bike but held back from asking me any questions. Unusual for Nicas.

I continued along the Pan-American, which followed the summit of a broad and airy ridge, resembling Pennine moor land. I felt strangely at home, expecting to see woolly sheep and cloth-capped Yorkshiremen at any moment. I could tell I was making progress in my journey. A high proportion of lorries had Costa Rica number plates, my next country after Nicaragua. I had crossed one side of my Central America map (Guatemala to Northern Nicaragua) and was now on the other side (Southern Nicaragua to Panama). Once I got to Panama, I would run out of Map.

The road drifted down to the pleasant town of Jinotepe, which had a huge statue of Pope John Paul II outside the church. When I asked the hotel receptionist why, she just said "Because it's a catholic church". Oh well, silly question I guess. The hotel was very large, but there were only a handful of people there. I asked for a west facing third floor room with a balcony, so I could enjoy watching the sunset over a beer. The hotel didn't stock beer, but the receptionist cheerfully directed me to a bar on the corner of the street. I knew it was a working men's bar the moment the lady behind the bar opened the fridge -

they only had litre bottles! So I had to take a giant litre bottle back to the hotel, hoping the receptionist wouldn't think I was an alcoholic. Fortunately, her head was buried in a newspaper. She didn't even notice me pop into the restaurant to 'borrow' a glass!

From Jinotepe a breezy twenty-six mile ride took me to Granada. Just before the city, going through deciduous woods, an iguana crossed the road in front of me. It was walking very slowly with an awkward gait, so I stopped for a look. It stopped and looked at me too, no doubt thinking my bike had an awkward gait. Then I met an ice-cream seller, his wares kept in a large cool box bolted to the front of his three-wheeled bike. I bought an ice-cream, and he told me he had cycled the six miles from Granada hoping to sell ice-creams to people on the road. I don't know what the profit margin was, but I was taken aback at the amount of effort he was prepared to go to in order to sell a few ice-creams. Needs must.

At the height of the simmering afternoon heat I entered Granada. Like León, it had no high rise flats or offices, only rambling old colonial style adobe houses. The Parque Central was well shaded with large trees, so it was relaxing to sit there for a while surveying the scene and deciding where to look for accommodation. The city felt different from León, maybe more upmarket, maybe a bit more American. I was falling into the Nicaraguan game of comparing the two cities. From the Parque Central, the Calle Calzada passes the cathedral and leads down to the shore of Lake Nicaragua. It is lined with a number of cafés and small hotels, so it seemed an ideal road to search for accommodation. I found a small family run hotel where

I took an upstairs room, which I could sit outside taking the air and watching the evening sun. The hotel also had a kitchen which residents could use and a well-stocked fridge full of beer at reception. It seemed perfect. I started to investigate the possibilities of visiting the island of Omotepe, in Lake Nicaragua.

᠅

Lake Nicaragua is the largest freshwater sea in the Americas after the Great Lakes. It is over a hundred miles long, and thirty-five miles wide. It has a reputation for rough water and high waves on account of the strong winds caused by the differences in temperature and climate between the Pacific and the Atlantic. Put simply, a lot of air moves from one side of the country to the other.

A ferry operates from the pier at Granada to the island of Omotepe. It is not a rapid ferry by any means. According to the schedule it leaves two afternoons a week, arriving in Omotepe the following day; the day after that it finally gets to San Carlos at the far end of the lake. From there it is possible to cross into Costa Rica. For a few days I got it into my head that I would take this route on my journey south.

However, my trips to the pier bore little fruit. The ferry service was interminably delayed. The guide books warn of turbulent seas making the passage slow, as the boat has to zigzag across the currents. It was reputed to be an ordeal. After several trips to the pier over the course of three days, I finally saw the boat. It was small, probably no bigger than Cal Mac's smallest Clyde Estuary boat. It had no more than two small passenger lounges, one on top of the other. The top one was first class, the lower one for the lower classes. There was an open deck for cargo. It was absurd to expect cabins with berths. It was running two days behind schedule, and some of the passengers who arrived on it seemed very relieved to be on terra firma again. I began to get second thoughts. There was actually little need for me to take this route as I could cycle round to the town of Rivas in a day, from where a shorter ferry route crossed over to the island. Plans to go on the lake were put on the back-burner for a while.

It was interesting to see the cargo being loaded onto the boat. A railway track had been laid along the pier, and there was a flat railway wagon on it. The cargo was loaded onto the wagon at the shore end of the pier, and then pushed all the way along the pier by two men. It was hard work and a sign of how cheap labour was. The passengers followed on foot. As I sat on the shore watching, a man came along the shoreline scavenging rubbish. He was carrying a couple of carrier bags full of flattened beer cans. He found a ball. Then he took off his shoes and socks and came over to chat to me. I saw that one of his socks had a giant hole from which his heel protruded.

"Is there much money in your country?" he asked.

"More than in this one." I replied.

"Are there cattle in your country?"

"Mainly sheep and deer. What were the Sandinista years like?"

"Bad. We had money, but there was nothing in the shops. The Sandinistas took most of the cattle."

That was a new one on me.

"Do you have Sandinistas in Scotland?"

"We have a socialist government. We have a free health system, and the government pays salaries to people over sixty-five."

The last piece of information stunned him into silence. There was still a lot to achieve in Nicaragua. The man continued on his way, after muttering that he was looking for some soap for a wash.

⚲

Feeling a bit uncertain about whether to leave Nicaragua by boat, or whether to continue south along the Panamericana, I settled into Granada for a few days. I had a good hotel room, sandwiched between two other rooms each occupied by a Canadian. To my right was Susan, a hemp farmer from Saskatchewan. Hemp can be planted, grown, and harvested in the space of six months, leaving the hemp farmer with spare time for the other six months of the year. Susan spent this time travelling, and was whiling winter away in the heat of Nicaragua. She knew where to get the best pizza in Granada, and wasted little time in taking me there.

Stephen, to my left, was a lecturer in Latin American history from Guelph. We quickly fell into discussions about various aspects of Latin American history as he was both well-travelled and well-read. I am the sort of person who knows a little bit about a lot of things, but am an expert in nothing. I enjoy the company of experts such as Stephen as I can learn from them free from the competitive pressure of two experts arguing.

We discussed the relative economic failure – or at least the poverty – of most of Latin America compared with Anglo-Saxon countries. Stephen attributed this largely to the Spanish colonial system of giving land to families who still, 500 years later, own it. They have little or no interest in improving the lives of their compatriots, so education is poor. The Spanish also used their colonies for plunder, to pay their debts and maintain an army, rather than invest to improve them and help them become self-sufficient.

Stephen had just been to the old convent, which is now an art museum. He recommended it, so the following morning I went along for a guided tour. It contains paintings, indigenous stone figures, and a display on the life of the poet Ruben Dario. My guide volunteered the information that things were better now than under the Sandinistas.

"Why?"

"Under the Sandinistas, all we had to eat was rice and beans. Now look at the range of foods in the shops."

What he said may be true for some people, especially here in slightly affluent Granada, but there are still many Nicas struggling on two dollars a day; eating nothing other than rice and beans. It was noticeable that the only supermarket in town was never really busy. Most people probably couldn't afford to shop there.

I needed to attend to some personal maintenance. I wanted another haircut, my first since Guatemala. I went into a barbers shop near the Parque Central and it was like stepping into a film set from the 1930's. A row of chairs faced a long wall covered in mirrors, and each was attended by a smart hairdresser in white jacket and well-pressed black trousers. At the far end a girl sat behind a small glass screen, where you went to pay afterwards.

What is there to say about a haircut? Well, as the hairdresser was about to finish, he pointed to a cut-throat razor and asked me if I wanted a shave. I hesitated. I have seen this done in cowboy films, but never had one myself. I dithered. Granada is in an earthquake zone, there was one due within the next two years. What would happen if the earth quaked as the barber was moving his blade swiftly across my throat?

I chickened out, I am ashamed to say, but at least I walked out of the shop with a trendy-looking Nicaraguan haircut.

When I got back to my hotel a man in his twenties on the pavement started talking to me. He had a wife and two children, and offered to give me a talk about the history of the city for twenty Córdobas. He had no tourist licence and was visibly poor; I had to admire him for

---

[7] You can now read it on the Internet at www.laprensa.com.ni

trying something. I gave him some money and forewent the historical tour.

The hot balmy evenings in Granada were ideal for wandering around the streets peeping into people's houses. Many left the doors wide open to maximise the benefit of drafts. The whole family would sit in a row on the wooden rocking chairs so typical of Nicaragua. Every house seemed to be furnished with them, they were lovely.

It was obvious to me that, fifteen years after the demise of the Sandinista government, the country was still much polarised on what they thought about their revolution. Everyone I spoke to was either for or against the Sandinistas. There was no middle ground. Each day in Granada I bought the newspaper "La Prensa", which is still owned and edited by the Chamorro family.[7] Every day, the editorial mentioned the Sandinistas. The usual train of thought was to mention something Hugo Chavez had done in Venezuela, mention his links with Fidel Castro, then mention Daniel Ortega, and then say how chaotic the world would be under a bunch of communists. Nicaragua should be saved from all of that. And so it went on, day after day. One morning the editorial lambasted a plan by the Mayor of Managua – a Sandinista – to erect a statue of Rigoberto López Perez to celebrate the fiftieth anniversary of his assassination of Anastasio Somoza. The editorial pointed out that Nicaragua is much divided. There are still people who remember the Somozas fondly. Is it appropriate to put a statue of López Perez in the capital amongst those of poets and great men like Bolívar? He wasn't even from Managua, the writer complained. Comparison was made with Costa Rica, where such things wouldn't happen. The writer concluded that Nicaragua should "move on". I reflected that in Costa Rica they have never needed to assassinate dictators.

⚲

Twelve miles from Granada is a volcanic crater lake called Laguna de Apoyo. I heard there was a hostel by the side of it invitingly called the Monkey Hut so I decided to cycle there for a night. The first few miles took me along the main dual-carriageway to Managua. It was a new experience cycling along a dual carriageway. There was little traffic apart from old American school busses labouring up the hills in the last gasp of their life. The turning to Laguna de Apoyo was not signposted and easy to miss. I encountered another ice-cream cycle, the man having pedalled out from Masaya with his box full of ice creams. His bike didn't have any gears, but for him it was a normal day's work to slowly pedal up and down the hills on this road, hoping to make a few pennies selling ice-creams. He was pedalling against time in the heat too, as the one I bought was getting soft.

Cycling up the crater rim was a long, uphill slog. The top yielded a view of a perfectly circular disc of blue, the sun sending silvery shimmers across the surface. Going down into the crater I was startled by a screaming sound. Howler monkeys. Distinctive to hear, but almost impossible to see. I stopped and scanned the thick trees for ages, but didn't get a glimpse of them. I could tell they were looking at me though, from the howling noise they were emitting.

The hostel was an alpine building set in its own grounds, with a resident warden called Toby. He was leaving at the end of the month, and a notice at reception advertised his job. Toby wanted to move to León, where there are bookshops. There were none in Granada. I think he had hit the nail on the head in respect of comparing the two cities – León had culture, whereas Granada did not. I contemplated applying for his job, but my target of getting to Panama was more appealing. Maybe like Toby I didn't find Granada thrilling enough, so I set off from the Monkey Hut the following day intending to bypass the city and head straight for Rivas, some way along the Pan American Highway.

Cycling through some woods I met a bit of pandemonium at the side of the road. A group of boys were getting excited about something up a tree, and they were attacking it with catapults and anything else they could lay their hands on. Stopping to watch, I saw a terrified animal like a giant squirrel jumping from branch to branch at the top of the tree. I asked them what they were aiming to do. They wanted to kill it so they could eat it. Talking to me was distracting them a bit, and I hoped this might enable the unfortunate animal to escape. In a poor country it really wasn't my place to be judgemental about their plans so I pedalled on, thinking about some men who had earlier told me they ate turtle eggs. They could tell I didn't approve, but "mind your own business" was written over their faces. It's fine to have principles about what we eat when we can go to a supermarket and buy anything we want. In Britain choosing to be vegetarian can be an affluent indulgence. In Nicaragua, killing a wild animal to eat is a virtual necessity for some people.

The scenery I went through was flat and fertile. The fertility varied according to the irrigation. At one place, there was rice growing in wet fields on one side of the road, yet the ground on the other side was parched brown. I couldn't quite understand it. Perhaps it was one land for the rich, one land for the poor. There was a steady wind all day, either in my face or to my left side. Psychologically it made me keep going, as I was afraid to stop and lose time. Just before Rivas a man driving a 4x4 stopped in front of me, and told me he was a keen cyclist too. He asked me a lot about my journey, and recommended a small family run hotel in Rivas called the Hospedaje Lidia.

I liked Rivas immediately. The Parque Central was a hive of activity, with a pizza restaurant on one corner where you could sit outside on the pavement watching the town go by as you waited for your pizza to arrive. The town had a warren of fascinating streets where just about anything could be bought. The Hospedaje Lidia was easy to find, and the friendly ladies who ran it sat in rocking chairs in a front room through which you had to pass to get in. I was given a very basic room which had all I wanted – a bed, and told to wheel my bike round to the gate at the back so they could let me in. The communal showers were very clean. Lying on my bed in my clean, showered state, I heard American voices coming from the room next door.

They belonged to Marcus and Ben, two young Californians who both had black moustaches. They were travelling together through the Americas, using a combination of busses and short flights, and ultimately heading for Argentina. Well, where else is there to go once you decide to see the Americas? We went for a beer at a bar across the road, where the waiter was a pest as he kept coming over to practice his English.

Rivas is a lively place because ferries cross from there to Omotepe, and I had revived my plan to spend a few days on the island, and then catch the other ferry to San Carlos, gateway to Costa Rica. Marcus and Ben were going that way the next day, and I decided to go too. In the morning, after a sturdy breakfast at the *hospedaje*, they took a taxi to the pier, about three kilometres out of town. I followed by bike. When I arrived there were a lot of people milling about, but no ferry. It was cancelled because of the high winds. It hadn't run for three days. Notwithstanding this, a rather sanguine policeman said it was worth waiting around as they might decide to operate the ferry later. Marcus popped out of a café like a cuckoo out of a clock to tell me they were waiting to see what happened. They had giant back-packs and were somewhat marooned there as a result. Anchored to the spot may be a better description. I went for a walk along the beach while I decided what to do next.

Nursing a coffee in a café overlooking the choppy lake and Omotepe, I came to the conclusion that I didn't want to hang around. The wind was still strong; there was no telling how many more days it could be like this. The excitement of possibly entering Costa Rica by way of San Carlos waned a little when I realised that it was mentioned in all the guide books and as a result everyone was going that way. There had been little traffic on the Pan American, and it had a good hard shoulder which I could nip onto when big lorries came by. I decided to be unconventional and enter Costa Rica on the main road.

First, I wanted to see a place called San Juan del Sur.

☹

From Rivas a well maintained road leaves the Pan American and heads down to the Pacific coast. At the end of it is a charming bay with a large beach, surrounded by hills and rocks. At the side of this bay sits San Juan del Sur.

San Juan del Sur has long been known to North Americans. Before the construction of a canal, land passage across Nicaragua was a favoured route between the two coasts of the United States. The arrival point on the Caribbean side was San Juan del Norte, a small port at the mouth of the San Juan River. From here, boats could navigate upstream to San Carlos on Lake Nicaragua. Crossing the lake, all that was then needed was a twelve mile land-hop to San Juan del Sur, on the Pacific coast. The route was busy in the nineteenth century, establishing San Juan del Sur in the minds of the United States.

Since the demise of the Sandinista government in 1990, Nicaragua has become more acceptable in the minds of Americans. It is a safe country, probably the safest in Central America. It is cheaper than neighbouring Costa Rica, long a favourite destination for retiring Americans. San Juan del Sur is slowly beginning to exploit these factors. Many Americans now live here, and American run businesses have sprung up to serve their needs. The most notable are estate agents – or real estate as they call it.

I arrived in the town expecting to see expensive condominiums and large flash cars. It quickly became evident to me that most of the people retiring here would struggle to afford to live in the United States. Falling share income, plus spectacular crashes like Enron, has left a number of Americans with pensions that are very small. Such people can live well in Nicaragua. The town has a bit of a Wild West feel about it.

There is a range of hotels to choose from. I ignored one which advertised in English "Southern Hospitality", whatever that meant; I took a bright and breezy room on the top floor of the Hostal Elizabeth instead. The owner – Elizabeth - made me a cup of real coffee which I sat drinking on the veranda at the front, next to the pavement. The veranda became a favourite place for watching some of the slightly eccentric Americans go by. Some of them struggle to speak Spanish, even after living there for some years. An elderly couple had been living in the hotel for several years. They were beginning to have health problems, but couldn't afford treatment and were now detached from health resources. It seemed a sad way to end up.

A Canadian earned a living by building sceptic tanks. He knew all about the design, construction, and maintenance of them. He told me everything he knew, and showed me his photograph album of recent projects. He bored me in ten minutes. He had already bored the pants off other residents at the hotel, who relished the nick-name I coined for him - The Shit Expert.

Some of the Americans I spoke to were disillusioned about their own country. Gerry from California told me flatly that he thought Bush and the rest of the establishment had lied and cheated their way into power, by rigging the voting and counting systems. Being more explicit, he explained that the company which made the machines that counted the votes supported the Republican Party, and had rigged the machines to mis-count votes in the Republicans' favour.

Another man, Warren, told me that he was a member of the Republican Party even though he wasn't a Republican. "Why?" I asked. "Because the local county is controlled by the Republicans. If I want something done, or complain about something, they look at the list of party members. They only act on your behalf if you are a member."

I spent two days listening to and watching all this, at the same time keeping an eye on the weather to see if the wind abated. The first night I didn't sleep much. I lay in bed listening to the tin roof rattling in the strong wind, glad that I had not gone to Omotepe. In the morning Elizabeth told me this was the windiest time of the year. I decided that if the wind hadn't abated by Thursday, I would give it a miss. I had already received an email from Marcus saying they had abandoned their trip to Omotepe.

One afternoon I went for a bike ride to a small beach a few miles up the coast. It was good to be pedalling along amongst country people again. I stopped at a remote shack with beer posters on the wall. Two teenage girls inside were pleased to have my company for fifteen minutes while I drank the coldest Pepsi I have ever had. A cockerel wandered about the earth floor as if it owned the place.

Further on, I found a track that led down to a small village by a beach. After a swim I went to a *pulperia* for a drink. They only had warm beer, which was still better than nothing. I sat outside between two groups of teenagers. One group was doing their homework. They were having an animated discussion about a planning exercise, involving furniture and equipment. They were well-dressed; all had bikes, and obviously middle class. The other group was less well off. Ordinary Nicas. They sat there looking on in silence. I was in between the two groups. In front of me cattle and horses were forlornly grazing the bone-dry road. A calf was energetically suckling its mother, getting a bit more luck. This, I thought, was idyllic. Rural Nicaragua, the perfect place to chill out.

On the way back to San Juan, I passed a field that had been marked out into plots for sale. A notice in English gave details, including the availability of title insurance. When I got back to the town, I went into an estate agent to ask about this concept. Under the Sandinistas, some land was appropriated from its owners for redistribution. There are now some properties with two titles, and the insurance is simply a legal opinion on whether the pre-revolution title holder still has any valid claim on the land. It sounded a bit dodgy to me.

San Juan del Sur is certainly fascinating. I wish its residents well.

I went back to Rivas for another night. The Hospedaje Lidia was full, so I stayed somewhere else on the main road. Some Americans arrived shortly after me, from Omotepe. They had been stranded there for several days because there were no boats, and the crossing they finally made was still very rough. That nailed my decision to forgo a trip to Omotepe and head off down the Pan American to Costa Rica. We were on the first floor of the hotel, where the rooms all had their own toilet and shower. Nicas stayed on the ground floor, in cheaper rooms with shared facilities. Economic apartheid. I sat outside my room for a while watching the night sky. One of the Americans opened the door to put his shoes out to air. He seemed to have second thoughts. "Do you trust these people?" he asked me, thrusting his head in the direction of the Nicas downstairs. "What, because they're black?" I asked. "Of course I do." Attitude apartheid.

In the morning I bought my last copy of La Prensa. True to form there was an editorial about Ortega's proposal to tax oil company profits. Then came the predictable chain – Marx, Lenin, Cuba, Chavez, and the Sandinistas. The inferred conclusion seemed to be that rich people shouldn't pay tax. If that meant poor people remained poor, that was their problem, not rich people's problem. Yes indeed.

Riding towards the frontier I passed a fading sign that read *"Obras, no palabras. Arnaldo Alemán."* Works, not words. It was a claim by Alemán, president from 1996 to 2001. I reflected that it should perhaps have read "Money, not works." Alemán was a right-wing Somoza supporter who was elected after Violeta Chamorro's post-revolutionary government. Some saw this as the country finally turning its back on the Sandinistas. However, Alemán has subsequently been discredited with much corruption, and at the time of my visit was awaiting charges. His successor, Bolaños, tried to root out this return to corruption. After all they had suffered, Nicaraguans deserve better than a slide back into the ways of corruption.

A few miles from the frontier, I stopped at a shop. The owner wasted little time in telling me he didn't like the Sandinistas. They were dangerous and dictatorial he said. Ortega was no better than Somoza had been. Bringing me a Coca-cola, he fretted about recent strikes – busses in Managua and doctors had been on strike. People weren't earning enough to live on, and this would help the Sandinistas, and Ortega in particular, win the forthcoming elections in November 2006. He said this would be bad for Nicaragua as it would wreck relationships with the United States. That old fear of the United States, controlling much thought in Central America, was depressing. Suddenly, I wanted to go to Costa Rica.

In the event, Ortega won the November 2006 presidential election, with 38.59% of the vote. The Nicaraguan Liberal Alliance candidate, Eduardo Montealegre came second with 30.94 %. Montealegre had been part of the previous government under Bolaños, and was supported by the United States.

Ortega now imports oil from Venezuela and has aligned himself with Hugo Chavez in Latin American affairs. La Prensa continues to criticise him on any almost daily basis. The United States watches with concern, although of course is more pre-occupied with its own troubles over Iraq.

Nicaragua remains polarised. I was in the country for a month, and I did not meet anyone who sat on the fence. There are no fences in Nicaragua. In spite of all that, it is a wonderful country with tremendously warm and proud people. A country worth visiting and a country worth watching. They have a sense of humour too, best illustrated by quoting a notice on the door of a bank in Granada:-

"It is forbidden to enter the bank carrying guns." Bank robbers beware!

CHAPTER THIRTEEN

COSTA RICA

"Costa Rica is considered unique in Central America; prosperity has made it dull, but this is surely preferable to the excitements and urgencies of poverty."

This was Paul Theroux's view in "The Old Patagonia Express". His journey through the Americas in the 1970's was mainly by train. Half a century of no wars, no army, and little political strife has made Costa Rica unique in Central America. It still has trains too. I was curious to see for myself how different it was.

Arriving in the town of Liberia I could immediately write a list of things that were different in Costa Rica. It wasn't just the American voices in the streets, the shops quoting prices in US dollars, or the spat-out chewing gum marking the pavements. People looked more affluent. They were better dressed; women wore make-up and jewellery. What traffic there was tended to be small cars rather than *camionetas*. The middle class were apparent in this country.

I stayed in a backpackers' hostel, which may have been a mistake as my ears were quickly assailed by the sounds of travellers complaining at how expensive Costa Rica was compared with other Central American states. This really was a bit rich coming from people from affluent countries who seemed to feel that cheap travel was a god given right, rather than an unfortunate side effect of the world economic system. I retreated to my room for a while to escape.

The hostel organised excursions up the local volcano, Volcan Rincon de la Vieja. I made a reservation for the following day's trip, which included transport, maps, and a guide if we wanted one. We had to be up early to catch the best time for getting clear views, and sure enough a minibus was waiting outside at seven o'clock. The minibus took a rough lane up to the National Park centre. I noticed it was covered in loose stones, and sat there scrutinising it with a cyclist's eye, glad that I was in a vehicle.

At the National park office we were given a brief talk about the routes we could take. The ranger said it was too windy to go to the summit. A young Costa Rican with the unlikely name of Sven wanted to try for the summit anyway, and feeling adventurous I joined him. We set off through the thick forest pausing now and again to look at trees with interesting shapes. As we were looking at one which was impressively thick, it made an almighty creaking noise. We looked at each other, then without saying a word we belted away from it as fast as we could. We both thought it was going to fall in the wind. Once we were safely away it was us who fell about – laughing!

Climbing further we emerged from the forest into the wind. The path divided and Sven suggested taking the right hand fork as he had been there before and knew it was a good route. What he didn't mention was that the path was steep and exposed. I got nervous and wanted to turn back. I didn't want to jeopardise my aim of cycling to Panama by risking a fall in the mountains.

I said goodbye to Sven and went back to the junction to take the other path thinking it would be better. I got no further than a hundred yards when I was blown right off my feet by a blast of fresh air. I clung to a rock for dear life, knowing in an instant that I was going no further. The clouds parted and I saw the summit. I caught a glimpse of Sven striding along the ridge; maybe like Jesus he had created a miracle and stopped the hurricane in its tracks.

I picked my way back down through the forest, passing the creaking tree which was still standing. When I reached the visitor centre some of the other day trippers were resting on a lawn. The ranger came over to see how I was.

"I expect you're a bit tired" he said.

"No, today's my rest day."

Leaving Liberia the wind was behind me, and I relished such unusual luxury. I was away from the Pan Americana, on a road leading south-westwards into the peninsula of Nicoya. I passed the new International Airport which was rapidly acquiring all the accoutrements that go with international travel. Souvenir shops, car hire depots, smart restaurants and advert hoardings lined the road for at least a mile. I felt a bit out of place, having cycled there from half a continent away. It was a far world from Nicaragua, still fresh in my mind.

Nicoya is separated from the mainland by the Gulf of Nicoya. It was once part of Nicaragua until a referendum in 1824, shortly after independence, saw the people decide to switch to Costa Rica. There are popular beach resorts on the peninsula, but I steered a course through the middle, away from the crowds. I was treated to a rural journey through quiet villages and tranquil dairy pasture in valleys as flat as a pancake, but always with hills in the background. Occasionally the road would rise, giving good views of the Gulf of Nicoya. The town of Nicoya had a cool, shaded Parque Central – an excellent place for a long cool ice cream. After Nicoya a road peels off to the left, crossing back to the mainland by a bridge. Most traffic went this way, but I continued straight on down the peninsula. The road was quiet and there were an amazing number of pot-holes that didn't square with Costa Rican affluence.

A small turning was signposted to Puerto Jesus, three kilometres away. Intrigued by the name, I took a detour to see what it was like. The dirt road led to a very small village with a large school, and continued another kilometre to expire on a river bank. The river was almost dry and small boats were marooned on the mud, looking old and abandoned. A fisherman was cleaning his boat. I asked him if there was ever water in the river. "At 4 pm" he said, "when the tide comes in." He added that until the bridge was built 40 years ago, this had been the main route to the peninsular from San Jose – going via Puntarenas and then taking the ferry – God willing – to Puerto Jesus. At that time there were lodging houses in Puerto Jesus but now all that remained was peeling paint on tired timber. The fisherman said there was a hotel in the next town, Carmona, with a swimming pool. That sounded like a good idea, so off I went.

I passed a family sitting beside the road selling giant water melons. They tempted me to stop, but I couldn't eat a whole one, so the young daughter fetched a knife to halve the melon. Her father cut my half into small segments, and I found a shady spot under a tree to enjoy my feast. That's what I call a lunch.

On the outskirts of Carmona I saw the hotel the fisherman had described. I couldn't miss it really; there was a large swimming pool at the front with a chute dominating the view. The rooms were in small blocks set well back from the road. There was a bar behind the pool. I liked the surroundings and checked in for two nights.

Carmona was a bit run-down, with a very overgrown Parque Central. A woman in a café next to it showed me a track that led to the peak of Cerro Azul. The hills behind the town looked appealing so I followed it, occasionally having to pick my way through long grass and weeds. In a high village called Bella Vista I bought a much needed drink at a small *pulperia*. From there it was a short hop to the summit of Cerro Azul, covered in radio masts and surrounded by fencing. I squeezed through a hole in the fence, stealing panoramic views of the gulf, the green speckled islands in it, and the distant town of Puntarenas. The effort of getting up there had been worthwhile.

On the way down, passing through a small wood, I caught a glimpse of something black flying from one branch to another. I paused. Another flash of black. Then there were several. It was a group of monkeys, making their way with silky precision from branch to branch, tree to tree, going down the side of the hill. Their route took them across the road and I stood spellbound for ten minutes or so, watching their spectacular trapeze act. It was impressive how they used their tails for grip and balance.

Wandering down I pondered why I had been having negative opinions of Ticos, as Costa Ricans like to be called. In other countries I had been amongst people who didn't have very much, and were genuinely interested in the foreigner. Ticos had more. They also had a different attitude. I felt they were always on the lookout to rip you off or overcharge for something, such as restaurants that don't tell you the prices exclude tax or compulsory tips, or the internet café that tried to charge me for an hour instead of half an hour. I felt constantly under siege from people who didn't come over as being particularly friendly. When you think you are under siege, it affects your own attitude.

I got back to the hotel just in time to see Barcelona −v− Chelsea on the television behind the bar. When it finished I went up to my room. The couple next door were having beer on the veranda, and they gave me a bottle. A well timed gift after my negative thoughts about Ticos! We discussed the state of the roads and they were baffled by the mystery of where all the car tax revenues went.

Road surfaces were a controversial point in Costa Rica. It is the most affluent Central American state, and its citizens pay relatively high taxes. Why then, they ask, do we have to suffer such abysmally poor road surfaces? Where does all the money go? I wondered this too, and soon learnt that a good way to wind up Ticos is to point out that road surfaces in Nicaragua are considerably better. They tend to look down their noses at Nicaraguans, many of whom work in their country to earn higher wages than they could at home.

Another early morning swim. Yellow breasted jays hovered over the pool before diving in for a dip. It was idyllic but I wanted to move on. Passing through striking scenery I caught glimpses of the top of Cerro Azul. The road surface got worse. In places it disappeared completely, leaving me to bump along on stones and gravel. By now it was a dead end road, going only as far as the ferry pier at Playa Naranjo and a handful of small villages beyond. My goal was to take the ferry over the sea to Puntarenas.

Needing a break from the road surface, I stopped for lunch in Tepanto at a small open air restaurant surrounded by vibrantly flowering bushes, the sounds of birds making a welcoming backdrop. A pair of friendly van drivers sat at the next table. I was slowly warming to Ticos. They lack the spontaneous open-ness of Nicaraguans, but comparing the two was pointless, like trying to compare the French with the Spanish. They are different. The bill for my sumptuous meal was less than four pounds, hardly expensive.

On a full stomach progress was slow. Playa Naranjo was always round yet another bend. I passed a hotel. Then a second. After the third I arrived at the pier. That was it. Playa Naranjo is three hotels, a ferry pier, a bar and a filling station. Next to the pier is a small pebbly beach, on which a couple of small boats were aground. The village has no shop. What I have just told you about Playa Naranjo is far more than you will glean from a guide book, so cherish it! The hotel furthest from the pier was the cheapest and the best, having a swimming pool with little yellow birds constantly skimming the surface for insects. The rooms had no television or air-conditioning; a blessing as there was no noise to disturb me, except that I was woken up during the night by the couple in the next room having sex.

The ferry left at two o'clock in the afternoon. The hotel owners said I could stay in the hotel until then, so I spent the morning beside the hotel swimming pool. It was paradise. Yellow birds were continually flying around the pool, catching insects or skimming water. I noticed a bird with a plume and a bright red chest – a *carpintero* – making a nest in a hole in a dead tree. For hours the bird pecked out dead wood to make the hole gradually bigger. It took me a while to work out there were actually two *carpintero*s sharing the work, each taking a turn at enlarging the hole while the other flew around looking for food. When a bird of prey, such as a *pilote*, came overhead they hid behind the tree – the instinct for survival. My presence didn't seem to bother them.

Costa Rica is famous throughout the world for its population and variety of birds. There are said to be over 800 species of birds in the country, and the varieties I saw presented a rich tapestry of colour.

At mid-day the ferry arrived and I went down to the pier. I watched the manoeuvres to squeeze the vans and lorries onto the ferry to maximise the number that could be carried. In spite of that four were left behind. My bike was chained to a lifebelt locker leaving me free to wander around the ship. Grey skies and picturesque scenery made me think I was crossing to one of the familiar Scottish islands. The pier at Puntarenas had a row of shops eagerly expecting our custom after the deprivations of rural Nicoya. After plundering the bakers shop I set off to find lodgings.

Puntarenas is built on a sandy isthmus defiantly sticking out into the Gulf of Nicoya. It is a holiday resort, fishing town and ferry port rolled into one; a cross between Scarborough and Oban. Unlike Scarborough, it faces west so gives the visitor glorious sunsets. Many of the buildings are made of timber and a lot hadn't been painted for years, adding to the charm. I found a room in an old hotel across the road from the beach. The entire building was made of wood, dried out by years of sunshine. The concept of fire escapes hadn't been invented when it was built. If it went up in smoke, so would all the happy residents. Roast holidaymaker with chips; one of the hazards of world travel.

I spent two nights there so I could have a day on the beach. It was the weekend, an ideal time to watch Ticos enjoying themselves en masse.

I was still noticing people doing things I hadn't seen in other countries. Ticos read newspapers, gel their hair, and wear sunglasses. They use mobile phones, and many are overweight. Cafés have ride machines to amuse children. Spare coins jangle in their pockets. There were no street children making me feel guilty and nobody pestered me to buy artisan crafts or have my boots cleaned. I felt unwanted all of a sudden.

I had another reason to be in Puntarenas. On Sunday afternoon there was a train to San Jose, and I wanted to ride on it. I had managed to book a ticket on the Internet. Furthermore, the operators had agreed to make special arrangements for my bike. When I got on the train, I was to ask for Johnny.

The train service has recently been restored after an absence of over fifteen years, in a fit of environmental concern by the Costa Rican government. The main service is a commuter line in San Jose. On Sundays one of the trains makes the return trip down to Puntarenas for the benefit of day trippers. For many Costa Ricans it is a novelty to ride the train, and the service is popular.

Puntarenas station is a bit of a trek out of town. I found the train before I found the station. It was parked in a siding near a factory, having arrived from San Jose some time before. They have resumed the services on the cheap by taking the old rolling stock out of the sidings in which it had been gathering cobwebs since 1990. The coaches were built in Japan in 1960. They were very basic, with hard seats. The locomotive had been built in Chicago.

A young man of about twenty was dashing about the carriages sorting things out for the return journey. He was stripped to the waist, showing off his pectorals to two female train attendants who sat lapping up the attention. This was Johnny and he was in charge of entertainment.

Johnny was impressed with my journey and took some photos of me, commenting that I must have a good body after all the cycling. Hmmm, I wasn't so sure. He stowed my bike in the caboose and took me to a seat reserved for me in the front carriage, near the engine. The train squeaked its way forward into the station. Some buses arrived from Puntarenas beach, disgorging their laughing passengers into the train.

After a lot of whistling for scurrying latecomers we noisily pulled out. People watched from the doorways of their homes. I opened the window and leaned out for a better look. The occupants of the small wooden houses were looking at the train, and at my head leaning out of the window looking at them. I felt like Paul Theroux.

After an hour we arrived in Orotina. The train went along the centre of the main street and stopped next to the Parque Central, causing a certain amount of chaos to road traffic. We were bombarded with people selling fruit, nuts, and drinks. Passengers assembled feasts and gorged themselves.

When we left Orotina it was almost dark; the cue for Johnny to start the entertainment. He appeared dressed in drag, feathers protruding from unlikely parts of his body. He had a megaphone and to my horror used this to amplify his dreadful singing. The Ticos loved it. I sat there wincing, hoping he couldn't see the awful look on my face after his kindness with my bike. To say he was an extrovert would be the understatement of the century. I was dreading that he would pounce on me and tell everyone through the megaphone about my bike ride. I shrank as small as I could and concentrated on peering at the darkness beyond the window.

He stopped singing and started a quiz. Thank god for that, I was saved from humiliation. By now the train was winding its way tortuously through mountains so I kept my face glued to the window looking at the dark shadowy views. I opened the window to get a closer look at the looming mountain silhouettes on the other side of the valley. The train picked its way along a narrow hillside ridge, clinging on for dear life.

Approaching the city, the other passengers gave Johnny a huge round of applause. A stewardess told me to shut the window as we were going through some rough suburbs where children threw things at the train. Surviving that, we arrived in the majestically decaying station in San Jose and Johnny reappeared dressed in civvies to tell me I could collect my bike from the caboose.

The crowds melted away from the station leaving me and my bike alone in a strange, dark city. It was the first capital city I had visited since starting my ride six months earlier. I felt uneasy in the gloom. I had a hostel reservation but wasn't sure where the hostel was, so I began to flag down passing taxis. The first two refused to take a bike. The third agreed, provided I removed the front wheel and all the bags. I sat in the front with the driver who was very amiable.

He dropped me at my hostel, the front door to which was up a flight of steps. I couldn't carry the bike and all my bags in one go, so I went up to reception carrying what I could, leaving the rest on the pavement. At reception there was a bit of confusion over my booking which distracted me. Remembering my remaining bags I dashed downstairs to see the red taxi disappearing round the corner. One of my bags was missing. I counted again to double-check. No, there was definitely one missing. A man walking his dog asked me if I was looking for a black bag.

"Yes, have you seen it?"

"The taxi driver put it in his boot and drove off."

"Did you get his number?"

"No."

"Thank you."

It was one of my panniers, containing all my spare clothes, my toiletries, the tent, a spare tyre, and – tragedy – my films. In an act of mad carelessness I had no clothes other than those I was standing in; worse, all the photographs I had taken since leaving Creel were lost. This was the lowest low point I could possibly imagine. A trough. A depression as deep as the Atlantic. I felt angry and despairing. I wanted to go home.

The lady who ran the hostel gave me some soap and toothpaste and put me in the best room they had. Acts of kindness help smooth ripples. The ripples, though, were giant waves of emotion. I had been through so many poor countries, travelling amongst people who had nothing, not even shoes to wear. I had been robbed in the richest country in Central America by a man wealthy enough to run a taxi. If he had been the poorest man in Nicaragua I wouldn't have felt so bad. What annoyed me most was that he had no need for my worn clothes and rolls of exposed film. It was so pointless.

Worst of all, I began to hate Costa Rica.

This was a real test of my principles. Normally I do not use the word "hate". I think it is negative, destructive, and the start of a chain that can lead to extremes. Hitler encouraged people to hate the Jews. Extreme political forces encourage people to hate others because of their race or colour. In Northern Ireland powerful people nurtured mutual hatred between Protestants and Catholics leading to thirty years of mindless and meaningless bloodshed. I don't let myself hate anyone or anything. It achieves nothing. Life is too short for that.

I had to manage my emotions. I reasoned with myself that I couldn't blame a whole country for one stupid greedy taxi driver. I could be robbed anywhere, even in my home town. Rationally, I knew I had no reason to hate Costa Rica, but my head needed to convince my heart. I was annoyed with myself too for deviating from my coastal route by my silly desire to ride on a train.

However, the train ride wasn't my only reason for being in San Jose. The following morning I had an appointment to meet Jac.

⚲

Several years ago I did Spanish classes at the Centro Lorca Español in Glasgow, with the intention of learning Spanish for my fanciful dream of cycling through Central America. Jac was in the same class and during a coffee break she said she had a house in San Jose which I would be welcome to visit if I were ever there. She was planning to move there for her work as an artist. At the time I had no concrete plans, but we maintained contact.

As I pedalled my way southwards from Mexico, I emailed Jac to report on my progress. She encouraged me on my way. Gradually I began to realise that the prospect of having a coffee with someone I already knew was another good a reason to detour to San Jose. I hadn't seen anyone I knew for almost six months.

Jac met me at my hostel and took me to a café she frequented that served astonishingly perfect coffee and had an alluring range of unhealthy, fattening cakes. When we sat down I blurted out my story of the missing bag. Well, I had to explain why I was still wearing yesterday's clothes! You always think it's obvious when you wear the same shirt as the day before, like when you unexpectedly go directly to work from a place other than home.

Jac was sympathetic and understanding. She gave me advice about where to go to buy socks, underwear and t-shirts. We arranged to meet again, after my enforced shopping trip. I had a social life once again and I was beginning to cheer up.

The streets of San Jose were lively with a wide range of shops. You could buy anything imaginable. The trouble was, I didn't see any clothes I particularly liked, and resented having to buy some through need. Collecting my thoughts over a coffee at one of the popular stand-up cafés, it dawned on me that I also needed a new pannier to replace the stolen one as I couldn't cram everything in the one I had left. Shopping was more complicated than I had bargained for. I had to go back to the hostel to research where the bike shops were.

The next day I visited four bike shops and heard the same story. No-one buys panniers in Costa Rica because they are too expensive and, anyway, Ticos don't go touring by bike. This shouldn't have surprised me as I hadn't seen any touring cyclists anywhere in Central America apart from Europeans. I was downhearted.

I contemplated buying a small rucksack and devising a way of fixing that to my carrier. Then I met Jac again and had an Idea.

Her husband, Alan, was in Glasgow and would be flying to Costa Rica the following week. Would he, I wondered, be able to go into a bike shop in Glasgow, buy a pannier, and bring it with him on the flight? I sounded out Jac and she agreed to ask Alan. To my delight he saw Operation Pannier as a challenge he simply couldn't resist, and almost by return of email confirmed that he had been to a shop in the West End and bought me two panniers. Yes, two. Panniers come in pairs of course. I was as chuffed as a dog with two tails. All I had to do was for Alan to arrive.

In my enforced wait I grew to like San Jose. It was pleasant to sit in the sun outside the Theatre Nacional. One afternoon while I was there a young man, Jose Carlos, approached me and asked if I would check his English homework. He had written a well argued article about illegal fishing. I gave him an impromptu English lesson for an hour, and we met again the following day. He wanted to go to the United States to work in medicine, but the possibility was slim now because of visa restrictions. We discussed other possibilities such as Canada and even Cuba. He had a positive view of Costa Rica – the mountains, the wildlife and the beaches. I felt he would be happier staying there.

One day I tried cycling to the crater of Volcan Irazú. The volcano lies to the north of Cartago, about thirty miles from San Jose, and rises to the dizzy height of 3,432 metres above sea level. It last erupted in 1963. According to one guide book, the journey is "almost entirely uphill". I'm glad they warned me, I wouldn't have known!

I didn't make it. I struggled uphill for twenty-three miles, stopping more and more frequently to rest. Stops became longer than cycling interludes. I accepted defeat just below the cloud line, and freewheeled down again to a restaurant called the Mirador de Ganado – The View of Cattle – for a well earned beer.

In spite of of the restaurant's rather specific name there were no cattle to be seen anywhere. There were no customers to be seen either, apart from me, and the slightly bored waiter hovered around making conversation. He liked Costa Rica because "we have freedom". He liked the President, but couldn't say why. He liked the CAFTA agreement as it would allow Costa Rica to export goods to the United States. He had a rosy view of life, which clearly wasn't going to be cluttered up with cattle.

When I got back to San Jose Jac suggested going to the pictures. There was a multiplex cinema on the outskirts of town and she conjured up a programme from the depths of the local paper. One of the films was Brokeback Mountain, a story about two cowboys in Wyoming who start a homosexual relationship while stuck on a mountainside all summer long watching cattle. This would make up for my disappointment at not seeing any cows at the View of Cattle Restaurant, so we agreed to go and see it. Jac phoned for a taxi while I tried to make myself look presentable with my limited wardrobe. I hadn't been to the cinema for months and I was excited.

The Costa Rican audience was excited too. A deeply conservative country, the idea of homosexuality was a boundary-pusher for many. The two cowboys touch for the first time. Giggles. They get together in bed for the first time. Gasps. The wife of one of them catches them kissing. More giggles. I found these reactions startling. The storyline is very moving – love, intolerance, screwed up lives - yet many in the audience could only see it as something to chuckle over. The forces of conservatism were hard at work, making fun of the consequences of being slightly different from whatever is "normal".

🚲

I still wanted to see the deep azure lake in the crater of Volcan Irazú. Jac suggested I went on the daily bus the municipal transport company operates. It isn't aimed at tourists; it stops in all the villages on the way, going as far as the crater because it happens to be at the end of the road.

It chugged its way slowly up the road I had toiled on with my bike the day before. Past the Mirador de Ganado where there were still no cattle. Past the point where I had expired in exhaustion. Not, however, past the National Park ticket office. The bus stopped as I had to buy an admission ticket. There was a price list on a wooden board above the door.

Costa Ricans 500 Colones

Foreigners 3,500 Colones.

Five hundred Colones is about a dollar. Reading the sign almost gave me a colonic irrigation on the spot. I was staggered. In Nicaraguan museums I had occasionally been asked to pay 50% more or maybe even double, recognising the abundant wealth of a rich foreigner. A factor of seven was totally outrageous. Having got so far I wasn't inclined to turn back, and they knew that. I was cornered and conned in one fell swoop. I paid up and got back on the bus, feeling a tad indisposed towards the Costa Rican government, who were responsible for this little bit of Market Pricing. I felt it was giving a message to Ticos that it was OK to overcharge foreigners.

At the crater rim it was cloudy, not a view in sight, not even of stray cattle. I went to the café and enjoyed one of the tastiest coffees I have ever had. One thing I will say about Ticos – they certainly know how to make coffee. The clouds lifted and I traipsed back to the rim. A great circular stadium of nature lay in front of me. Rock, ash, water, trees. Grey, blue, black, green. A stone tumbled down the slope and splashed into the lake. I could see nothing man-made, apart from the wooden fence holding me back.

Before long it was time to go back. The bus made its way down through the villages to Cartago from where we took the motorway back to San Jose. When I returned to the hostel I learnt that Alan had arrived from Glasgow and I could collect my new panniers the following day. Yippee!

☿

Collecting the panniers was my long awaited Exit Pass. After nine days in San Jose I wanted to turn the pedals again. A route would take me back down to the coast near Puntarenas, so my rail tour hadn't diminished the amount of cycling I would do. I said goodbye to Jac and Alan and made my way through the city streets. It wasn't long before I was on the old road to Orotina. It was quiet as a motorway had been built on the other side of the valley.

I returned to the pleasure of stopping at idiosyncratic village *pulperias*. In one I sat on a bar stool with my drink, watching baby chicks wandering to and fro. The owner called his wife from the kitchen to meet me. She appeared carrying a can of beer in a paper bag. She explained that they didn't have an alcohol licence but sometimes supplied cans of beer "under the counter" to neighbours as a personal favour. They came out of the kitchen fridge, not the one in the shop, so the transaction was nothing to do with the business. No doubt the local policeman sometimes needs a beer!

I stopped in Ciudad Colón to ask a man trimming his hedge the way. As he turned to me, I saw he had blue eyes. He introduced himself as Günter from Cologne. I said I like Germany and he replied "So do I" which made me laugh. He had lived in Costa Rica for thirty-two years, and said "They are thieves and liars, but it's still worth living here in spite of that!"

🚲

One of the advantages of cycle travel over bus or car is that you see all sorts of unexpected things by the side of the road. Pushing the bike up a hill, I heard a rustling noise in the leaves in the v-shaped concrete drainage channel that lined the road. I stopped to see what it was. The first thing I saw was its tail, and I thought "Oh no, a snake". I stood back a metre or so, just in case.

It was working its way steadily downhill, so I gingerly followed it. Then it emerged from the leaves - an armadillo! It had been making so much noise in the leaves that it hadn't heard me; it just stood there looking around. I stood as still as I could. It had a very small head with a pinkish face. After a while, it scurried up the hillside, into the trees, and out of my life. It was an experience that bus tourists would never get. I have never seen an armadillo in the wild before.

Shortly after this brush with nature I was in Orotina, which I remembered from the train ride. I found a good guest house at the end of the main street. The lady in charge brought me a cold beer as I stepped out of the shower, with sublimely perfect timing.

🚲

From Orotina I went down to the coast. Crossing a bridge over a wide river I saw people peering over the parapet. I peered myself and saw crocodiles. A dozen or so were languishing on the mud, looking deceptively peaceful. Oddly, nobody was bathing in the cool waters. At Parrita a dirt road went along the coast for about twenty-five miles. I emailed Gavin and Leo for advice about it, as they had come this way. They had no problems, adding as an afterthought that they had done it in the rainy season. I wished I had too as it was unbelievably dusty. Every vehicle that passed threw up a great dust cloud that reached every part of me and my bike. Fortunately there were plenty of places to stop for a break. At one, the girl said she didn't like living there because of all the dust. I think my arrival brightened up her day.

The tarmac returned at Dominical. I cheered with elation. Dominical is a low key surfing resort with plenty of budget accommodation. I looked at a number of rooms. At one place the owner – on learning that I had come from Mexico - showed me a '*cuartito*' which had a '*bañito*' which really made me *laughito*. We were sharing a joke about the Mexican tendency to use diminutives. They add "-ito" to more or less any word at will, turning a "*cuarto*" or room, into a "*cuartito*", or little room.

I went for a *cuartito* in a small family run place, with a view out of the window onto a big bush with bright red flowers. It had a chair and table where I could sit writing my diary, and watch the hummingbirds hovering about the red flowers. It was perfect. I stayed there for two nights, as I wanted a rest day.

The bike needed a good clean after the grimy road. I went to the filling station in the village armed with a toothbrush and empty bottle, so I could buy some diesel to clean the chain and gears with. I cycled directly up to the pump, and one of the two 20-year old boys working there made a joke about filling the bike. I explained what I wanted to do, and they showed me a shaded corner where I could work.

I accidentally dropped the toothbrush into the plastic bottle full of diesel, and couldn't get it out. I went to the boys to see if they had a knife, to cut the bottle, and one of them went into the workshop to fetch a proper can designed for such tasks.

When I finished, they let me wash my hands in the workshop. The bike shone like a new pin, and the helpful boys got a good tip. Happiness should be shared.

My mileage tally was now 3,785 and I expected something to go wrong with the bike any time. The gears had slipped a couple of times, usually a sign that the chain is starting to wear. I was surprised the chain had lasted so well, to be honest. I kept my fingers crossed, hoping I would still make it to Panama City. I calculated it was 325 miles from Dominical, plus detours, so I reckoned my policy of letting sleeping dogs lie could continue a bit longer. I had a specific finishing point in mind, the Panama Canal at Balboa. I started dreaming about hotels selling champagne – there had to be one somewhere near the canal!

I left Dominical at seven in the morning, early for a Sunday. I was getting into the habit of starting early to avoid the worst of the afternoon heat. I was astonished to see lots of red legged crabs on the road. At first I thought they were spiders, but I could tell from the way they walked that they were crabs. I couldn't understand why they were on the road rather than the beach. They ran from side to side, making them hard to run over.

Shortly afterwards I passed a group of cyclists going the other way. They were members of a club out for a Sunday run. They had a support vehicle bringing up the rear. The driver stopped and gave me water and papaya which were much welcomed. The cyclists had come downhill from San Isidro and would return from Dominical in their support vehicle. Hah!

I re-joined the Panamericana at Palmar Norte, a desolate windswept town kept busy by the banana harvest. It was gloomy as thick grey clouds were gathering. It looked suspiciously like rain. I carried on. At two o'clock the heavens opened. I was passing through a little village called Venecia which had a shop with a very inviting roof overhanging at the front. I bought a tin of fish and some juice and sat under it watching the rain. There were two parrots in the garden and I amused myself by trying to get them to say "Hello" in English.

This was the first heavy rain I cycled in since Durango in October. Even though it was the dry season, such a run of good luck was remarkable. My waterproof jacket got some funny looks as most men in this part of the world simply take their shirts off when it rains.

I continued to Rio Claro, near the frontier with Panama. It was my last night in Costa Rica. There were no less than three hotels in this border town, and I checked in at the most expensive – costing about seven pounds.

I lay on my bed reflecting about Costa Rica. I was still trying to shake off a lingering feeling of stupidity over losing a bag in San Jose. However, the enjoyable cycling since leaving the metropolis had made up for that. The following morning I was on the road before eight; I swallowed up the last few miles of Costa Rica and breezed through the immigration and money changing formalities in twenty minutes. I was in Panama, my seventh country, with a pocket full of US dollars and a lot of miles under my belt.

CHAPTER FOURTEEN

HELP FROM THE
POLICE IN PANAMA

Until 1903 Panama was part of Colombia. When it became independent, no-one thought to change the clocks. It is still on Colombian time rather than Central American time, so I had to put my watch forward an hour.

Panama has a significant place in Scottish history, although not everyone is aware of this. Panama played a key part in the political union of Scotland with England in 1707. How was that? I hear you ask. I will explain.

In the 1690's Scotland and England were separate countries, albeit under one king, William the Third. England was reaping considerable profits from trading colonies around the world. As foreigners, Scots were excluded from this bounty and wanted a colony of their own. To facilitate this, in 1693 the Scottish Parliament created the grandiosely named Company of Scotland Trading to Africa and the Indies.

At the same time a Scot called William Paterson founded the Bank of England, earning himself a reputation for integrity and honesty in the process. Shortly afterwards he returned to Scotland and persuaded the trading company to support his idea of setting up a colony in Darien, part of what is now Panama. The directors spent two years trying unsuccessfully to raise finance in England, before resolving to raise the entire finance required - £400,000 – in Scotland.

The idea gripped the nation. The population of Scotland at the time was under a million, and every penny of spare cash was sunk into the scheme. It is remarkable that such a sum could be raised in so small a country. After months of preparation, five ships sailed out of Leith, near Edinburgh, in July 1698. They were carrying 1,200 Scottish volunteers (mainly men) and a considerable quantity of food, brandy and goods for trade.

They arrived on the coast of Panama on the first of November 1698 in a bay which they named Caledonia Bay. They built a settlement optimistically called New Edinburgh which they defended by building Fort St. Andrew on a hill overlooking it.

The project was a disaster. Numerous colonists died from malaria or yellow fever. The English were uncooperative and banned their ships from trading with them. The colony was badly organised and descended into anarchy; the goods taken there for trade included such useful necessities as woollen bonnets and clay pipes. They were unsaleable.

Accepting defeat, the dwindling number of survivors fled to Jamaica and New York in their remaining ships. Before news of the fiasco got through to Scotland a second group had set out from Greenock to join them. By the time they arrived in Caledonia Bay the place was deserted. They tried to start the settlement again but quickly succumbed for the same reasons. The colony was abandoned.

The failure of the scheme, which had soaked up so much investment from a relatively small population, virtually bankrupted the country. Queen Anne succeeded to the throne in 1702 mindful to encourage the political union of her two peoples. Scotland had lost heavily; such a loss could more easily be shared with England. The proposed Treaty of Union between the two nations included a clause dissolving the Darien Company, and recompensing the shareholders. It was a significant factor in convincing the Scottish Parliament to vote for union with England, and voting itself out of existence for almost three hundred years.

Caledonia is still marked today on maps, although some refer to it by the Spanish name "Punta Escocés" – Scottish Point. In 1998, three hundred years after its founding, the Panamanian government invited Britain to send an archaeological expedition to excavate the site. The jungle around New Edinburgh was cleared and many remains were uncovered, hardly disturbed in 300 years. The moat guarding Fort St Andrew was being used by indigenous people to shelter fishing boats, probably unaware of how it was made.

The scheme was a monumental own-goal for Scotland.

From the frontier a wide new dual carriageway stretched to the horizon. My first impression was that Panama looked even more affluent than Costa Rica. Perhaps the well maintained houses with neat gardens next to the dual carriageway weren't typical. Modern micro-buses zipped past every few minutes, with exhaust pipes sticking up in front of the windscreen, like old steam engine chimneys. The antiquated American school buses – ubiquitous in other countries, were absent. The road went gently uphill for several miles and I needed two *refrescos* at Santa Marta. The couple running the prim little shop had negative views of politicians, exclaiming that eight political parties was far too many. I was by now used to hearing negative views of politicians so I drank up and moved on to the town of David.

David had no distinguishing landmarks. There were a few modern hotels around the Parque Central, which had a corrugated iron fence around it protecting us from works. A man from whom I bought a water melon told me to go to Boquete, a pleasant town in the mountains with good hotels. After four days on the coastal plain I thought – why not climb another hill?

Climbing up to Boquete, I was frustrated that the best views, towards the Pacific, were behind me. The climb was steady without being steep, and I punctuated it with my favourite pastime – stopping for cool drinks. At one place, Tony came over to chat. He was forty-six and had just returned from working in the United States. He could tell I was European – not American – just by looking at me, which pleased me no end. He didn't like the United States, in particular its support for Israel. He was annoyed at how Jewish culture had infiltrated every aspect of American life, citing as an example the way the stars above the eagle on the back of a dollar bill were arranged in the pattern of the Star of David. I had never noticed that before. He experienced a lot of racism in the United States.

The shopkeeper was listening and said that a lot of Americans retire to Panama now. He thought it was going to change the country.

The road dipped downhill into Boquete, which lays flat on the floor of a crater 1,060 meters above sea level. Mountains, fresh air and cool breezes made it an oasis in the tropics. There was a vast array of hotels and I took a room with its own front door off the street and a fridge. It was perfect. I could come and go without passing reception, and keep a handy supply of food and drink in the fridge.

I saw an advert for guided walks in the local mountains. When I phoned, Fernando said he could take me to the top of Volcan Barú the following night, by the light of the full moon. It sounded exciting, as the volcano is the highest point in Panama – 3,478 meters – and one of the few places in the world where you can see the Pacific Ocean and the Atlantic Ocean at the same time. On a clear day. The advantage of going up in the night was that the sky was likely to be clearest when the sun rose. I couldn't contain my eagerness but first Fernando needed to come and see me to assess my fitness. When he arrived we got on instantly and he thought I would have no difficulty in reaching the summit. Flattery gets you everywhere. We agreed to leave that night at one a.m.

After his visit I went for a short hike up a road that climbed out of Boquete on the opposite side of the valley to Volcan Barú, hoping to get a preview of the mighty mountain. I stopped at a *pulperia*, and spoke to the man who ran it. Coincidences never cease to amaze me. The man was Fernando's brother, Roberto.

We sat together talking about the world in general and in particular Americans who retire to Panama. I raised the subject because I had seen a notice in English saying "Private property keep out".

Roberto didn't think much of them. "They come here expecting us to speak English. Prices go up as they can afford to pay more. Land prices are multiplying. Other Americans arrive to sell services to those already here, undermining employment prospects for Panamanians. They impose a different culture on us."

Apart from that, he was happy with his new neighbours!

It is a familiar story. I have heard it in Scotland about the English, in Denmark about the Germans, and in Spain about all other Europeans. The migration of retired people to cheaper places is becoming a world phenomenon.

> "Some people are now refusing to sell land to Americans because it jeopardises their children's and grand-children's futures."
>
> "Yes, but money talks. If I offered you a million dollars for this *pulperia*, what would you say?"
>
> Laughter.
>
> "It's not worth that!"

Roberto changed the subject to the British Royal Family. A popular conversation topic in every nook and cranny of the planet, for some reason. Prince Charles had just married Camilla. My opinion was sought. I said I was pleased that the couple had found happiness; it is a basic human need. There was much hilarity when I owned up to having Parker as my surname. No relation, I can assure you!

Fernando arrived at a quarter to one, as arranged. I had just woken up from a nap, thanks to my efficient body clock. It's funny how often my body clock wakes me up ten minutes before the alarm. We drove uphill in the moonlight, my mind full of expectation. We parked near the ranger station which was, oddly, closed. Fernando said we would check in on our way out, a procedure which would clear airport queues in a jiffy. The path was steep. At a clearing we stopped to look at the moonlit view. I asked Fernando what his views were of the Americans living there.

> "They are arrogant and tend to regard Panamanians as inferior. Local people are worried that with a population of only three million we could be outnumbered in our own country."

I asked him what he thought were the worst aspects of American immigration.

"Putting up signs telling people to keep off their property, refusing to learn Spanish, and expecting Panamanians to learn English."

His neighbours had just sold land to some Americans, and he thought they were just plain stupid to do so. Sometimes land was sold on to another buyer for a profit. He asked me how I would feel if I couldn't afford to buy a house in my own country because foreigners were buying them.

We talked about the Noriega years. General Noriega became President in 1983 after first taking control of the National Guard. He ruled the country with a tight fist, and used this strength to manipulate the economy and siphon piles of money into his bank accounts. He was into drug trafficking in a big way. Fernando described the country as a police state where everyone was afraid to do anything or protest.

Most of Fernando's clients were European. Something that surprised him about European culture was that when he went to see people about his mountain tours, they would invariably invite him into their rooms to talk – as I had done myself. Panamanians would never do that

Talking to Fernando took my mind off the long hard climb, made worse by the loose rocks lying on the path. It drizzled from time to time and I wasn't optimistic about seeing both the Oceans. When we saw the moon and stars they were as bright as Broadway adverts. A couple of hundred feet below the summit was a bothy in which a man was curled up in a sleeping bag. He had already been to the summit. From the bothy we made a final dash for the top, scrambling up the last stretch to save time on the twisting path. We reached the mast-covered plateau at six-fifteen, just as it was starting to get light. Fernando congratulated us on our timing – he had assessed my level of fitness correctly and we were about to see the sun rise.

Both Oceans were covered in banks of cloud. There was an opening through which we saw a hazy sun appearing, giving us the privilege of another day. We were surrounded in pink, white and orange cloud. Through gaps we caught glimpses of water. We had done it; we were on the highest point of Panama and could see both Oceans. It was freezing cold so we ran about to keep warm.

We descended quickly - not good for my old legs. It was my second experience of a fast descent in the hands of a guide. In some professions they want you to finish quickly so they get their money. I recovered from my exertions over a lasagne in the Pizza Place, the wall of which was covered with newspaper cuttings about the official encouragement of United States citizens to retire here. They get a Pensioners Visa if they can prove income of $500 per month. One writer said that Costa Rica had priced itself out of the market. Another said she employed a live-in housekeeper for $150 per month so they were contributing to local employment. The housekeeper will never be able to afford a house of her own.

I was in the supermarket buying some groceries when the lights went out. A power cut. An American howled "Haven't they heard of standby generators here?" It sounded like his new country was a challenge for him.

⚙

Panama is long and thin. It is like Scotland on its side. Most people live in the middle, in Panama City, Balboa and Colón. Either side of this "central belt" are long stretches of rugged unpopulated mountain and forest. After I left Boquete I cycled along a stretch of Pan-American Highway with no dots marked on my map. There was no obvious destination and it crossed my mind that I might have to camp. At about three I got to a village called Los Ruices, which had a *Transito* compound – traffic police. I went in for advice on accommodation along the road. The officers and some local teenagers were watching Real Betis v Real Madrid on TV. My arrival seemed more exciting than the football.

They said there was no accommodation before Santiago, forty miles further on. The sergeant in charge said I could stay at their compound if I wanted, but he thought I could make it to Santiago before dark if I got my skates on. His optimism encouraged me to try for it, giving me three hours to do forty miles. The first hill hammered home to me how tired I was, and I doubled back to the police compound to take up their offer.

The police base was on an isolated stretch of the road; they go there for three days at a time, staying in a dormitory with showers and a kitchen. There were three officers on duty - the sergeant and two constables. A local teenager stayed there helping with errands. I was given a bunk in their dormitory.

The football finished and they returned to their task of stopping vehicles to check documents. The phone rang.

The teenager shouted for the sergeant, who took the call. There had been a collision further along the road, and to my surprise the two constables flagged down a passing bus to get to the scene. I asked the sergeant if they had a patrol car. "Yes," he said, "but it needs repairing".

I went for a walk exploring some of the paths around the village. I popped into a *cantina* for a beer, and told the barman I was staying at the Police compound. He said the *Transitos* were all decent guys and I had nothing to worry about.

When I got back, the Panamanian Flag had been taken down for the night. The two bobbies were back from the accident which had been caused by a car swerving to avoid a hole in the road. They knew I had been for a beer - traffic police can smell beer on your breath from fifty yards. One of them was now off duty and went to get some hot take-away food and more beer.

We spent the evening comparing our cultures, and of course my salary with theirs. The sergeant had been in the police for twenty-two years.

> "That means you were in the police under the Noriega Dictatorship"
>
> "Yes" a constable said, "he used to clean Noriega's boots".

The sergeant described the American invasion in 1989 to oust and arrest Noriega, known as Operation Just Cause. He thought the American soldiers were trigger-happy, killing too many Panamanians in the process. Two thousand people were killed, many in poor areas of Panama City which were shelled from the sea.

It was clear the younger officers respected the sergeant's stories and advice. I felt comfortable in their company. The fact that two local teenagers were hanging around the compound was a sign that they were trusted by the community.

I noticed at bedtime that my odometer showed 3,997 miles!

⛇

In the morning I was awakened by the policemen getting up at five o'clock. I got up at five thirty so I could leave as soon as it was light, to avoid cycling in the worst of the heat. The Panamanian Flag was hoisted sharp at six, according to regulations. I thanked the sergeant, and asked if he wanted me to pay anything.

"No, it's part of my duty to make tourists safe."

He was a credit to Panama and a credit to the police especially. Travel guide books paint such a woeful picture of Latin American police that I was cheered to have such a positive experience.

The air was cool, the rising sun made the hills look enchanting, with - dare I say it - a little Scotch mist. I saw a tortoise on the road, and moved him off it into the sun. When the odometer clicked over to 4,000 I let out a cheer that could be heard in Scotland. It was priceless as I knew

I wouldn't be doing 5,000. I tried to calculate in my head if I was likely to do 7,000 kilometres.

Santiago had a disorganised main street with a modern cathedral at the top end. I celebrated my 4,000th mile with some Mexican beer and a pizza. How international we have become. The next day, I deviated from the Panamericana into the Peninsula de Azuero to the south of the main road. The junction at Santa Maria was a maze of buildings and badly signposted. I had to ask where the turning was.

A few miles later I was flagged down by a *Transito* on a motorcycle, who used a well-choreographed set-piece to stop me. "What now?" I thought.

> "I just wanted to check that you were going to Chitré. Are you exploring?"
>
> "Yes"
>
> "I thought I would check, as you might have been going to Panama City and taken the wrong turning."

The advice not to trust Latin American police was looking even shakier. I thanked him and off he went.

When I started my journey in northern Mexico, I had no return flight booked, no timescales, and no obligations. The freedom was wonderful. Now things were different as I had booked a flight from Panama City to Madrid. I had reserved a place on an excursion boat through the

Panama Canal. I had even made a reservation for a couple of nights in a plush hotel overlooking the Canal. Freedom had evaporated; my life was cluttered with plans, dates, times, and appointments. The end was nigh, my days were numbered.

I still had time to explore the lanes of the Peninsula de Azuero. It was dry as a bone. Fields miraculously supported cattle which inexplicably clung to life in the fiery heat. It looked like a desert, but is in fact an ancient sea marsh dehydrated by the effects of El Niño and thousands of years deforestation. In Chitré I ventured into a *cantina* to ask if I could take a glass of beer into the restaurant next door, which didn't have any. The barman said I could bring my meal into the bar if I wanted. I perched on a bar stool to eat, constantly trying to stop grains of rice dropping into my boots. I was glad I hadn't put clean socks on. Local men were discussing the second hand car market. Then one of them noticed me.

> "What brings you to Chitré?"

> "I'm cycling from Chihuahua to Panama." I said casually, as if I had come to deliver double-glazing leaflets.

> "Are you retired?"

> I told him my age.

> "You don't look it, how long do people live in Scotland?"

> "It depends on whether they smoke."

Or whether they drink, live in damp houses, and are poor; I added under my breath.

🚲

At the village shop in Los Pozos a man was assembling brooms imported from El Salvador. The heads were in one carton, the handles in another. It was a good job they had arrived together. I said I had come through El Salvador. He asked me if it was safe. What could I say? I had come all the way from Chihuahua safely. In Mexico, people had expressed doubt and disbelief about my journey. I was often told I wouldn't make it. I wished I could send them postcards to show it was possible. Now the ride was nearly behind me, questions were more specific.

> "How did you cross frontiers, do you have a passport?"
>
> "Do you get punctures?"
>
> "Have you had any problems?"
>
> "Where do you sleep?"

Staying in hotels for seven months was a clue to my relative affluence, which had often been disguised by my chosen mode of transport. In poor countries only poor people cycle. I recently read that in Britain a bicycle is now seen as a must-have accessory for affluent people. A token gesture to pretend you care about the environment.

🚲

I cycled past a gigantic advert thanking Omar for the Canal. It was dated 1999.

Lieutenant Colonel Omar Torrijos seized power in a military coup in 1968. He was a staunch nationalist and was determined to achieve Panamanian control of the Canal. After years of intensive negotiations he signed a treaty with President Carter in 1977, handing control back to Panama by 2000. It was a remarkable achievement given the determination of the United States to secure an American-controlled canal in the first place. They nearly lost the race to the French.

The Gold Rush and the acquisition of large parts of Mexico in the 1850's spurred the United States to look for a solution to the long sea journey round South America. The tantalisingly narrow Central American isthmus had to be crossed by mule – dangerous, slow, and hopelessly inefficient in the jungle.

A railway across Panama opened in 1855, built by an American company to carry goods and people between the two oceans. In 1876 a US government commission recommended a canal route through Lake Nicaragua. In the same year a French entrepreneur called Wyse realised that the railway company's concession did not include a canal construction right, and purchased one from the government of Colombia, then called New Granada. He thought the existence of the railway would make it easier to survey and construct a canal.

Surveyors sent from France reported that they could barely see through the trees.

Meanwhile another Frenchman called Ferdinand de Lesseps was basking in the success of constructing the Suez Canal. It is entirely at sea level and has no locks to delay ships. De Lesseps saw the opportunity of extending his reputation by building a similar canal through Panama. He insisted it too would have no locks, and be cut through whatever land was in its way.

He decided on a sea level route without any definitive survey work. The highest point of the route was 330 feet above sea level, and de Lesseps brushed this aside by saying a ditch would be dug through it. It would be some ditch! It was typical of the way he dismissed problems.

France was fanatical with enthusiasm for his venture. Vast sums of money were raised to finance the work. Men were recruited and work began in 1881.

It was found that instead of being rock, much of the ground was soil which became mud in the heavy rain of Panama. Landslides were frequent and the sides of the cut couldn't be stabilised. De Lesseps' solution was to insist on gentler gradients to the sides, which would make each bank almost a mile wide. He was headstrong and could never be persuaded to build a canal with locks. Since that time surveys have shown that the two oceans have different sea levels – the Pacific is several inches higher than the Atlantic. It is interesting to speculate what might have happened had he succeeded in building a sea level cut.

Costs escalated but still France invested heavily in the company. Costs weren't the only problem. The French workers – like the Scottish colonists before them – were dying in their thousands from malaria and yellow fever. The link between mosquitoes and malaria had yet to be established and no precautions were taken.

Money and people were poured into the problem for several years, to no avail. It was worse than putting your finger into the proverbial dyke to stop a flood. In 1888 the scheme was finally abandoned as de Lesseps could raise no more money to sink into the Panamanian mud. By then 22,000 people had died of disease and 1,200 million Francs had been lost.

Like the Scots in 1699, the French had met their Waterloo in Panama.

I had time make a final detour up into some mountains. El Valle is a small spa town in a volcanic crater twenty-eight kilometres north of the Panamericana. The brightly painted Cabañas De Colores lived up to their name and the owner gave me three nights for the price of two, a variation of the marketing tactic of British supermarkets who now sell two of everything for the price of three, to see if you are awake.

A local man showed me the path to a peak on the rim of the crater, called Pico del Indio because its shape resembles the face of a sleeping Indian. He was returning home from a morning's work tending the garden of a millionaire. "He doesn't pay much" the man said. "They never do, that's why they're millionaires" I replied. There was a path along the rim making it easy to wander around looking at the town from different angles. On the way down I slipped into a *pulperia* for some fruit juice. The shop owner happily gave me his views of all the Americans living in his country. Fine, he said, they bring in money and are good news. I ventured onto the subject of General Noriega. Even in a small place like El Valle, he said, you couldn't go out at night because the state police ran a curfew. Times were hard. I wondered afterwards how I would feel if tourists in Britain asked my opinion of Margaret Thatcher. I would tell them all right, but my views may not be typical. She was after all elected more times than I care to remember.

After my exertions I went to relax in one of the thermal pools heated by volcanic water. It was soothing to watch the hummingbirds and redwings. I mulled over different aspects of Panama as I lay there in the hot water, all sorts of minerals allegedly improving my complexion and general well-being. Some people were having mud painted over their face and body. It was supposed to make them look more attractive, but I wasn't going to let myself be fooled by that one. My wrinkles are still here to prove it!

In the night I was awoken by severe itching. It couldn't be bed bugs as the place was spotless; it was my third night there anyway. I had a long shower and that cured it. I reckoned the minerals in the thermal bath were to blame. I slept soundly until some workmen arrived in a clatter at seven thirty to build another cabaña. I said goodbye to the owner, her dog and her cat, and returned downhill to the Panamericana. It was surprisingly quiet. Near San Carlos a turning was signposted to Playa El Palmar. I took it, as I fancied a swim in the sea.

It was a surfing village, so there were a number of places to stay. At one, a man was sitting on the veranda with his dogs. He showed me a comfortable looking room in his house. He was 60 and his doctor had told him to stop surfing as he had heart problems. He was continuing to surf to prove his doctor wrong. As no-one is immortal, it will be his doctor who will one day be able to say "See, I was right"!

His son arrived, and the two of them immersed themselves into a conversation about surfing which was totally unintelligible to me. A different language. I felt out of place and wandered off to find somewhere else. Later in the evening I was walking around San Carlos when I saw two touring cyclists. I waved at them to stop. They were Canadians, cycling from Vancouver to Argentina with twice as much luggage as me. What was more amazing was that they had heard about me! Shopkeepers had mentioned me when they had stopped for drinks. I had no idea I was becoming a celebrity in Panama. They thought Central America wasn't "real" Latin America and they were keen to reach South America. They singled out El Salvador as being americanised. I can see their point as I had noticed that Salvadoreans really bought into the idea that eating chicken nuggets washed down with Pepsi was the height of sophistication.

Meeting them unsettled me a bit. They were going through Colombia, and I had read an article in the Miami Herald saying how safe Colombia is becoming. The country intrigued me and I was thinking – why stop now? Pedalling has been my life for six months, what do I do next?

Another day, another stretch of road – dual carriageway now, another *abarrote* to stop at. The man in charge, Nacho, was talkative. To my surprise he asked me about the Channel Tunnel – he wanted me to confirm that such a thing actually existed. When I described it he was surprised at its length. I made his day by telling him I had been through it myself, as he had never met anyone who had.

I brought up Panamanian politics, explaining that I had found Nicaragua a much divided country. He explained that in Panama there were so many parties, with inevitable coalition governments, that it was not easy for people to become polarised. He thought Nicaragua a very unlucky country, so many natural disasters and wars. It looks destined to be poor.

Nacho had an opinion about General Noriega too. The country was much safer under his rule. There was less freedom but more security. He mentioned the *pandilleros* controlling urban life and said they couldn't have existed under Noriega because he controlled everything. Yes, I thought, maybe he controlled things through *pandilleros* called the secret police.

I left him and continued to La Chorrera. Drivers in the congested town were impatient of me, and I got shouted at for going the wrong way down a one-way street. It was going to be my last overnight stop before arriving at the canal, and I dithered a bit about which hotel to stay in. The two in the centre were unappealing and I ended up taking a room in a cheap dive further out. The bar next door had Vila Real –v- Inter Milan on TV. At half time I woke up to the fact that the woman running the hotel said the price was ten dollars for twelve hours. At first, the significance of this had gone over my head. Then I thought – hang on, this means I will have to leave at four o'clock in the morning. When the match finished, I went straight back for clarification.

> "Yes, it's ten dollars for twelve hours. If you want more, you have to pay more."
>
> "What kind of hotel is this, you pay to sleep in a hotel?"

The penny was dropping. The owner saw the funny side and said I could stay until seven o'clock without paying more. At that point a taxi arrived and out stepped a businessman and a girl wearing a very tight mini-skirt. They vanished quickly into one of the bedrooms. I had inadvertently stumbled into a house of ill-repute.

It was amusing to watch some of the comings and goings during the evening. The woman who came to do the nightshift saw I was alone in my room and came along for a chat. She was unmarried and had three children. She thought it was better to work and have financial independence than live off a man's salary. She said there were a lot of single mothers in Panama, especially since the American invasion to see off Noriega.

I said goodbye to her in the morning and pedalled sadly into my last day on the road. The dual carriageway was boring. After sixteen miles I went up a slip road into Arraijan to look for something to eat. A café up a flight of stairs had a terrace overlooking the road and the filling station opposite. I ordered a breakfast asking as an afterthought if there was any fruit juice. After first saying no, the lady in charge sent her daughter to buy a bag of oranges. Ten minutes later, freshly squeezed juice was placed in front of me, like a gift for the king. It was gorgeous.

I confided in the lady that I was planning to cycle across the Puente de Las Americas, the high suspension bridge crossing the canal. She said it swayed from side to side. I was nervous about it – Gavin and Leo had told me it was a horrendous start to their first day cycling, all those months ago. I remembered that I had sometimes visited friends living on the top floors of high-rise blocks in Glasgow, which also sway in the wind. It didn't reduce my apprehension.

She wished me good luck for the final leg of my journey. I rounded a bend and saw the towers of a bridge. Then a car park and viewing station on the left. I glanced down at the silvery water. It was the Panama Canal. I had almost made it. Traffic was thundering past me, impatient to get into the capital. I put my head down and braced myself for the horror of the bridge.

I heard a loud whistle. I looked, it was a policeman. He was shouting at me to stop. For a moment it flashed through my mind to ignore him and pedal on, regardless. Then I remembered that Panamanian policemen are armed. I stopped and waited for a gap in the traffic so I could cross over and speak to him.

He told me it's forbidden to cycle across the bridge. I said I was from Europe and had cycled here all the way from Chihuahua in Mexico. I had come over four thousand miles to cycle over this bridge, and I wasn't going to give in lightly. He phoned his boss to see if he could get me permission to cross. I heard him say I was cycling round the world. I don't remember saying that, exactly. I also noticed there were two gaps in his bullet holder, making me glad I had stopped. We stood there patiently waiting for the answer.

While we were waiting, constable Escobar kept his hand firmly on my handlebar. He gripped it as if he had made an arrest. I wasn't going to make a run for it, but he didn't know that. We chatted about our families as a diversion.

Then his boss called back. I was going to be escorted over the bridge. I had to wait for a patrol car. Wow!

After about twenty minutes a police pick-up truck arrived, and the driver told me to get in the back with my bike. "Hang on to that" he said, pointing to a metal handle. Hang on I did, as we went round the block so he could change direction to get onto the bridge.

I hung onto the bike and the handle for dear life as we roared across. The bridge was narrow. Traffic was intense and scary. I was glad the police had saved me from it, glad I had set a rule about 'No rules'. It would be a bad ending to be flattened by a bus after 4,387 miles or – more impressively - 7,058 kilometres. He dropped me on a roundabout. I was in Balboa.

My hotel was a short distance away, on the bank of the canal. I had made it, achieving my dream of seeing a slice of Mexico and the countries of Central America. I checked in, wheeled my bike into the lift, and luxuriated in my room. I had a bottle of Spanish Cava in the fridge, some chocolates, a balcony with a view of the canal, and football on TV - Milan v Lyon. I was ready to celebrate and rest.

The room also had a BATH - you know, one of those things you can fill with hot water and lay in. I didn't think they existed in Central America. While the bath filled and the cava chilled, I stood on the balcony watching the ships make their way into the canal. Soon I would be on one myself.

CHAPTER FIFTEEN

FINALE

The morning arrived for my boat trip. The other passengers waiting at the pier were almost entirely elderly, there were hardly any backpackers. The $149 fare had no doubt priced them off, which is a pity as it is a rare experience to be able to see a wonder of the world at close quarters. It's possible to work your way through as a line handler on a yacht, but it can take several days or weeks - plus an element of good luck - to organise. For backpackers who relish the challenge of earning themselves a free ride, this is ideal.

Over forty ships a day pass through the canal, smaller ones have to share the locks to maximise the number that can go through in a day. Our ship was small, so we had to wait over an hour for the two vessels we were booked to share the locks with. Passenger ships can't share locks with ships carrying dangerous goods.

While we were waiting a huge container ship dwarfed us as it went by. We stood on the upper deck and watched it slide gently into the first of the Miraflores Locks. Its entry was controlled by a series of locomotives on tracks either side of the lock. A cable from each locomotive is secured to the ship and kept tight so the ship goes centrally in without knocking the side walls. The ships go in under their own power; they are not pulled by the locomotives, which look tiny in comparison with the mass of a container ship. A locomotive has only been pulled into the water twice; each time because the pilot's instructions were misunderstood.

When our turn came, we shared the lock with a small freighter which entered the lock first. We followed and tied up behind it. A luxury yacht came in and tied up to our side. Some of us peered down onto it, no doubt envious. I noticed people on a lower deck were talking to the yacht's skipper, so I went down to listen to the conversation.

The skipper was an employee of the boat's owner, an American millionaire who used the boat occasionally to entertain business associates to lunch. He would fly in with his guests, then fly off again soon after lunch. The fee for the yacht to go through the canal was $1,000 and it had to be booked a year in advance through shipping agents. You couldn't simply turn up at Miraflores and buy a ticket.

After Miraflores the canal heads towards the hills. The Gaillard Cut, the initial works of which had defeated the French, takes the canal through the highest part of the peninsula. It is deep and narrow, though not of course as deep as originally planned by De Lesseps; it is 85 feet above sea level. Large ships are not allowed to pass in opposite directions as the combined water turbulence could knock them of course, and damage the banks.

Our boat had a guide who gave an informative commentary. He said the canal employees are paid at the same wage rates as when it was American owned, to try to maintain the same standards set by the United States. The Panamanian constitution was amended so the rules of the previous administration could be continued. The canal revenues are over $1 billion per year, and the canal company transfers a significant proportion of the profits to the government which is used for social and health projects. The major user of the canal was now China, rather than the United States, with Japan and Chile also being significant users. The latter didn't surprise me, given the amount of Chilean wine we now drink in Britain.

After the Gaillard Cut, the canal passes Gamboa. Our boat stopped at the pier to let some people off who were returning to Balboa. Most of us stayed on board for the rest of the journey. We were delayed there by a build up of traffic which meant that we had lost our original timeslot. Shortly after leaving Gamboa the canal widened noticeably. It entered Lake Gatún, a broad expanse of water ringed by trees. The navigation channel is marked with posts. As we crossed Lake Gatún the sun started to go down, making ghostly silhouettes of the giant ships we passed.

Gatún Locks took us down to sea level again. In the darkness I stared at the Atlantic Ocean, scarcely believing that I had been on the Pacific only that morning. Our boat made its way across the bay to the city of Colón. We didn't stay long; a fleet of busses was waiting to take us back to the safety of hotel rooms in Balboa.

歲

The canal is important to Panama, a big part of its life. I found many Panamanians had an opinion about it, of one sort or another. One café owner thought the transfer of ownership to Panama had been bad for the economy as the country had lost the spending power of all the Americans who used to work and live in the Canal Zone. What he said didn't really add up, as the wages previously paid to Americans are now paid to Panamanians. The country is also getting the toll income, so it must be better off on that count too.

Others were very positive about it, as it made Panama important in the world. Generally people liked the idea that the canal was Panamanian owned, and appreciated the value of the social and infrastructure programmes brought about by the income.

The boat tour guide had told us the dimensions of the locks, which govern the size of ships that can use the canal. Therein lies a problem. The canal is too small for new generations of super-ships built to take containers piled high on their decks like sandwiches on a buffet counter. To survive, the canal must be enlarged.

Omar Torrijos's son Martin became president in 2004. He commissioned a study into the consequences of making it bigger. There was concern not only of the finances, but also of the effect it would have on water usage and the environment, particularly in the catchment area of Lake Gatún. A scheme to widen the canal locks was put to a national referendum. It will cost $5 billion and take several years to complete.

They had little choice but to vote yes, and work has now begun. They must be competitive to survive. You have to admire the shrewdness of United States too, for agreeing to "surrender control" of an asset which was almost at the end of its useful life. They have neatly avoided the bill for widening it – the money now has to be raised by a small country. The United States has shown renewed interest in a route through Nicaragua, now that it no longer owns Panama. Perhaps they were shaken a bit when China agreed to fund some new cranes at Miraflores. The region will continue to be interesting for years to come.

Two days later I returned to Colón by train. The railway between Panama City and Colón survives because of the canal it helped to construct. Ships heavily laden with containers can't always pass above the lock-gate sills as they draw too much water. The solution is to unload enough containers for the ship to bob up and pass over the sill into the lock. While the ship is going through the canal, the containers are taken across by train, and re-loaded in Colón. The railway is still owned by an American company and has been modernised. A passenger train leaves Panama City every morning, returning from Colón in the evening. It is a good way to get another look at the canal as it passes close by it for much of the way. The ride takes about an hour.

The fare is high – considerably higher than the bus. There are two classes of carriage, Business Class and Tourist Class, which oddly enough describe their users very accurately. In spite of the high fares it attracts enough regular users to fill four Business Class coaches.

The regulars work mainly in the banking and shipping sectors.

The business users on the train illustrated the contrasts of Panama City. Going from the canal into the city you pass rows and rows of blocks of flats that are poor and ugly. Doorways with no doors, window frames without windows. The ugliness emphasised a poverty which is sometimes mistakenly romanticised by an image of pretty little huts with thatched roofs. Many black people lived in this district, some of them descendants of people imported to build the railway and the canal.

Further along is the banking district, and along the sea front block after block of luxury apartments. In this city the poor and the rich have one thing in common – sea views. It won't be long though before the poor get moved on and their "real estate" developed to its maximum potential.

Panama hasn't heard the last of General Noriega either. Imprisoned in Miami since 1989, his prison term is about to come to an end. He wants to return to Panama, but is facing extradition to France to face drugs-related charges there. If he returns to Panama, there are outstanding murder charges. His return might awaken too many unhappy memories of a dark period in Panama's history.

Panama remembers its history; whether Spanish, Scottish or French. The ruins of the original Spanish settlement at Panama La Vieja are now being restored in conjunction with the Spanish government. New Edinburgh has been excavated. The obstinate Frenchman is remembered too; a statue of Ferdinand de Lesseps enjoys a prominent position in the Old Town. How different things might have been had he succeeded; and for that matter if the Scottish colony had too.

Although my cycle ride was over, I couldn't stop cycling. I pedalled out of Panama City on the Darien road to the airport and caught my plane home. I flew with Air Madrid, and the flight was awful. A few months later Air Madrid went bust.

BIBLIOGRAPHY.

"A Concise History of Mexico" by Brian Hamnet, Cambridge University Press, 1999.

"Bicycling Mexico" by Ericka Weisbroth and Eric Ellman, Hunter Publishing (USA) 1990.

"Villa – Soldier of the Mexican Revolution" by Robert Scheina, Potomac Books inc. 2004.

"A Short Account of the Destruction of the Indies" by Bartolomé de Las Casas, originally published 1552 in Spain. First English version published by Penguin in 1992, reprinted 2004.

"Mexico" by Katharine and Charlotte Thompson, Cadogan Guides 1991.

"The Old Patagonian Express" by Paul Theroux. First published in Britain by Hamish Hamilton, 1979.

"El Salvador – Nation of the Modern World" by Alastair White, Ernst Benn Limited 1973.

"Salvador" by Joan Didion, Granta Books 1983.

"The Panamericana" by Simon Calder, Vacation Work 2000.

"Nicaragua" by Carol Wood, Ulysses Travel Publications (Canada) 1999.

"Nicaragua – The Threat of a Good example", Oxfam 1985.

"Post-war Reconstruction in Central America" by Patricia Ardón, Oxfam 1999.

"The Floating Brothel" by Sian Rees, Headline Publishing 2001

"So Far from God" by Patrick Marnham, Bloomsbury Classics 1996.

"Central America – Wrestling With US power" by Understanding Global Issues, 1999.

"The Golden Isthmus" by David Howarth, Collins 1966.

Lonely Planet and Rough Guides.

www.casa-alianza.org The website of Casa Alianza.

Spanish Words Used in the Text.

Note that some of these words are not used in Spain.

abanico (Nicaragua and Costa Rica)	electric ventilation fan in room. In standard Spanish an abanico is a hand-held fan.
abarrote (Mexico)	small general shop
alcalde	town mayor
amiga	a girl-friend
barranca	canyon
bienvenidos	welcome
buenos dias/buenas tardes/buenas noches	good morning/good afternoon/good night
camioneta	pick-up truck, or any vehicle used to carry standing passengers in the back.
campesino	rural worker
cantina	public bar
chiste	a joke
colectivo	small minibus
comedor	basic restaurant
encomienda	land allocated by Spanish Crown in 16th Century, with certain rights and privileges.
espectacular	spectacular, impressive

fuera de juego	off-side (in football)
gasolinera	filling station
hospedaje	small hotel
mestizo	mixed race people, Spanish/ Indigenous Indian
Migración	immigration office
muchacho	equivalent to the northern English 'lad'.
palapa	small restaurant on a beach, usually roofed over with tree branches.
pandilleros (Central America)	urban gang members
plaza	small square in a town
pulperia (Central America)	small general shop
quesadilla	cheese filled tortilla
rato	chat or small party
refresco	cold drink
regalo	present, gift.
Reino Unido	United Kingdom
tacos	savoury tortilla snacks, usually containing meat, onion, chili, chopped mint.

taqueria	stall in a street selling tacos
tonto	crazy or mad
topes (Mexico)	speed humps
Transito	traffic police
tuc-tuc (Guatemala)	3-wheeled scooter taxi.
tuctuquero (Guatemala)	tuc-tuc driver
zocalo (Mexico)	central square or plaza
pase, or pase usted	come in
seguro	certain, sure

Indigenous words

huipiles (Guatemala)	loose fitting blouse, often hand woven by the wearer.

Printed in the United Kingdom
by Lightning Source UK Ltd.
129725UK00001B/79-165/P